SINGAPORE

THE MINI ROUGH GUIDE

There are more than one hundred and fifty
Rough Guide travel, phrasebook, and
music titles, covering destinations from
Amsterdam to Zimbabwe, languages from
Czech to Vietnamese, and musics from
World to Opera and Jazz

Forthcoming titles include

Alaska • Copenhagen
Ibiza and Formentera • Iceland

Rough Guides on the Internet

www.roughguides.com

Rough Guide Credits

Text editor: David Price
Series editor: Mark Ellingham
Production: Julia Bovis and Katie Pringle
Cartography: Melissa Flack and Edward Wright

Publishing Information

This third edition published November 2000
by Rough Guides Ltd, 62–70 Shorts Gardens,
London, WC2H 9AH

Distributed by the Penguin Group:

Penguin Books Ltd, 27 Wrights Lane, London W8 5TZ
Penguin Putnam, Inc., 375 Hudson Street, New York 10014, USA
Penguin Books Australia Ltd, 487 Maroondah Highway,
PO Box 257, Ringwood, Victoria 3134, Australia
Penguin Books Canada Ltd, 10 Alcorn Avenue,
Toronto, Ontario, Canada M4V 1E4
Penguin Books (NZ) Ltd,
182–190 Wairau Road, Auckland 10, New Zealand

Typeset in Bembo and Helvetica to an original design by Henry Iles.
Printed in Spain by Graphy Cems.

320pp, includes index
A catalogue record for this book is available from the British Library.

ISBN 1-85828-566-6

SINGAPORE

THE MINI ROUGH GUIDE

by Mark Lewis

ROUGH
GUIDES

We set out to do something different when the first Rough Guide was published in 1982. Mark Ellingham, just out of university, was travelling in Greece. He brought along the popular guides of the day, but found they were all lacking in some way. They were either strong on ruins and museums but went on for pages without mentioning a beach or taverna. Or they were so conscious of the need to save money that they lost sight of Greece's cultural and historical significance. Also, none of the books told him anything about Greece's contemporary life – its politics, its culture, its people, and how they lived.

So with no job in prospect, Mark decided to write his own guidebook, one which aimed to provide practical information that was second to none, detailing the best beaches and the hottest clubs and restaurants, while also giving hard-hitting accounts of every sight, both famous and obscure, and providing up-to-the-minute information on contemporary culture. It was a guide that encouraged independent travellers to find the best of Greece, and was a great success, getting shortlisted for the Thomas Cook travel guide award, and encouraging Mark, along with three friends, to expand the series.

The Rough Guide list grew rapidly and the letters flooded in, indicating a much broader readership than had been anticipated, but one which uniformly appreciated the Rough Guide mix of practical detail and humour, irreverence and enthusiasm. Things haven't changed. The same four friends who began the series are still the caretakers of the Rough Guide mission today: to provide the most reliable, up-to-date and entertaining information to independent-minded travellers of all ages, on all budgets.

We now publish more than 100 titles and have offices in London and New York. The travel guides are written and researched by a dedicated team of more than 100 authors, based in Britain, Europe, the USA and Australia. We have also created a unique series of phrasebooks to accompany the travel series, along with an acclaimed series of music guides, and a best-selling pocket guide to the Internet and World Wide Web. We also publish comprehensive travel information on our Web site: **www.roughguides.com**

Help us update

We've gone to a lot of trouble to ensure that this Rough Guide is as up to date and accurate as possible. However, things do change and all suggestions, comments and corrections are much appreciated, and we'll send a copy of the next edition (or any other Rough Guide if you prefer) for the best letters.

Please mark letters "Rough Guide Singapore Update" and send to:

Rough Guides, 62–70 Shorts Gardens, London, WC2H 9AH, or Rough Guides, 4th Floor, 345 Hudson St, New York NY 10014.

Or send email to: mail@roughguides.co.uk
Online updates about this book can be found on
Rough Guides' Web site (see opposite)

The author

After graduating from the University of Bristol, Mark Lewis spent a year teaching English in Singapore, during which time he regularly contributed book reviews to the *Singapore Straits Times*. Having spent the best part of the next year exploring Southeast Asia, he returned to England and began work on the first edition of this guide. Co-author of the *Rough Guide to Malaysia, Singapore & Brunei*, and of the *Rough Guide to Vietnam*, Mark is currently the Features Editor of *Computer Weekly* magazine.

Acknowledgements

Mark Lewis would like to thank his wife Susie and his family for their love and support.

Readers' letters

Thanks to all the people who wrote in with comments on the previous edition of this guide, in particular: Patricia Harrison, Peter Herd, William M. Newlands and David Paterson.

CONTENTS

The Guide

Listings

CONTENTS

Contexts

CONTENTS

MAP LIST

Introduction

Singapore is certainly the handiest and most marvellous city I ever saw, as well planned and carefully executed as though built entirely by one man. It is like a big desk, full of drawers and pigeon-holes, where everything has its place, and can always be found in it.

W. Hornaday, 1885

Despite the immense changes the past century has imposed upon the tiny island of **Singapore**, natural historian William Hornaday's succinct appraisal is as valid today as it was then. Since gaining full independence from Malaysia in 1965, this absorbing city-state has been transformed from a sleepy colonial backwater into a pristine, futuristic shrine to consumerism. Yet visitors prepared to peer beneath the state's squeaky-clean surface will discover a profusion of age-old buildings, and values and traditions that have survived the profound social and geographical change. The island has not been overwhelmed by development – even as you make your way in from the airport, you'll be struck immediately by Singapore's abundance of parks, nature reserves, and lush, tropical greenery.

Singapore's **progress** over the past three decades has been remarkable. Lacking any noteworthy natural resources, its early prosperity was based on a vigorous free trade policy, in place since 1819 when Sir Stamford Raffles first set up a British trading post here. Later, mass industrialization bolstered the economy, and today the state boasts the world's second busiest port after Rotterdam, minimal unemployment, and a super-efficient infrastructure. Almost the entire population has been moved from unsanitary kampungs (villages) into new apartments, and the average per capita income is over US$16,000. Yet none of this was achieved without considerable compromise – indeed, the state's detractors claim it has sold its soul in return for prosperity.

Put simply, at the core of the Singapore success story is an unwritten bargain between its **government** and population that critics describe as soft **authoritarianism**. The loss of a certain amount of personal freedom has been accepted in return for levels of affluence and comfort that would have seemed unimaginable thirty years ago. But as the nation's youth (who don't remember a time before the improvements they take for granted) begin to find a voice, public life should become increasingly, if gradually, more liberal and democratic.

Whatever the political ramifications of the state's economic success, of more relevance to the five million annual visitors is that improvements in living conditions have resulted in a steady loss of the state's **heritage**, with historic buildings and streets bulldozed to make way for shopping centres. Singapore undoubtedly lacks the personality of some Southeast Asian cities, but its reputation for being sterile and sanitized is unfair. Shopping on state-of-the-art Orchard Road is undoubtedly a major draw for many tourists, but elsewhere can still be found the dusty temples, fragrant medicinal shops, and colonial buildings of old Singapore, neatly divided into historical enclaves.

Much of the city's fascination springs from its **multicultural population**: of the 3.87 million inhabitants, 77 percent are Chinese, whose shops, restaurants and temples are found across the island, fourteen percent are Malays, and seven percent are Indians, with the remaining two percent made up of other ethnic groups. This diverse ethnic mix textures the whole island, and often turns a ten-minute walk into what seems like a hop from one country to another. One intriguing by-product of this ethnic melting pot is **Singlish**, or Singaporean English, a patois which blends English with the speech patterns, exclamations and vocabulary of Chinese and Malay. Another is the amazing range of mouthwatering **cuisines** on offer in the city. Inevitably, the greatest emphasis is on Chinese, Malay and Indian foods, but your trip to Singapore will give you the opportunity to sample Thai, Vietnamese, and any number of other Asian specialities.

The entire state is compact enough to be explored exhaustively in just a few days. Forming the core of downtown Singapore is the **Colonial District**, around whose public buildings and lofty cathedral the island's British residents used to promenade. Each surrounding area has its own distinct flavour, ranging from the aromatic spice stores of **Little India**, to the tumbledown backstreets of **Chinatown**, where it's still possible to happen upon calligraphers and fortune tellers, or the **Arab Quarter**, whose cluttered stores sell fine cloths and silks. **North** of the city, you'll find the country's two **nature reserves** – Bukit Timah Nature Reserve and the Central Catchment Area – and the splendid **Singapore Zoological Gardens**. In the **west** of the island, the East meets Disneyworld at **Haw Par Villas**; while the **east coast** features good seafood restaurants, set behind long stretches of sandy beach. In addition, over fifty islands and islets lie within Singaporean waters, all of which can be reached with varying degrees of ease. The best day-trips, however, are to **Sentosa**, the island amusement arcade which is linked to the south coast by a short causeway (and cable car), and to **Pulau Ubin**, off the east coast, whose inhabitants continue to live a kampung life long since eradicated from the mainland.

When to visit

Singapore is just 136km north of the equator, which means that you should be prepared for a hot and sticky time whenever you go. **Temperatures** are uniformly high throughout the year, but it's the region's humidity levels which make the heat really uncomfortable – a good downpour is the only thing that really clears the air. Be prepared for **rain** during your stay – November and December are

	C°		RAINFALL
	AVERAGE DAILY		AVERAGE MONTHLY
	MAX	MIN	MM
Jan	31	21	146
Feb	32	22	155
March	32	23	182
April	32	23	223
May	32	23	228
June	32	23	151
July	31	22	170
Aug	31	22	163
Sept	31	22	200
Oct	31	22	199
Nov	31	22	255
Dec	30	22	258

usually the coolest, and the wettest, months, but rain can fall all year round. On average, June, July and August record the lowest annual rainfall. Otherwise, the only other consideration is the possibility of coinciding with one of the island's many **festivals** (see p.237), of which the liveliest and most extensive is Chinese New Year in January/February.

BASICS

Getting there from Britain and Ireland

There are regular daily flights to Singapore from Britain and connecting flights from Ireland to all major British airports. It's a highly competitive route and the cheapest return tickets, available through discount agents, can be as low as £400 in the low season (Jan–June).

If you want to see more of Southeast Asia on your trip to Singapore you could consider buying an **open-jaw** ticket which allows you, for example, to fly into Bangkok, travel overland to Singapore and then fly home from there. There's also the option of a **round-the-world ticket** (RTW), if Singapore is just one stop on a longer itinerary. Additionally, an increasing number of **package holidays** are available, including fly-drive deals and city breaks. Although usually not the cheapest way of travelling, these can be worthwhile if your time is limited.

The Singapore Tourism Board (STB) is based at First floor, Carrington House, 126–130 Regent St, London W1R 5FE
℡ 020/7437 0033; ⓦ www.newasia-singapore.com

ROUTES AND FARES

The quickest and most comfortable way to reach Singapore from Britain is to fly **nonstop** with Singapore Airlines, British Airways, Royal Brunei or Qantas from London Heathrow (SIA also from Manchester) – a journey time of some thirteen hours. Many other scheduled airlines offer **indirect** flights, which typically touch down at their own national hubs, and maybe elsewhere, en route to the final destination. These flights take longer (17–22 hours) but work out far cheaper. Add-on costs from other British airports are around £60 return to London.

There are no nonstop flights from **Ireland** to Singapore; airlines will quote you through-fares via British airports. Alternatively, you could take advantage of the cheap air fares between Ireland and Britain and pick up an onward flight from London with another airline.

Discounted **fares** start from around £520 for nonstop flights and £400 for indirect in low season, but you should be prepared to add to that a couple of hundred pounds in the high-season months of July, August and December. The cheapest tickets will be with airlines such as Air India (via Delhi), KLM (via Amsterdam), Finnair (via Helsinki), Pakistan International Airlines (via Karachi), Turkish Airlines (via Istanbul), Thai International (via Bangkok), Gulf Air (via Bahrain), Kuwait Airways, or Aeroflot (via Moscow and Dubai).

There's a list of reliable **discount flight agents** on p.6, or consult the ads in the national weekend papers (particularly the *Guardian, Daily Telegraph, Observer* and *Sunday Times*), London's *Evening Standard* newspaper or *Time Out* magazine, or major regional newspapers and listings magazines.

If you are a **student** or **under 26**, you may be able to get further discounts on flight prices – consult usit Campus or STA (see p.6) in the first instance – but for this part of the world, there's little difference between a youth fare and a regular discounted one.

Increasingly you'll find good-value flights on the **Internet**: *www.lastminute.com*, *www.cheapflights.co.uk* and *www.ebookers.com* are worth checking out for special offers.

AIRLINES AND DISCOUNT FLIGHT AGENTS

Airlines

Aer Lingus ☎ 0645/737 747;
Ⓦ *www.aerlingus.ie*

Aeroflot ☎ 020/7355 2233;
Ⓦ *www.aeroflot.com*

Air India ☎ 020/8560 9996;
Ⓦ *www.airindia.com*

British Airways
☎ 0345/222111, Dublin
☎ 1800/626 747;
Ⓦ *www.british-airways.com*

British Midland
☎ 0870/607 0555;
Ⓦ *www.iflybritishmidland.com*

Finnair ☎ 020/7408 1222;
Ⓦ *www.finnair.com*

Gulf Air ☎ 020/7408 1717;
Ⓦ *www.gulfairco.com*

KLM ☎ 08705/074 074;
Ⓦ *www.klm.com*

Kuwait Airways
☎ 020/7412 0006;
Ⓦ *www.kuwait-airways.com*

Malaysia Airlines (MAS)
☎ 0870/607 9090;
Ⓦ *www.mas.com.my*

Pakistan International Airlines
☎ 020/7499 5500;
Ⓦ *www.fly-pia.com*

Qantas ☎ 0345/747767;
Ⓦ *www.qantas.com.au*

Royal Brunei Airlines
☎ 020/7584 6660;
Ⓦ *www.bruneiair.com*

Ryanair ☎ 0870/156 9569,
Dublin ☎ 01/609 7800;
Ⓦ *www.ryanair.com*

Singapore Airlines
☎ 0870/608 8886;
Ⓦ *www.singaporeair.com*

Sri Lankan ☎ 020/8759 4048

Thai International ☎ 0870/606 0911; Ⓦ *www.thaiair.com*

Turkish Airlines
☎ 020/7766 9300;
Ⓦ *www.turkishairlines.com*

Discount flight agents

Bridge the World
☎ 020/7911 0900.

Flightbookers
☎ 020/7757 2444.

Joe Walsh Tours
Dublin ☎ 01/671 8751;
Cork ☎ 021/277 959.

North South Travel
☎ 01245/608 291.

STA Travel ☎ 020/7361 6262;
Ⓦ www.statravel.co.uk

Trailfinders
London ☎ 020/7938 3366,
Dublin ☎ 01/677 7888;
Ⓦ www.trailfinders.co.uk

Travel Bag ☎ 020/7287 5558.

Travel Bug
London ☎ 020 7835 2000,
Manchester ☎ 0161/721
4000; Ⓦ www.flynow.com

usit Campus ☎ 0870/240 1010;
Ⓦ www.usitcampus.co.uk

usit Now
Belfast ☎ 028/9032 4073,
Dublin ☎ 01/602 1600;
Ⓦ www.usitnow.ie

ROUND THE WORLD AND OPEN-JAW TICKETS

The cheapest **round-the-world tickets** start from around £750 in low season (departing Jan–June & Sept to early Dec). A typical one-year open ticket would depart from and return to London, taking in Singapore, Bangkok, Bali, Sydney, Auckland, Tahiti, Los Angeles and New York, allowing you to cover the Singapore–Bangkok and Los Angeles–New York legs overland. STA, usit Campus and Trailfinders all specialize in RTW tickets.

Open-jaw tickets which allow you to fly into one airport and out of another without having to retrace your steps, are calculated in different ways by different airlines, but you can expect to pay at least the highest of the two return fares you are combining. Flying into Bangkok and out of Singapore, reckon on around £500, although it's well worth shopping around for deals on these tickets. For details of the overland sector see "Getting there from Southeast Asia", p.21.

GETTING THERE FROM BRITAIN AND IRELAND

PACKAGES AND ORGANIZED TOURS

There are many **package holidays** and **organized tours** available to Singapore, and the main operators are listed below; all also offer trips further afield into Malaysia and beyond. For **city breaks**, five nights in Singapore, including flights but with room-only accommodation in a three-star hotel, cost around £700 (£900 in high season), rising to £900–1100 for two weeks.

Specialist operators can also arrange itineraries which include a ride on the extremely swish **Eastern & Oriental Express** train between Singapore and Bangkok (see box on p.22 for more details).

Several companies offer **fly-drive packages** to Singapore and into Malaysia, offering different levels of organization along the way. A standard fourteen-day route, starting in Singapore and visiting Melaka, Kuala Lumpur, the Cameron Highlands, Penang, Kota Bharu and Kuantan, costs £1000–1200, including return flight, the use of a small car and accommodation in three-star hotels.

SPECIALIST TOUR OPERATORS

Abercrombie & Kent Travel
ℑ020/7730 9600;
ⓌWwww.abercrombiekent.com
Top of the range tailor-made tours.

Bales Worldwide
ℑ01306/885991;
ⓌWwww.balesworldwide.com
Tailor-made trips

incorporating the Eastern & Oriental train journey from Singapore to Bangkok.

British Airways Holidays
ℑ01293/723710.
Five-night city breaks starting from £700.

Eastern & Oriental Express
ℑ020/7928 6000.

Tours including one of the most exclusive train journeys in the world.

Kuoni Travel ☏ 01306/740500.
Tailor-made tours.

Magic of the Orient
☏ 01293/537700.

Specialists in tailor-made tours starting at £640 for a five-night city break.

Thomas Cook Holidays
☏ 01733/563200.
Good selection of fly-drive holidays and city breaks.

Getting there from the USA and Canada

S
ingapore is one of the world's great air hubs, with competition among a large number of carriers making it one of the cheapest Southeast Asian destinations to reach **from North America**.

Singapore is roughly halfway around the world from the **east coast** of the USA, which means that whether you plan on flying east or west you're going to have a long flight with at least one stopover. The eastbound (transatlantic) route is more direct and a bit faster – about 21 hours' total travel time – which makes it cheaper than flying west. From the **west coast**, it's faster and cheaper to head west (over the Pacific) – Los Angeles to Singapore takes as little as nineteen hours – although flying via Europe may suit your itinerary better and doesn't cost much more.

Air fares from North America to Southeast Asia are highest from around early June to late August, and again from early December to early January. All other times are considered low season. The price difference between high season and low season is only about $200 on a typical round-trip fare, but bear in mind that you will have to make your reservation further in advance during the high season. Remember that flying on weekends ordinarily adds about $100 to the round-trip fare; price ranges quoted below assume midweek travel.

Local **travel agents** should be able to access airlines' up-to-the-minute fares, although in practice they may not have time to thoroughly research all the possibilities; occasionally you'll turn up better deals by calling the **airlines** direct (be sure to ask about seasonal promotions).

Most consistently, your best bet will be to try specialist travel agents. These are the outfits you'll see advertising in the Sunday newspaper travel sections, and they come in several varieties. **Consolidators** buy up large blocks of tickets to sell on at a discount. They don't normally impose advance purchase requirements (although in busy periods you'll want to book ahead to be sure of getting a seat), but they often charge very stiff fees for date changes; note also that airlines generally won't alter tickets after they've gone to a consolidator, so you can only make changes through the consolidator. **Discount agents** also deal in blocks of tickets off-loaded by the airlines, and typically offer a range of other travel-related services such as insurance, youth and student ID cards, car rentals, tours and the like. They tend to be most worthwhile to students and under–26s. Discount **travel clubs**, offering money off air tickets, car rental and the like, are an option if you travel a lot. Most charge annual membership fees. The **Internet** is also a useful resource. Try Ⓦ *www.cheaptickets.com* or Ⓦ *www.lastminute.com* for deals, last minute specials or just to compare prices.

Always be aware that the pool of travel companies is swimming with sharks – never deal with a company that demands cash upfront or refuses to accept payment by credit card.

The Singapore Tourism Board (STB) has offices in the USA at Twelfth floor, 590 Fifth Ave, New York, NY 10036 Ⓣ 212/302-4861; Two Prudential Plaza, 180 N Stetson Ave, Suite 2615, Chicago, IL 60601 Ⓣ 312/938-1888; 8484 Wiltshire Blvd, Suite 510, Beverly Hills, CA 90211 Ⓣ 323/852-1901; and in Canada at 2 Bloor St West, Suite 404, Toronto, Ontario M4W 3E2 Ⓣ 416/363-8898; Ⓦ *www.singapore-usa.com*

ROUTES AND FARES

Singapore Airlines offers the most frequent departures, with **direct flights** originating in New York (eastbound via Frankfurt or Amsterdam), Los Angeles/San Francisco (westbound via Tokyo, Taipei or Hong Kong) and Vancouver (westbound via Seoul). However, **indirect flights** on other airlines – or a combination of airlines – might not add much time to your journey, and if you go through a consolidator you might be able to get a free stopover each way. The airlines that fly to Singapore are too numerous to list here: see opposite for some of the major carriers.

If you're planning to travel in several Asian countries, consider making Hong Kong or Bangkok your first stop;

you'll save about $200 over the fare to Singapore and from Bangkok you can travel overland by train to Singapore – see "Getting There From Southeast Asia" (p.21).

From **New York**, you'll pay $900 direct round-trip in the low season, $1100 in the high season; from **Washington**, **Miami** or **Chicago**, $1000/$1250; from **Houston**, $950/$1100; from **Los Angeles**, **San Francisco** or **Seattle**, $800/$1000; from **Toronto** or **Montréal**, CDN$2200/$2400; and from **Vancouver**, CDN$2000/$2300.

AIRLINES AND FLIGHT AGENTS

Airlines

Air Canada ☎1-888/247-2262;
Ⓦwww.aircanada.ca

Air France
USA ☎1-800/237-2747,
Canada ☎1-800/667-2747;
Ⓦwww.airfrance.fr

British Airways
USA ☎1-800/247-9297,
Canada ☎1-800/668-1059;
Ⓦwww.british-airways.com

Canadian Airlines
Canada ☎1-800/665-1177,
USA ☎1-800/426-7000;
Ⓦwww.cdnair.ca

Cathay Pacific
USA ☎1-800/233-2742,
Canada ☎1-800/555-1212;
Ⓦwww.cathay-usa.com

Finnair ☎1-800/950-5000;
Ⓦwww.finnair.com

ËVA Airlines ☎1-800/695-1188; Ⓦwww.evaair.com

Japan Air Lines
☎1-800/525-3663;
Ⓦwww.japanair.com

KLM/Northwest
USA ☎1-800/374-7747,
Canada ☎1-800/361-5073;
Ⓦwww.klm.com

Korean Airlines ☎1-800/348-5000; Ⓦwww.koreanair.com

Malaysia Airlines
☎1-800/552-9264;
Ⓦwww.malaysiaair.com

Philippines Airlines
☎1-800/435-9725;
Ⓦwww.philippineair.com

GETTING THERE FROM THE USA AND CANADA

PIA (Pakistan International Airlines)
☎1-800/221-2552;
🖳www.fly-pia.com

Singapore Airlines
☎1-800/742-3333;
🖳www.singaporeair.com

Thai International
USA ☎1-800/426-5204,
Canada ☎1-800/668-8103;
🖳www.thaiair.com

United Airlines
☎1-800/538-2929;
🖳www.ual.com

Agents, consolidators and travel clubs

Air Brokers International San
Francisco ☎1-800/883-3273;
🖳www.airbrokers.com

Council Travel New York
☎1-800/226-8624;
🖳www.counciltravel.com

Educational Travel Center
Madison, WI
☎1-800/747-5551 or
☎608/256-5551;
🖳www.edtrav.com

Flight Centre Vancouver, BC
☎1-877/321-4255;
🖳www.flightcentre.com

Gateway Express Edina, MN
☎612/831-3525;
🖳www.gatewayexpress.com

High Adventure Travel Inc.
San Francisco ☎1-800/350-
0637 or 415/912-5600;
🖳www.airtreks.com

Last-Minute Travel Club
Woburn, MA
☎1-800/LAST-MIN;
🖳www.lastminutetravel.com

Moment's Notice Brooklyn, NY
☎212/486-0500;
🖳www.moments-notice.com

Overseas Tours Millbrae, CA
☎1-800/323-8777.

STA Travel New York
☎1-800/777-0112;
🖳www.sta.com

Travel CUTS Toronto
☎1-800/667-2887 or 416/979-
2406; 🖳www.travelcuts.com

Worldtek Travel New Haven,
CT ☎1-800/243-1723;
🖳www.worldtek.com

RTW TICKETS AND COURIER FLIGHTS

If Singapore is only one stop on a longer journey, you might want to consider buying a **round-the-world ticket (RTW)**. Some travel agents can sell you an "off-the-shelf"

RTW ticket that will have you touching down in about half a dozen cities (Singapore is on many itineraries); these tickets can also be tailored to your needs but are apt to be more expensive. Plan for $1380 for a RTW ticket travelling for example New York–Hong Kong–Singapore–(overland on your own)–Bangkok–Delhi–London–New York.

Most airlines operating in this part of the world offer so-called **Circle Pacific** fares, allowing four (or sometimes more) stopovers in the course of a round trip between North America and Asia or Australasia. However, fares run to around $1800 – not very economical unless you have some really obscure stopovers in mind, and plan to travel right across Australia as well. Otherwise, you'll probably find it's cheaper to have a discount travel agent put together a ticket with your intended stops.

A further possibility is a **courier flight**, although the hit-or-miss nature of these makes them most suitable for the single traveller with a very flexible schedule. Courier flights to Singapore come up regularly, but most departures are from Los Angeles – figure on paying around $300, maybe less if it's a last-minute deal. Contact the Air Courier Association (☎1-800/282-1202), or Now Voyager (☎212/431-1616).

PACKAGES AND ORGANIZED TOURS

Packages to Singapore can include five-star city breaks, sightseeing excursions and opulent splendour aboard the Eastern & Oriental Express train. Inevitably, these packaged journeys are more expensive and less spontaneous than they would be if done independently, but for the traveller with more money than time they offer a convenient and hassle-free experience.

The **Eastern & Oriental train journey** between Bangkok and Singapore (see box on p.22 for more information) is the ultimate in luxury: tours start at $3600 and invariably throw in several days' worth of side trips along with the two-night train journey. **Fly-drive** packages, starting at around $1800, include neighbouring Malaysia and allow you to keep costs down by giving you more independence.

Note that your local travel agent should be able to book any tour for you at no additional cost. For a list of North American tour companies, see the box below.

NORTH AMERICAN TOUR OPERATORS

Abercrombie & Kent 1520 Kensington Rd, Oak Brook, IL 60521 ☎ 1-800/323-7308; Ⓦ www.abercrombiekent.com
Deluxe tours built around the Eastern & Oriental Express.

Adventures Abroad Suite 2148-20800, Westminster Highway, Richmond, BC, Canada V6V 2W3 ☎1-800/665-3998; Ⓦ www.adventures-abroad .com
Small-group adventure tours to Singapore and other spots in Southeast Asia.

Asian Pacific Holidays 90101 Reseda Blvd, Suite 227, North Ridge, CA 91324 ☎ 1-800/825-1680; Ⓦ www.asianpacificholidays .com

Off-the-beaten-path tours throughout Southeast Asia

Japan & Orient Tours 3131 Camino del Rio North, Suite 1080, San Diego, CA 92108 ☎ 1-800/377-1080; Ⓦ www.jot.com
City breaks, fly-drives, Eastern & Oriental Express.

Pacific Bestour 228 River Vale Rd, River Vale, NJ 07675; ☎ 1-800/688-3288; Ⓦ www.bestour.com
City breaks, Eastern & Oriental Express.

TBI Tours 53 Summer St, Keene, NH 03431 ☎ 1-800/221-2216; Ⓦ www.generaltours.com
Offers a variety of packages in Singapore.

GETTING THERE FROM THE USA AND CANADA

Vacationland 150 Post St,
Suite 680, San Francisco, CA
94108
℡ 1-800/245-0050;
Ⓦ www.vacation-land.com

Extensive range of city
breaks, fly-drives, regional
tours, sightseeing add-ons,
plus golf itineraries.

Getting there from Australia and New Zealand

Singapore is not only one of the main Southeast Asian gateways but also one of the main stops on the way from Australasia to Europe, so there are plenty of airlines and routes to choose from. Direct flights are not always the cheapest and it's well worth taking advantage of a **stopover** en route – Asian airlines fly via their home base giving you a perfect opportunity to explore a bit more of the area. If you want to visit Singapore as part of a wider trip there are several good-value options worth considering such as: an **open-jaw ticket** that allows you to fly you into one country and out of another, and travel overland in between; multi-stop **Circle Asia** fares; **Round-the-World** (RTW) tickets; or flying somewhere else first – like Thailand, Malaysia or Indonesia – and continuing **overland** from there. For example, you could take the train from Malaysia (Kuala Lumpur to Singapore only takes six hours – see "Getting there from Southeast Asia", p.21 for details).

The Singapore Tourism Board (STB) has offices in Australia at Eighth floor, St Georges Court, 16 St Georges Terrace, Perth, WA 6000 ⓣ 09/3235 8578; and Level 11, AWA Building, 47 York St, Sydney, NSW 2000 ⓣ 02/9290 2888; and in New Zealand at Third floor, 43 High St, Auckland ⓣ 09/3581191; ⓦ *www.newasia-singapore.com*

ROUTES AND FARES

Tickets purchased direct from the airlines are usually expensive – more than likely you'll be quoted the published rate. **Fares** to Southeast Asian destinations are very competitive so whatever kind of ticket you're after it's best to shop around. The flight agents listed on p.18 can fill you in on all the latest deals and any special limited offers. If you're a student or under 26, you may be able to get a discounted fare; STA is a good place to start. Fares are seasonally rated, with prices for flights usually higher during Christmas and New Year and mid-year periods; generally high season is mid-May to end-Aug and Dec to mid-Jan, shoulder March to mid-May and Sept to mid-October and low the rest of the year – with a difference of around A/NZ$200 between each. Airfares from east coast Australian gateways are all pretty much the same (common rated on most airlines, with Ansett and Qantas providing a shuttle service to the point of departure); Perth and Darwin are A$100–200 cheaper. From New Zealand you can expect to pay NZ$150–300 more from Christchurch and Wellington than from Auckland.

Malaysian Airlines (MAS), Singapore Airlines, Royal Brunei, Qantas, Ansett and Garuda all have regular services **from Australia** to Singapore. On the whole, fares to Singapore from Brisbane, Sydney or Melbourne and Cairns are roughly between A$599 low season and A$799 high season for a single and A$899–1199 for a return depending on which airline you choose. The real bargains are often with Middle Eastern airlines keen to fill flights for the leg to Singapore before they head for home; Egypt Air, for example, flies twice a week from Sydney for $A589.

From New Zealand, Air New Zealand, British Airways, Garuda, Qantas and Singapore Airlines and Malaysian, among others, fly to Singapore and Kuala Lumpur, with fares starting at NZ$799 low season and NZ$1099 high season for a single and NZ$1299–1499 for a return.

AIRLINES AND FLIGHT AGENTS

Airlines

Air New Zealand Australia
ⓣ 13/2476, New Zealand
ⓣ 0800/737 000 or 09/357 3000; ⓦ www.airnz.co.nz

Ansett Australia Australia
ⓣ 13/1414 or 02/9352 6444, New Zealand ⓣ 09/379 6409; ⓦ www.ansett.com.au

British Airways Australia
ⓣ 02/8904 8800, New Zealand
ⓣ 09/356 8690; ⓦ www.british-airways.com

Egypt Air Australia
ⓣ 02/92326677; ⓦ www.egyptair.com
No NZ office.

Garuda Australia ⓣ 1300/365 330, New Zealand ⓣ 09/366 1855 or 0800/128 510.

Malaysia Airlines Australia ⓣ 13/2627, New Zealand ⓣ 09/373 2741 or 008/657 472; ⓦ *www.malaysiaairlines.co.my*

Merpati Australia ⓣ 08/8981 5229. No NZ office.

Qantas Australia ⓣ 13/1313, New Zealand ⓣ 09/357 8900 or 0800/808 767; ⓦ *www.qantas.com.au*

Royal Brunei Airlines Australia ⓣ 07/3221 7757; ⓦ *www.bruneiair.com* No NZ office.

Singapore Airlines Australia ⓣ 13/1011, New Zealand ⓣ 09/303 2129 or ⓣ 800/808 909; ⓦ *www.singaporeair.com*

Thai International Australia ⓣ 1300/651 960, New Zealand ⓣ 09/377 3886; ⓦ *www.thaiair.com*

Discount flight agents

Anywhere Travel Sydney ⓣ 02/9663 0411; ⓔ *anywhere@ozemail.com.au*

Budget Travel, Auckland ⓣ 09/366 0061 or 0800/808 040.

Destinations Unlimited Auckland ⓣ 09/373 4033.

Flight Centres Australia ⓣ 02/9235 3522, New Zealand ⓣ 09/358 4310); ⓦ *www.flightcentre.com.au*

Northern Gateway Darwin ⓣ 08/8941 1394; ⓔ *oztravel@norgate.com.au*

STA Travel Australia ⓣ 13/1776, fastfare telesales ⓣ 1300/360 960, New Zealand ⓣ 09/309 0458, fastfare telesales ⓣ 09/366 6673; ⓦ *www.statravel.com.au* ⓔ *traveller@statravelaus .com.au*

Student Uni Travel Sydney ⓣ 02/9232 8444; ⓦ *www.sydney@backpackers .net*

Thomas Cook, Australia ⓣ 02/9231 2877, direct telesales ⓣ 1800/801 002, New Zealand ⓣ 09/379 3920; ⓦ *www.thomascook.com.au*

Trailfinders Sydney ⓣ 02/9247 7666.

Travel.com.au Sydney ⓣ 02/9262 3555; ⓦ *www.travel.com.au*

usit Beyond Auckland ⓣ 09/379 4224 or 0800/788 336.

PACKAGES AND ORGANIZED TOURS

Package holidays to Singapore are numerous and good value, especially if you just want a relaxing break around the pool. As well as flights and accommodation, most companies also offer a range of itineraries that take in the major sights and activities. Bookings are usually made through travel agents who carry a wide selection of brochures for you to choose from. An organized tour is worth considering if you're after a more energetic holiday, have ambitious sightseeing plans and limited time, are uneasy with the language and customs or just don't like travelling alone.

City stays, **fly-drive** options and **coach tours** are offered by a whole host of operators through your travel agent, including Ansett Australia Holidays, Creative Tours, Asian Explorer Holidays, Qantas Holidays, Singapore Asian Affair Holidays and Venture Holidays; most can also arrange add-on trips to resort islands, cruises from Singapore, air passes, rail travel and can book accommodation in regional Malaysia. Sample city-break prices are four nights in Singapore from A$999/NZ$1150, with the exact price depending on the level of accommodation chosen. Package holidays departing from Perth or Darwin, where available, generally cost about A$200 less per person. Extended journeys from Singapore cater to all tastes – from those in search of thrills and adventure to those who simply prefer to tour in a group. Most of the specialists listed below can organize activities that may be difficult to arrange yourself like whitewater rafting, diving, cycling and trekking.

Most organized tours don't include air fares from Australasia.

SPECIALIST TOUR OPERATORS

Abercrombie & Kent
Melbourne ☎03/9699 9766 or 1800/331 429 (also Sydney & Brisbane),
Auckland ☎09/579 3369;
Ⓦ*www.abercrombiekent.com*
Upmarket tours of Southeast Asia including travel on the Eastern & Oriental Express (see p.22).

Adventure Specialists Sydney ☎02/9261 2927.
Overland and adventure tour agent companies including Intrepid and Peregrine.

The Adventure Travel Company Auckland ☎09/379 9755.
One-stop shop for adventure travel; agents for Intrepid, Peregrine, and a host of others.

Adventure World Sydney ☎02/9956 7766 or 1800/221 931,
Auckland ☎09/524 5118;
Ⓦ*www.adventureworld.com.au*
Agents for a vast array of international adventure travel companies.

Always Padi Travel Sydney ☎1800/259 297;
Ⓦ*www.padi.com*
All-inclusive dive package holidays to prime dive sites in the region.

Intrepid Adventure Travel
Melbourne ☎1300/360 667;
Ⓔ*info@intrepidtravel.com.au*
Small-group tours with the emphasis on cross-cultural contact and low-impact tourism.

Peregrine Adventures
Melbourne ☎03/9662 2700;
Ⓦ*www.peregrine.net.au*
Small-group adventure travel company offering a range of graded trips.

San Michele Travel Sydney ☎02/9299 1111 or ☎1800/222 244.
Customized rail tours throughout Southeast Asia, as well as city breaks, sightseeing trips and cruises out of Singapore.

Silke's Travel Sydney ☎1800/807 303, 1800/807 860, 02/9380 5835 or 02/9380 6244; Ⓦ*www.silkes.com.au*
Specially tailored packages for gay and lesbian travellers.

Getting there from Southeast Asia

f you are not too restricted by time, it can work out cheaper to get a flight to another Southeast Asian city and then continue your journey from there. Flights to **Bangkok** can often be particularly good value, and from there, as well as from **Jakarta** and **Hong Kong**, there are frequent daily flights to Singapore. It's obviously longer, but cheaper, to travel overland by train from Bangkok – the main line runs down the west coast of Malaysia and ends in Singapore.

FROM THAILAND

The cheapest way of getting to Singapore from Thailand is to catch the bus from Bangkok, though taking a train is a more comfortable option. Trains depart from Bangkok's Hualamphong station (book at least a day in advance at the station ticket office) four times a day for Hat Yai, where the line divides. One daily train goes south via the Malaysian border town of Padang Besar to Butterworth,

THE EASTERN & ORIENTAL EXPRESS

If you've got money to burn, there's no more luxurious way to cover the 1900km between Bangkok and Singapore than on the sumptuous **Eastern & Oriental Express**, a fairy-tale trip that unashamedly re-creates the pampered days of the region's colonial past. Departing once or twice weekly from Bangkok (and Singapore), the Express takes 41 hours to wend its unhurried way between the two cities, stopping at Butterworth, Ipoh and KL en route. At Butterworth, passengers disembark for a whistle-stop tour of Penang by bus and trishaw. On board, guests enjoy breakfast in bed, lunch, tea and dinner, all served by attentive Thai and Malaysian staff in traditional or period garb. There are two bars (one in the observation carriage at the rear of the train) as well as two luxurious restaurant cars serving Western and Oriental cuisine of a high standard; fortune-tellers, Chinese opera singers and musicians keep you entertained. Many guests dress up lavishly for the occasion so be sure to have smart clothes with you or you'll feel decidedly uncomfortable.

The two-night trip costs from US$1350 per person. Bookings can be made in Bangkok through Sea Tours Co. Ltd, c/o *Tong Poon Hotel*, 130 Rong Muang, Soi 4, Rama VI Rd (℡ 662/2468661); in Singapore at E&O Services, 32-01/3 Shaw Towers, 100 Beach Road (℡ 3223500); or contact the specialist tour operators on p.7, p.14 and p.20 before leaving home.

Kuala Lumpur and Singapore in 28 hours (£60/US$90 one-way).

There are also three daily flights from Bangkok on Thai Airways to Singapore (£250/US$375). From Phuket, there's one flight daily (£160/US$240), and also one daily from Hat Yai (£150/US$225).

Tickets are available from travel agents in Bangkok; students and under-26s will probably be able to undercut these prices by booking through STA, 14th floor, Wall Street Tower, 33 Suriwong Rd (☏ 02/236 0262).

FROM INDONESIA

There are daily Garuda flights from Jakarta to Singapore (£76/US$114 one-way; 3hr). From other Indonesian regions you'll need to take an internal flight to Jakarta first. In addition, ferries run through the day from Pulau Batam in the Riau archipelago (accessible by plane or boat from Sumatra or Jakarta) to Singapore – a thirty-minute trip; £8/US$12).

FROM MALAYSIA

Regular flights connect the major Malaysian airports with Singapore (£65/US$98 from KL with MAS), and there are four trains a day from Kuala Lumpur. Buses link Singapore with all large towns and cities in peninsular Malaysia and represent the most affordable means of reaching the city-state. From KL expect to pay the equivalent of £11/US$16.

GETTING THERE FROM SOUTHEAST ASIA

Visas and red tape

British citizens, and those of the Republic of Ireland, the United States, Canada, Australia and New Zealand, don't need a **visa** to enter Singapore. Regulations change from time to time, though, so check with the embassy before departure. You'll normally be stamped in for fourteen days, although you can be given one month on request. Extending your stay for up to three months is perfectly possible, at the discretion of the Immigration Department (see p.263); extensions beyond three months are not unknown, but are less common. If you have any problems with extending your stay, there's always the option of taking a bus up to Johor Bahru, across the border in Malaysia, and then coming back in again.

CUSTOMS

Upon entry from anywhere other than Malaysia you can bring into Singapore one litre each of spirits, wine and beer duty-free; duty is payable on all tobacco. There are no restrictions if you're coming from Malaysia.

Many goods for sale in Singapore are duty-free, including electronic and electrical items, cosmetics, cameras, clocks, watches, jewellery, and precious stones and metals, but you should bear in mind how much you are allowed to take home with you free of charge.

British customs allow £136 worth of goods to be brought into the country **duty-free**. Above this, duty is calculated according to the kind of goods. **Americans** can take home up to $400 worth of goods purchased overseas duty-free. If you carry back between $400 and $1000 worth of stuff you'll have to pay 10 percent of the value in duty; above $1000, the duty depends on the items. Duty is not payable on antiques or original works of art. You can also send home packages from abroad duty-free if they're valued at less than $50. **Canadians** are exempt from paying duty on up to CDN$300 worth of goods after spending seven days out of the country (or $100-worth after a trip lasting 2–6 days). Travellers returning to **Australia** can bring in $400 worth of gifts duty-free (for under-18s, this is reduced to $200), not including personal purchases such as clothing which don't incur duty. **New Zealand** permits $700 worth of gifts. In both countries, certain goods must be declared for inspection and may be prohibited: these include cordless phones purchased overseas (some Asian brands are incompatible with local systems), artefacts containing wood or other plant material (wooden carvings, spears, ornamental knives, skins, seeds, etc), and foodstuffs.

SINGAPOREAN EMBASSIES AND CONSULATES ABROAD

Australia 17 Forster Crescent, Yarralumla, Canberra, ACT 2600 ☏06/273 3944.

Canada Suite 1305, 999 Hastings St, Vancouver, BC V6C 2W2 ☏604/669-5115.

Indonesia Block X/4 Kav No. 2, Jalan H.R. Rasuna Said Kuningan, Jakarta 12950 ☏021/520 1489.

Ireland *No office, contact London.*

VISAS AND RED TAPE

Malaysia 209 Jalan Tun Razak,
Kuala Lumpur 50400
℡ 03/261 6277.
New Zealand 17 Kabul St,
Khandallah, Wellington, PO
Box 13-140 ℡ 04/479 2076.
UK 9 Wilton Cres, London
SW1X 8SA ℡ 020/7235 8315.

USA 3501 International Plaza
NW, Washington, DC 20008
℡ 202/537-3100; 2424 SE
Bristol, Suite 320, Santa Ana
Heights, CA 92707
℡ 714/476-2330.

Health

The levels of **hygiene** and **medical care** in Singapore
are higher than in much of the rest of Southeast
Asia, and with any luck, the most serious thing
you'll go down with is a cold or an upset stomach. **Tap
water** is drinkable throughout the island and all food for
public consumption is prepared to exacting standards.
Drinking excessive amounts of alcohol is a more likely
cause of diarrhoea than the food you may eat, as in a tropical climate your tolerance level is likely to be much lower
than it would be at home.

Medical services are excellent, with staff almost everywhere speaking good English and using up-to-date tech-

niques. **Pharmacies** are well stocked with familiar brand-name drugs; pharmacists can also recommend products for skin complaints or simple stomach problems, though if you're in any doubt, it always pays to get a proper diagnosis. Opening hours are usually Monday to Saturday 9.30am–7pm. **Private clinics** are found throughout the city – your hotel or the local tourist office will be able to recommend a good English-speaking doctor. A visit costs around $10–20, not including the cost of any prescribed medication. Don't forget to keep any receipts for insurance claim purposes.

For a list of hospitals and clinics in Singapore, turn to Directory, p.263. In a medical emergency, dial ☎ 995.

INOCULATIONS

There are no inoculations required for visiting Singapore, although the immigration authorities may require proof of a yellow fever vaccination (administered within the last ten years) if you're arriving from an endemic country.

However, it's a wise precaution to visit your doctor or local immunization clinic no later than four weeks before you leave to check that you are up to date with your polio, typhoid, tetanus and hepatitis A inoculations.

If you are travelling on from Singapore to other destinations in Southeast Asia, it is likely that you will require further protection, particularly against malaria. Singapore is malaria-free, but you must start taking any course of tablets one week before you plan to move on.

For inoculation advice in the **UK** call up the 24-hour MASTA Travellers Health Line (☎ 0891/224100). In the **US**, contact New York's Travelers Medical Center

HEALTH

(☎212/982–1600); in **Canada** contact the International Association for Medical Assistance to Travellers (☎519/836–0102). In **Australia** and **New Zealand**, contact your nearest vaccination centre.

Since there are no reciprocal health agreements between Singapore and any other country, it's essential to arrange travel insurance before you leave home, which will cover you for medical expenses incurred.

Money, banks and costs

S ingapore is one of the more **expensive** Asian cities, especially for accommodation. The city affords few savings for special groups – senior citizens do not get reductions, although an ISIC card might occasionally pay dividends for students. However, you will find that **bargaining** is a way of life throughout Singapore, especially when shopping or renting a room for the night – it's always worth trying to haggle, though note that you don't bargain for meals. Most tourist attractions offer discounted entrance fees for children.

CURRENCY

The currency is the Singapore dollar, written simply as $ and divided into 100 cents. Notes are issued in denominations of $1, $2, $5, $10, $20, $50, $100, $500, $1000 and $10,000; coins are in denominations of 1, 5, 10, 20 and 50 cents, and $1. The current exchange rate is around $2.50 to £1 and $1.65 to US$1. All prices given in the guide are in Singapore dollars, unless otherwise stated.

COSTS

If money is no object, you'll be able to take advantage of hotels, restaurants and shops as sumptuous as any in the world. On the other hand, with budget dormitory accommodation in plentiful supply, and both food and internal travel cheap in the extreme, you could survive on less than £10/US$16 a day. Upgrading your lodgings to a private room in a guesthouse, eating in a restaurant and having a beer or two gives a more realistic daily budget of £20/US$32 a day.

TRAVELLERS' CHEQUES AND CARDS

The safest and most convenient method of carrying your money is as **travellers' cheques** – either sterling or US dollar cheques are acceptable, though check with your bank for the latest advice before you buy. Available at a small commission from most banks, and from branches of

American Express and Thomas Cook, these can be cashed at Singaporean banks, licensed moneychangers and some hotels, upon presentation of a passport. Some shops will even accept travellers' cheques as cash.

Major **credit cards** are widely accepted in the more upmarket hotels, shops and restaurants throughout the region, but beware of the illegal surcharges levied by some establishments – check before you buy something with a card that there's no surcharge; if there is, contact your card company and tell them about it. Banks will often advance cash against major credit cards, and with American Express, Visa and Mastercard, it's possible to withdraw money from **automatic teller machines (ATMs)** in Singapore – get details from the companies direct before you leave home.

EMERGENCY CASH

Having **money wired** from home is never convenient or cheap. Western Union and MoneyGram both offer a reliable service using a combination of post offices, American Express offices and their own local offices. Charges depend on the destination and the amount being transferred. Funds should be available for collection within minutes of being sent.

Transferring money from bank to bank can take anything from two to seven working days and incurs a small fee in Singapore and a larger one back home. You'll need, first, to supply your home bank with details of the local branch to which the money should be sent, after which it'll be issued to you upon presentation of some form of ID.

BANKS

Singapore **banking hours** are generally Monday to Friday 10am–3pm and Saturday 9.30–11.30am, outside of which you'll have to go to a moneychanger in a shopping centre, or to a hotel. Major banks represented include the Overseas Union Bank, the United Overseas Bank, the OCBC, the Development Bank of Singapore, Standard Chartered Bank, Hong Kong Bank and Citibank. No black market operates in Singapore, nor are there any restrictions on carrying currency in or out of the state. This means that rates at moneychangers are as good as you'll find in the banks.

Opening hours, holidays and festivals

Shopping centres are open daily 10am–9.30pm, while offices generally work Monday to Friday 8.30am–5pm and sometimes on Saturday mornings (see opposite for banking hours). In general, Chinese temples open daily from 7am to around 6pm, Hindu temples 6am–noon and 5–9pm, and mosques 8.30am–noon and 2.30–4pm; specific opening hours for all temples and museums are given in the text.

As there are so many ethnic groups and religions found in Singapore, your visit could easily coincide with a **festival**. Bear in mind that the major festival periods will make traffic on the island heavier and crossing into Malaysia much slower. Over Ramadan in particular, transport networks and hotel capacity are stretched to their limits, as countless Muslims engage in *balik kampung* – the return to one's home village. Chinese New Year causes similar problems. Some, but by no means all, festivals are also public holidays (when everything closes); check the list below for those. For full details on Singapore's festivals see p.237.

Most of the festivals have **no fixed dates**, but change annually according to the lunar calendar; the Islamic calendar shifts forward relative to the Gregorian calendar by about ten days each year, so that, for example, a Muslim festival which happens in mid-April one year will be nearer the beginning of April the following year. We've listed rough timings, but for specific dates each year it's a good idea to check with the local tourist office.

PUBLIC HOLIDAYS

January 1 New Year's Day
January/February Chinese New Year (2 days)
February/March Hari Raya Haji
March/April Good Friday
May 1 Labour Day

May Vesak Day
August 9 National Day
November Deepavali
December Hari Raya Puasa
December 25 Christmas Day

THE GUIDE

THE GUIDE

Introducing the city

The diamond-shaped island of **Singapore** is 42km from east to west at its widest points, 23km from north to south, and linked to **Malaysia** by two causeways. Ever since Sir Stamford Raffles first landed on its northern bank in 1819, the area around the Singapore River, which strikes into the heart of the island from the south coast, has formed the hub of the city.

Singapore's **central** or **downtown districts** lie within a three-kilometre radius of the mouth of the river. Although buses do run between these districts (see bus routes information on p.47), you might prefer to explore the whole central region on foot. You'll need at least two days to do justice to the historic enclaves, and experiencing Singapore's commercial mecca, Orchard Road, can occupy several days. Bear in mind that you are in the tropics: apply sun screen and stay out of the midday sun. And beware, strolling through the remaining pockets of old Singapore entails negotiating uneven five-foot ways (the covered pavements that front Singapore's old shophouses) and yawning storm drains.

The telephone code for Singapore is 65.

At the very heart of the city, on the north bank, the **Colonial District** has a cluster of buildings that recall the days of early British rule: Parliament House, the Cathedral, the Supreme Court, the Cricket Club and, most famously, **Raffles Hotel**. Moving west, **Fort Canning Park** has several attractions, including the **Singapore History Museum**. From here, it's a five-minute stroll to the eastern end of **Orchard Road**, the main shopping area in the city. North from Fort Canning Park, you soon enter **Little India**, whose main drag, Serangoon Road, is around fifteen minutes' walk from Raffles Hotel. Ten minutes southeast of Little India, Singapore's traditional **Arab Quarter** sits at the intersection of North Bridge Road and Arab Street. South, across the river, the monolithic towers of the **Financial District** cast long shadows over **Chinatown**, whose rows of shophouses stretch for around a kilometre, as far as Cantonment Road.

Downtown Singapore is probably where you'll spend most of your time, but the rest of the island has its attractions too. The super-efficient bus and underground train networks link the city centre with the suburbs to the north, east and west, while cable cars provide a dramatic means of reaching the island theme park of **Sentosa**, off the southern coast. The area north of downtown Singapore is the island's suburban heartland, home to the **Zoological Gardens** as well as vast new towns; allow at least half an hour for bus trips out to this region. Aside from the infamous jail near **Changi** Village, the eastern district is primarily of interest as the jumping-off point for boats to the sleepy island of **Pulau Ubin**. The west of the island boasts a clutch of good theme parks, most notably **Jurong BirdPark**, in addition to Singapore's industrial zone and port.

For a map of Singapore island, see colour map 1.

INTRODUCING THE CITY

Arrival

Most people's first glimpse of Singapore is of **Changi airport**, and a telling glimpse it is. Its two terminals, connected by the Skytrain monorail, are modern, efficient and air-conditioned – Singapore in microcosm. You might also arrive via the 1056-metre-long causeway from the Malaysian city of Johor Bahru, or by boat from the Indonesian archipelago. Wherever you arrive, the well-oiled infrastructure means that you'll have no problem getting into the centre.

BY AIR

Changi airport is at the far eastern end of Singapore, 16km from the city centre. As well as duty-free shops, money-changing and left-luggage facilities, the airport boasts a 24-hour post office and telephone service, hotel reservations counters, day rooms, saunas, and business and Internet centres. There's also a *McDonald's*, a *Swenson's* ice-cream parlour and, in Terminal One's basement, a food centre – the cheapest and most authentically Singaporean option. But the likelihood is that you'll barely get the chance to take in Changi – baggage comes through so quickly that you can be on a bus or in a taxi within fifteen minutes of arrival. Be sure to pick up one of the free maps and weekly *This Week Singapore* guides that the Singapore Tourism Board (STB) leaves at the airport.

Getting into the city from the airport

Singapore's underground train system (MRT – Mass Rapid Transit) doesn't yet extend as far as the airport, so you'll have to take either a taxi or a public bus into the centre.

The **bus** departure points in the basements of both terminals are well signposted, but make sure you've got the right money before you leave the concourse, as Singapore bus drivers don't give change; take the #36 (every 10min, 6am–midnight; $1.50). The bus heads west to Stamford Road before skirting the southern side of Orchard Road. Ask the driver to give you a shout at the Capitol Cinema stop for Beach Road, and at the YMCA stop, where you need to cross over Bras Basah Park if you are staying in Bencoolen Street. Another option is to take a **MaxiCab** shuttle into town. These six-seater taxis depart every fifteen minutes, or when full, and will take you to any hotel in the city for a flat fare of $7 (children $5). MaxiCabs are equipped to take wheelchairs.

Taxis from the airport levy a $3 surcharge on top of the fare. Again, the taxi rank is well signposted, and a trip into downtown Singapore costs around $15 and takes twenty minutes. There are also **car-rental** agencies at the airport (see p.260), though you'd be advised not to travel around Singapore by car (see "City transport", p.48).

BY BUS

Buses stop at one of three terminals in Singapore. Local buses from **Johor Bahru (JB)** in **Malaysia** arrive at Ban San Terminal at the junction of Queen and Arab streets, from where a two-minute walk along Queen Street and a left turn along Rochor Road takes you to Bugis MRT station. Buses from elsewhere in Malaysia and from **Thailand** terminate at one of two sites, Lavender Street Terminal and the Golden Mile Complex. Lavender Street Terminal, at the corner of Lavender Street and Kallang Bahru, is around five minutes' walk from Lavender MRT. Alternatively, walk a short distance in the other direction to the end of Jalan Besar and hop on bus #139 if you're heading for the guesthouses on Bencoolen Street. Bus #145 passes the Lavender Street Terminal on its way down North Bridge and South Bridge roads. From the Golden Mile, take any bus along Beach Road to Raffles City to connect with the MRT. You'll have no trouble hailing a cab at any terminal.

BY TRAIN

Trains from Malaysia end their journey at the **Singapore Railway Station** on Keppel Road, southwest of Chinatown. You haven't officially arrived in Singapore until you step out of the station – which is owned by Malaysia – as the "Welcome to Malaysia" sign above the main entrance testifies. The grounds of Singapore's rail system were sold lock, stock and barrel to the Federal Malay States in 1918, though recently the Singapore government has been buying back segments of it piecemeal. From Keppel Road, bus #97 travels past Tanjong Pagar MRT station and on to Selegie and Serangoon roads, or you can usually find a cab in the forecourt.

BY SEA

Boats from the **Indonesian archipelago of Riau** dock at the World Trade Centre, off Telok Blangah Road, roughly 5km east of the centre. From Telok Blangah Road, bus #97 runs to Tanjong Pagar MRT. Bus #65 goes to Selegie and Serangoon roads, via Orchard Road, or take bus #166 for Chinatown. Boats also dock at the Tanah Merah Ferry Terminal, linked by bus #35 to Bedok MRT station.

It's also possible to reach Singapore by boat from **Malaysia**. Bumboats from Kampung Pengerang on the southeastern coast of Johor moor at Changi Village, beyond the airport, from where bus #2 travels into the centre, via Geylang, Victoria and New Bridge roads. Swisher ferries from Tanjung Belungkor, also in Johor, dock at the Changi Ferry Terminal a little way east of Changi Village, from where you'll have to take a taxi – either all the way into town, or into Changi Village to connect with bus #2. Finally, ferries from Tioman Island dock at the new Tanah Merah Ferry Terminal (see p.39).

With so many of Singapore's shops, restaurants and offices located in vast high-rise buildings and shopping malls, deciphering addresses can sometimes be tricky. The numbering system generally adhered to is as follows: 02-15 means room number 15 on the second floor; 10-08 is room 8 on the 10th floor. Bear in mind that in Singapore, ground level is referred to as 01, or the first floor.

Departure

International flights take off from Changi airport in the far east of the island. Boats to Malaysia and Indonesia push off from one of three points along the southern coast, and buses and trains access Malaysia via the causeway in the far north of the island. The recently completed second causeway links Tuas in the west of the island with Geylang Patah, 20km west of Johor Bahru, but buses and trains still use the original link.

BY AIR

There are good deals on plane tickets from Singapore to **Australia**, **Bali**, **Bangkok** and **Hong Kong**. However, if you're planning to head for either **Malaysia** or **Indonesia** by air, it might be worth going to JB (see below), across the causeway, or Batam, the nearest Indonesian island (see "Boats" below), and buying a flight from there.

Allow plenty of time for getting out to the airport (45–60 min), especially during the morning and evening rush hours. Bus #36 (daily 6am–midnight; $1.50) runs frequently down Orchard Road and Bras Basah Road en route to Changi. Taxis cost $12–15.

For Changi airport flight enquiries, and the addresses and telephone numbers of airlines, travel agencies and the Malay, Indonesian and Thai consulates in Singapore, see "Directory", pp.259–266.

BY ROAD

The easiest way across the causeway to **Johor Bahru** is to get the #170 JB-bound **bus** from the Ban San Terminal (every 15min; 6am–12.30am; $1.20) or the plusher air-con Singapore–Johor Express (every 10min; 6.30am–11.30pm; $2.40), both of which take around an hour (including border formalities); both stop at JB bus terminal. From the **taxi** rank next to the terminal, a car to JB (seating four) costs $30. The Singapore–KL (Kuala Lumpur) Express leaves from the Ban San Terminal daily at 9am, 1pm, 5pm and 10pm (6hr; $23). For other destinations, go to either the Lavender Street Terminal or the Golden Mile Complex.

At peak hours (6.30–9.30am and 5.30–7.30pm) and at weekends, the roads leading to the causeway seethe with cars and trucks – all full of petrol, after a law passed in the early 1990s banned Singaporeans from driving out of the country on an empty tank. Previously, people crossed into Malaysia, filled up with cut-price fuel and then headed home; now, signs line the roads approaching the causeway requesting that Singaporean cars top up to three-quarters of a tank or risk a $500 fine.

BY TRAIN

You can make free seat reservations up to one month in advance of departure at the information kiosk (daily 8.30am–2.30pm & 3–7pm; ☎2225165) in the train station. There are air-conditioned trains to KL at 8am, 2.45pm and 10.10pm. These trains all stop at JB, along with an additional service at 6.10pm which terminates there. For information on the **Eastern and Oriental Express** to Bangkok, see p.22.

BY BOAT TO MALAYSIA

From Changi Point bumboats run to **Kampung Pengerang** in Johor. Boats leave when they're full (daily 7am–4pm; $5 one-way) and the trip takes 45 minutes. A newer, more reliable service departs for **Tanjung Belungkor**, also in Johor, daily at 7.30am, 11.30am, 4pm and 8pm from the new Changi Ferry Terminal. Run by Ferrylink (☎5453600), the service takes 45 minutes and costs $20, or $32 return; check in one hour before departure. Finally, from the Tanah Merah Ferry Terminal, there's an 8.30am service (March–Oct daily except Wed; $140 return) to **Tioman Island**. Information and tickets from Auto Batam (☎5427105). Again, check in one hour before departure.

BY BOAT TO INDONESIA

Boats to **Batam** in the Riau archipelago depart half-hourly throughout the day from the World Trade Centre (7.30am–7pm; $17 one-way), docking at Sekupang, from where you take a taxi to Hangnadim airport for internal Indonesian flights. There are also four boats a day ($49 one-way) from the Tanah Merah Ferry Terminal to **Tanjung Pinang** on Pulau Bintan, from where cargo boats leave three times a week for Pekanbaru in Sumatra. Information and tickets are available from either Dino Shipping (℡2769722) or Bintan Resort Ferries (℡5424369). From Kijang Port, south of Tanjung Pinang, there are boat services to Jakarta.

Information and maps

The Singapore Tourism Board (STB) maintains three **Tourist Information Centres**. One is at Tourism Court, 1 Orchard Spring Lane (Map 5, B7; Mon–Fri 8.30am–5pm, Sat 8.30am–1pm; toll-free ℡1-800/736 2000); another at Liang Court Shopping Centre, Level 1, 177 River Valley Rd (Map 3, D5; daily 10.30am–9.30pm; ℡3362888); and the third at 01-35 Suntec City Mall, 3 Temasek Blvd (Map 4, I12; daily 8am–8pm; toll-free ℡1-800/3325066).

The best available **map** of Singapore Island is the 1:22,500 Nelles *Singapore*, though the *Singapore Street Directory*, from all Singapore bookshops, is essential if you have to rent a car.

A number of publications offer **"what's on"** listings and recommendations. Two of these – *Where Singapore* and *This Week Singapore* – are available free at hotels all over the island. The "Life!" section of the *Singapore Straits Times* has a decent listings section, but best of all are *8 Days* magazine, which is published weekly and costs $1.50, and the newer *IS*, a free paper published fortnightly.

SINGAPORE ON THE INTERNET

www.gov.sg The offical Web site of the Singapore government.

www.newasia-singapore.com The Singapore Tourism Board's official site, featuring tour planner, attractions, current events, a virtual "tour" of the island and an accommodation search by price range.

www.makansutra.com Quirky Web site maintained by the foodies who annually publish the *makansutra* food guide to Singapore. Carries fascinating essays about the cultural and culinary facets of eating out in Singapore.

straitstimes.asia1.com.sg The *Singapore Straits Times* on the Internet.

City transport

All parts of the island are accessible by **MRT** (the underground rail network) or **bus**, and fares are reasonable so that there's little to be gained by renting a car. However you travel, it's best to avoid the rush hour (roughly 8–9.30am and 5–7pm) if at all possible; outside these times, things are relatively uncongested. The annually updated *Transitlink Guide* ($1.50), available from bus interchanges, MRT stations and major bookshops, outlines every bus and MRT route on the island in exhaustive detail. Singapore also has thousands of easily available and affordable **taxis**.

THE MRT (MASS RAPID TRANSIT) SYSTEM

Singapore's **MRT** system was officially opened on March 12, 1988, and currently boasts 48 stations, with more under construction. In terms of cleanliness, efficiency and value for money, the system is second to none – compared to

London's tubes or New York's subways, a trip on the MRT is a joy. Nor is there any possibility of delays owing to a passenger falling onto the line – the automatic doors dividing the platform from the track open only when trains are stationary. The system has two main lines: the north–south line, which runs a vaguely horseshoe-shaped route from Marina Bay up to the north of the island and then southwest to Jurong, and the east–west line, connecting Boon Lay to Pasir Ris. Trains run every four to five minutes on average, daily from 6am until midnight. For information, pick up the free *MRT Handy Guide* from any station, or call the MRT Information Centre on ☏1-800/3368900 (toll-free).

For a plan of the MRT system, see colour map 9.

A no-smoking rule applies on all trains, and eating and drinking are also outlawed. Signs in the ticket concourse seem to indicate that there is a ban on hedgehogs as well. In fact, they mean "no durians" – not an unreasonable request if you've ever spent any length of time in a confined space with one of these pungent fruits.

Tickets and fares

Tickets cost between 60c and $1.60 for a one-way journey. Change machines will break $1 and $2 notes; larger notes can be changed at the information counter. The **Transitlink Farecard** – a stored-value card that's valid on all MRT and bus journeys in Singapore, is sold at MRT stations and bus interchanges for $12 (including a $2 deposit). The cost of each journey you make is automatically deducted from the card; any credit on the card when you leave Singapore will be reimbursed at a Farecard outlet. The **Tourist Day Ticket** is also available for $10 from most MRT stations. The ticket allows you to take up to twelve bus or MRT rides a day, regardless of distance travelled – though you'd have to do an awful lot of travelling to make this ticket pay.

BUSES

Singapore's **bus network** is slightly cheaper to use than the MRT system, and far more comprehensive – there are several routes which are particularly useful for sightseeing (see box). Two bus companies operate on the roads of Singapore: the **Singapore Bus Service (SBS)** and **Trans-Island Bus Services (TIBS)**. Most buses charge distance-related **fares** ranging from 60c–$1.20 (70c–$1.50 for air-con buses). Others charge a flat fare, displayed on the destination plates on the front of the bus. Change isn't given, so make sure you have the correct fare. For bus route information, call toll-free ☏1-800/2872727 (SBS) or ☏4825433 (TIBS).

If you are in town for a while, buy a **Transitlink Farecard** (see p.45), which you insert – picture side down – into the validator as you board; press a button to select your fare, which is deducted from the stored value. Another ticket option is the **Tourist Day Ticket** (see p.45), though this is not a very cost-effective means of travel. Neither is the Singapore Trolley, a mock-antique bus that loops between the Botanic Gardens, the Colonial District, the Singapore River and Suntec City throughout the day. One day's unlimited travel is $14.90; call ☏3396833 for more details.

TAXIS

There are more than ten thousand **taxis** on the streets of Singapore, so you shouldn't have any trouble hailing a cab, day or night; they come in various colours, but are clearly

USEFUL BUS ROUTES

Below is a selection of handy bus routes; note that many of the services from the Orchard Road area actually leave from Penang Road or Somerset Road:

#2 passes along Eu Tong Sen Street (in Chinatown) and Victoria Street (past the Arab Quarter) en route to Changi Prison and Changi Village.

#7 runs along Orchard Road, Bras Basah Road and Victoria Street; its return journey takes in North Bridge Road, Stamford Road, Penang Road and Somerset Road en route to Holland Village.

#36 loops between Orchard Road and Changi airport.

#65 terminates at the World Trade Centre, after passing down Jalan Besar, Bencoolen Street, Penang Road and Somerset Road.

#97 runs along Stamford Road to Little India, then on to Upper Serangoon Road; returns via Bencoolen Street and Collyer Quay.

#103 runs between New Bridge Road Terminal (Chinatown) and Serangoon Road (Little India).

#124 connects Scotts Road, Orchard Road and North Bridge Road with South Bridge Road and New Bridge Road in Chinatown; in the opposite direction, travels along Eu Tong Sen Street, Hill Street, Stamford Road and Somerset Road.

#139 heads past Tai Gin Road, via Dhoby Ghaut, Selegie Road, Serangoon Road and Balestier Road.

#167 passes down Scotts Road, Orchard Road and Bras Basah Road, Collyer Quay, Shenton Way and Neil Road (for Chinatown).

#170 starts at the Ban San Terminal at the northern end of Queen Street, passing Bukit Timah Nature Reserve and Kranji War Cemetery on its way to JB in Malaysia.

CITY TRANSPORT: BUSES • TAXIS

marked "TAXI". All cabs are **metered**, the fare starting at $2.40 for the first kilometre and rising 10c for every 240 metres. However, there are **surcharges** to bear in mind, notably the 50 percent charged on journeys between midnight and 6am. Journeys from Changi airport incurs a $3 surcharge, and there's a $3 surcharge for taxis booked over the phone. More confusingly still, the Singaporean government has introduced an Electronic Road Pricing programme (ERP) in order to relieve congestion within the city's Central Business District (CBD) at peak times, and these electronic tolls will be reflected in your bill, depending upon the time of day.

Singapore's taxis have in-built speed monitors. If you hear a persistent chiming noise your driver is breaking the 80kph expressway speed limit.

On the whole, Singaporean taxi drivers are friendly, but their English isn't always good, so it's a good idea to have your destination written down (in English) if you are heading off the beaten track. If a taxi displays a red destination sign on its dashboard, it means the driver is changing shift and will accept customers only if they are going in his direction. Finally, tourists with wheelchairs should note that the TIBS Taxis company (☎4811211) has ten wheelchair-accessible cabs.

RENTING CARS AND BIKES

The Singapore government has introduced huge disincentives to driving in order to combat traffic congestion. If you want to drive into the CBD (see above) you'll have to buy a stored value **CashCard** to cover the electronic tolls that are now automatically levied. What's more, **parking** is expensive: you need to purchase coupons from a licence booth, post office or store. In fact, the only real reason for renting a car in Singapore is to travel up into Malaysia, and even

SINGLISH: AN INTRODUCTION

Upon first hearing the machine-gun rattle of Singaporean English, or **Singlish**, you could easily be forgiven for thinking you're listening to a language other than English. Pronunciation is so staccato that many words are rendered almost unrecognizable – especially monosyllabic words such as "cheque" and "book", which together would be spoken "che-boo". In contrast, in two-syllable words the second syllable is lengthened, and stressed by a rise in tone: ask a Singaporean what they've been doing, and you'll variously be told "wor-king", "shop-ping", and "slee-ping".

But it's the unorthodox rhythms of phrasing that make Singlish so memorable. Conventional English syntax is twisted and wrung, and tenses and pronouns discarded. If you ask a Singaporean if they've ever seen Michael Jackson, you might be answered "I ever see him", while enquiring whether they've just been shopping might yield "go come back already".

Responses are almost invariably reduced to their bare bones, with single-word replies often repeated for stress. Request something in a shop and you'll hear "have, have", or "got, got" (a Singaporean customer might respond with "where got?" – meaning "where is it?"). In a restaurant, if you ask whether the kitchen can rustle you up a sandwich, the reply will be either "can, can" or "cannot".

Suffixes and exclamations drawn from Malay, Hokkien and English complete this patois, the most distinctive being "lah", as in "okay lah", and "so cheap one lah" (which translates as "this is really inexpensive, isn't it?"). Also commonly heard, are "is it?" (pronounced "eezeet?"), which expresses "really?" and "ah", which means "yes" if on its own and accompanied by a nod of the head, but can imply a question if set at the end of a phrase.

If Singlish still has you totally baffled, you might try raising your eyes to the heavens, and crying either "ay yor" (with a drop of tone on "yor") or "Allama" – both expressions of annoyance or exasperation.

then it's far cheaper to rent from a company based over the causeway (in JB), as Singaporean firms levy a $25 Malaysia surcharge. If you're still keen on driving in Singapore itself, rental companies are listed on p.260.

Bike rental is possible along the East Coast Parkway, where the cycle track that skirts the seashore is always crowded with Singaporeans in full cycling gear. Expect to pay around $4–8 an hour for a mountain bike, and bring some form of ID to leave at the office. The dirt tracks that crisscross Pulau Ubin, off Changi Point at the eastern tip of the island, are ideal for cycling – a day's rental at one of the cluster of shops near the jetty again costs $4–8, though the price doubles during the school holidays (June, Nov & Dec). Finally, there's a range of bikes – including tandems – available for rent next to the ferry terminal on Sentosa Island ($2–5 an hour), which provide by far the best way to see the island.

ORGANIZED TOURS

If you're pushed for time, there are several reputable companies in Singapore offering **sightseeing tours**. The main operators are listed on p.266, or ask at your hotel or the tourist office. Tours vary according to the operator, but four-hour city tours typically take in Orchard Road, Chinatown and Little India, and cost around $30. Specialist tours are also available – on Raffles, horse racing, Singapore by night, World War II sights, even an "In Harmony with Feng Shui" tour – costing $30–$80 per person. For more details, contact the STB. For nature and bird-watching trips, contact R. Subharaj at 8 Jalan Buloh Perindu (☎7874733), whose outings range from three-hour birding sessions ($20) to personalized nature tours spanning Singapore and Malaysia, for around $600 a day for up to five people. Members of the Registered Tourist Guides

Association (☎3392110) charge $25–50 an hour (minimum 4hr) for a personalized tour.

Trishaws – three-wheeled bicycles with a carriage on the back – were once a common form of transport in Singapore, though they're a bit of an anachronism these days. You'll still see a few trishaws providing a genuine service around Little India and Chinatown, but most drivers now congregate on the open land below Bugis Village (p.63) from where they'll give you a 45-minute sightseeing ride for $25–40.

BOAT CRUISES

Fleets of **cruise boats** ply Singapore's southern waters day and night. The best of these, the Singapore River Cruises, cast off (every ten minutes; 9am–11pm) from Boat Quay, Clarke Quay, Raffles' landing site and Riverside Point Landing Steps for a $10 cruise on a traditional bumboat, passing the old **godowns** where traders once stored their merchandise. Several cruise companies also operate out of Clifford Pier, offering everything from luxury catamaran trips around Singapore's southern isles, to dinner on a Chinese sailing boat. A straightforward cruise will set you back around $20, and a dinner special $35–50. Cruise companies include Eastwind (☎5333432), Singapore Riverboat (☎3389205), Singapore River Cruises (☎3366111) and Watertours (☎5339811). If you don't relish the idea of an organized cruise, you can haggle with a **bumboat** man on Clifford Pier: if you're lucky, he'll take a group around the southern isles for $25 an hour.

It is also quite possible to **charter** your own boat, but you'll fork out up to $1000 a day for the privilege. Charter companies include Amaril Cruises (☎4759688), J & N Cruises (☎2707100), Fantasy Cruises (☎2840424) and Pacific Seacraft (☎2706665).

The Colonial District

The British left Singapore an impressive legacy in the stately nineteenth-century piles of the **Colonial District**. From the Bencoolen Street/Beach Road area, it's an easy jaunt on foot to survey the fruits of grandiose empire building; if you're coming from further afield, you'll need to take the MRT to either Raffles Place or City Hall MRT stations.

As the colony's trade grew in the last century, the Singapore River became its main artery, clogged with the traditional cargo boats known as bumboats, with painted eyes, as though they could see where they were going. The boats ferried coffee, sugar and rice to the river bank warehouses (godowns), where coolies loaded and unloaded sacks. These days, with the bumboats all but gone, the river is quieter, cleaner and inevitably less fascinating, though both banks are undergoing a profound commercial revitalization, as new restaurants and bars move into formerly abandoned buildings.

The heart of the Colonial District is the immaculately groomed grass of the **Padang** ("field" in Malay), which stretches out below **St Andrew's Cathedral** towards the river. To the south of the Padang are the **Empress Place Building**, **Parliament House** and the **Singapore Cricket Club** – the epitome of the colonizers' stubborn refusal to adapt to their surroundings. To the north is the grand old **Raffles Hotel**, beyond which a string of nineteenth- and twentieth-century churches leads to Singapore's famous entertainment centre, **Bugis Village**. Also in the north of the district are shops and restaurants of the **CHIJMES** complex, the **Singapore Art Museum** and the **Singapore History Museum**. Heading west from the Padang, you pass **City Hall** and the **Supreme Court** before climbing the slopes of **Fort Canning Hill**, ten minutes' walk from the Padang, and one of the few hills in Singapore not lost to land reclamation.

THE PADANG AND AROUND

Map 3, H5. City Hall MRT.

Earmarked by Raffles as a recreation ground shortly after his arrival, such is the symbolic significance of the **Padang** that its borders have never been encroached upon by speculators and it remains much as it was in 1907, when G.M. Reith wrote in his *Handbook to Singapore*: "Cricket, tennis, hockey, football and bowls are played on the plain . . . beyond the carriage drive on the other side, is a strip of green along the sea wall, with a foot-path, which affords a cool and pleasant walk in the early morning and afternoon." Once the last over of the day had been bowled, the Padang assumed a more social role: the image of Singapore's European community hastening to the corner once known as Scandal Point to catch up on the latest gossip is pure Somerset Maugham. Today the Padang is kept as pristine as ever by a bevy of gardeners mounted on state-of-the-art lawnmowers.

Land reclamation has widened the Padang to the east, but much of the waterside **Esplanade Park** is presently off-limits, while work continues on the ambitious **Theatres by the Bay** project, aimed at making Singapore the arts capital of the East by the end of the millennium.

As an April Fool's Day joke, the Straits Times reported in 1982 that the Padang was to be sold off for development; the ensuing public outcry jammed the newspaper's switchboard.

Singapore Cricket Club

Map 3, H6. City Hall MRT; bus #97 or #167.

The brown-tiled roof, whitewashed walls and dark green blinds of the **Singapore Cricket Club**, at the southwestern end of the Padang, have a nostalgic charm. Founded in the 1850s, the club was the hub of colonial British society and still operates a "members only" rule, though there's nothing to stop you watching the action from outside on the Padang itself. The Singapore Rugby Sevens are played here, as well as a plethora of other big sporting events and parades; a timetable of forthcoming events is available at the club's reception. Eurasians, who were formerly ineligible for membership of the Cricket Club, founded their own establishment in 1883, the **Singapore Recreation Club**, which lies across on the north side of the Padang, and is presently undergoing profound renovations.

The Supreme Court and City Hall

Map 3, H5–G6. City Hall MRT; bus #124 or #166.

Just to the west of the Cricket Club, Singapore's Neoclassical **Supreme Court** (formerly the site of the exclusive *Hotel de L'Europe,* whose drawing rooms allegedly provided Somerset Maugham with inspiration for many of his Southeast Asia short stories) was built between 1937 and 1939, and sports a domed roof of green lead and a splendid, wood-panelled entrance hall – which is as far as you'll get unless you're appearing in front of a judge, as it's not open to the public. Next door is the older **City Hall**, whose uniform rows of grandiose Corinthian columns lend it the austere air of a mausoleum. Wartime photographs show Lord Louis Mountbatten (then Supreme Allied Commander in Southeast Asia) on the steps announcing Japan's surrender to the British in 1945. Fourteen years later, Lee Kuan Yew chose the same spot from which to address his electorate at a victory rally celebrating self-government for Singapore. Nowadays, rather less dramatic photographs are taken on the steps as newlyweds line up to have their big day captured in front of one of Singapore's most imposing buildings.

St Andrew's Cathedral

Map 3, H4. Services Sunday 7, 8 & 11am, 2, 5 & 7pm. City Hall MRT; bus #97 or #167.

St Andrew's Cathedral, on the west side of the Padang on Coleman Street, gleams even brighter than the other buildings nearby. The third church to be built on this site, the cathedral was constructed in high-vaulted, Neo-Gothic style, using Indian convict labour, and was consecrated by Bishop Cotton of Calcutta on January 25, 1862. Its exterior walls were plastered using Madras *chunam* – an unlikely composite of eggs, lime, sugar and shredded coconut husks which shines brightly when smoothed – while the small cross behind the pulpit was crafted from two fourteenth-century nails salvaged from the ruins of Coventry Cathedral in England, which was destroyed during World War II.

THE PADANG AND AROUND

THE SEPOY MUTINY

Plaques on the west wall of St Andrew's Cathedral commemorate the victims of one of Singapore's bloodiest episodes, the **Sepoy Mutiny** of 1915. The mutiny began when a German warship, *Emden*, was sunk by an Australian ship off the Cocos Islands: its survivors were brought to Singapore and imprisoned at Tanglin Barracks, at the western end of Orchard Road. With almost all of Singapore's troop contingent away in Europe fighting the Kaiser, the Muslim Punjabi soldiers of the **Fifth Light Infantry**, known as sepoys, were sent to guard the prisoners. Unfortunately, these men's allegiance to the British had recently been strained by the news that Turkey had come out against the Allies in Europe. A rumour that they were soon to be sent to Turkey to fight fellow Muslims upset them still further, and the German prisoners were able to incite the sepoys to mutiny. In the ensuing rampage through the city on February 15, 1915, the sepoys killed forty other soldiers and civilians before they were finally rounded up by some remaining European sailors and a band of men led by the Sultan of Johor. All were court-martialled and the resultant executions saw 36 sepoys shot before huge crowds. As for the Germans, they took the opportunity to effect an escape. Nine of them finally got back to Germany via Jakarta and one, Julius Lauterbach, received an Iron Cross in recognition of his daring and rather convoluted flight home through China and North America.

Closed-circuit TVs have been installed, which allow the whole congregation to view proceedings up at the altar – a reflection of the Chinese fascination with all things hi-tech, since the cathedral's size hardly requires it.

- -

During the Japanese invasion of Singapore, the cathedral became a makeshift hospital; the vestry was an operating theatre and the nave a ward.

- -

Victoria Concert Hall and Victoria Theatre

Map 3, G7–H7. Raffles Place MRT; bus #97 or #167.

To the south of the Padang, across the road from the Cricket Club, are two fine examples of colonial architecture, the **Victoria Concert Hall** and adjoining **Victoria Theatre** – the venues for Singapore's most prestigious cultural events (see pp.232 & 236 for details). The theatre was completed in 1862 as Singapore's town hall while the concert hall was added in 1905 as a tribute to the monarch's reign. During the Japanese occupation, the clock tower was altered to Tokyo time, while the statue of Raffles that once stood in front of the tower narrowly escaped being melted down. The newly installed Japanese curator of the National Museum (where the statue was sent) hid the statue and reported it destroyed. A copy of the statue can be seen by the river at **Raffles' landing site**, where, in January 1819, the great man apparently took his first steps on Singaporean soil. Sir Stamford now stares contemplatively across the river towards the business district. The Singapore River cruise boats (see p.51) depart from a tiny jetty a few steps along from Raffles' statue.

Empress Place Building

Map 3, G7–H7. Raffles Place MRT; bus #97 or #167.

In the very south of the Colonial District, towards Cavenagh Bridge, you'll find **Empress Place Building**, a robust Neoclassical structure named after Queen Victoria and completed in 1865. It served for ten years as a courthouse before the Registry of Births and Deaths and the Immigration Department moved in. Latterly, it has housed cultural exhibitions, and when renovations are completed the building will reopen with a permanent **Asian Civilization** collection, whose focus upon the island's

THE PADANG AND AROUND

Indian and Malay heritage will complement the Asian Civilization Museum in Armenian Street (see p.66): ask at the STB for further details. The pyramid-shaped time capsule in the grounds in front of the building, sealed in 1990 as part of Singapore's silver jubilee celebrations, contains "significant items" from Singapore's first 25 years of independence.

The tall obelisk in front of Empress Place Building commemorates the visit of James Dalhousie, Governor of India, in 1850.

Parliament House

Map 3, G6. City Hall MRT; bus #124 or #166.

Southwest of the Padang on Parliament Lane, the dignified white Victorian building ringed by fencing is **Parliament House**, built as a private dwelling for a rich merchant by Singapore's pre-eminent colonial architect, the Irishman George Drumgould Coleman. It is sometimes possible to watch Singapore's parliament in session from up in the Strangers' Gallery – call ☏3368811 for details. The bronze elephant in front of Parliament House was a gift to Singapore from King Rama V of Thailand (whose father was the king upon whom *The King and I* was based) after his trip to the island in 1871 – the first foreign visit ever made by a Thai monarch.

RAFFLES HOTEL

Map 3, I2. City Hall MRT; bus #56 or #171.

The lofty halls, restaurants, bars, and peaceful gardens of the legendary **Raffles Hotel**, probably the most famous hotel in the world and almost a byword for colonialism, prompted

THE HISTORY OF RAFFLES HOTEL

This most inherently British of hotels started life as a modest seafront bungalow belonging to an Arab trader, Mohamed Alsagoff. After a spell as a tiffin house, the property was bought in 1886 by the enterprising Armenian Sarkies brothers, who eventually controlled a triumvirate of quintessentially colonial lodgings: the *Raffles*, the (still extant) *Eastern and Oriental* in Penang, and the *Strand* in Rangoon.

Raffles Hotel opened for business on December 1, 1887 and quickly attracted some impressive guests. It is thought that **Joseph Conrad** stayed in the late 1880s; certainly **Rudyard Kipling** visited soon after this, though the hotel was far from sumptuous. "Let the traveller take note," wrote Kipling, "feed at *Raffles* and stay at the *Hotel de l'Europe*". The hotel enjoyed its real **heyday** during the first three decades of the new century, when it established its reputation for luxury and elegance – it was the first building in Singapore with electric lights and fans.

In 1902, a little piece of Singaporean history was made at the hotel, according to a (probably apocryphal) tale, when the last **tiger** to be killed on the island was shot inside the building. Thirteen years later another *Raffles* legend, the **Singapore Sling** cocktail, was created by bartender Ngiam Tong Boon.

The rich, famous and influential have always patronized the hotel, but it is its literary connections of which the hotel is proudest. **Herman Hesse**, **Somerset Maugham**, **Noel Coward** and **Günter Grass** all stayed at *Raffles* at some time – Maugham is said to have written many of his Asian tales under a frangipani tree in the garden.

During **World War II**, when the Japanese swept through the island, the hotel became the invading officers' quarters. After the Japanese surrender in 1945, *Raffles* was a transit camp for liberated Allied prisoners. Postwar deterioration earned it the affectionate but melancholy soubriquet "grand old lady of the East" and the hotel was little more than a shabby tourist diversion when the government finally declared it a **national monument** in 1987. A \$160-million facelift followed and the hotel reopened on September 16, 1991.

RAFFLES HOTEL

Somerset Maugham to remark that it "stood for all the fables of the exotic East". But after its renovation a decade ago, *Raffles* now gets a very mixed reception. Though it retains much of its colonial grace, the shopping arcade that now curves around the back of the hotel lacks finesse, selling *Raffles*-related souvenirs, exclusive garments, leatherware and perfume. Still, if you're in Singapore, there's no missing *Raffles* and, if you can't afford to stay here, there are other ways to soak up the atmosphere. A free **museum** (daily 10am–9pm), located upstairs, at the back of the hotel complex, is crammed with memorabilia, much of which was recovered in a nationwide heritage search that encouraged Singaporeans to turn in souvenirs that had found their way up sleeves and into handbags over the years. Otherwise, a Singapore Sling in *The Bar and Billiards Room* – one of thirteen food and beverage outlets in the hotel – will cost you around $17.

ALONG BRAS BASAH ROAD

The area around Raffles Hotel was long a focal point for expatriate life. To the south, on the plot of land now occupied by the shops and hotels of soaring **Raffles City**, stood the Raffles Institution, a place of learning founded by Raffles himself, and built by George Drumgold Coleman in 1837. West along Bras Basah Road, the **CHIJMES** complex, a delightful piazza-style restaurant venue is crafted from the remains of a former convent.

Raffles City

Map 3, H3–I3. City Hall MRT.
Raffles City is a huge development that sits beside the intersection of Bras Basah and North Bridge roads and

comprises two enormous hotels – one of which is the 73-storey *Westin Stamford* – a multi-level shopping centre and floor upon floor of offices. Completed in 1985, the complex was designed by Chinese-American architect I.M. Pei (the man behind the Louvre's glass pyramid) and required the highly contentious demolition of the venerable Raffles Institution, established by Raffles himself and built in 1835 by George Drumgould Coleman. The **Westin Stamford** holds an annual vertical marathon, in which hardy athletes attempt to run up to the top floor in as short a time as possible: the current record stands at under seven minutes. Lifts transport lesser mortals to admire the view from the *Compass Rose* bar and restaurant on the top floor.

The imposing Singapore War Memorial stands on the open land east of Raffles City; comprising four seventy-metre-high white columns, it's known locally as the "chopsticks".

The CHIJMES complex

Map 3, H2. City Hall MRT; bus #171 or #190.

Along **Bras Basah Road** west from *Raffles Hotel*, you'll find one of Singapore's newest and most aesthetically pleasing eating venues, the **CHIJMES** complex. Based around the Neo-Gothic husk of the former Convent of the Holy Infant Jesus (from whose name the complex's acronymic title is derived), CHIJMES is a rustic version of London's Covent Garden, whose lawns, courtyards, waterfalls, fountains and sunken forecourt give a sense of spatial dynamics that is rare indeed in Singapore. CHIJMES' shops and boutiques open from 9am to 10pm, the restaurants and bars from 11am to 1am.

ALONG BRAS BASAH ROAD

SINGAPORE ART MUSEUM

Map 3, G1. Tues & Thurs–Sun 9am–5.30pm; Wed 9am–9pm; $3 including free tour (Tues–Fri 11am & 2pm, Sat & Sun 11am, 2pm & 3.30pm); ⊤ 3323222. City Hall MRT; bus #171, #190 or #197.

The new **Singapore Art Museum**, at 71 Bras Basah Rd, is a long-overdue replacement for the tired art wing of the National Museum. The art museum has a peerless location in the venerable St Joseph's Institution, Singapore's first Catholic school, whose silvery dome rang to the sounds of school bells and rote learning until 1987. Though extensions have been necessary, many of the original rooms survive, among them the school chapel (now an auditorium), whose holy water receptacles, stations of the Cross and mosaic floor remain intact. In the school quad, the former gymnasium, glass sculptures by the American designer Dale Chihuly sprout off the walls like luminescent mushrooms.

The Art Museum's rolling schedule of visiting collections brings work by such acclaimed artists as Marc Chagall and the sculptor Carl Milles to Singapore. But greater emphasis is placed on contemporary local and Southeast Asian artists and art work. Indeed, the museum's real strength lies in the mapping of the Asian experience – from Bui Xian Phai's *Coalmine*, an unremittingly desolate memory of his labour in a Vietnamese re-education camp, to Srihadi Sudarsono's *Horizon Dan Prahu*, in which traditional Indonesian fishing boats ply a Mark Rothko-esque canvas. Montien Boonma's *The Pleasure of Being, Crying, Dying and Eating* comprises a tall stack of ceramic bowls decorated with jawbones and fronted by a scattering of broken pottery. The **E-Mage Multimedia Gallery** gives background to the ASEAN artists and art works featured.

Outside the museum, the souvenir shop stocks prints and postcards, and there's a classy branch of *Dôme*, where you can have a coffee under the watchful gaze of a statue of the seventeenth-century saint, John Baptist de la Salle, which stands over the museum's porch.

WATERLOO STREET

Map 4, E9–D13. City Hall MRT; bus #171, #190 or #197.

Semi-pedestrianized **Waterloo Street** is at its best on Sundays, springing to life as worshippers throng to its temples and churches. The modern **Kuan Yim Temple**, named after the Buddhist goddess of mercy, may not have the cluttered altars, dusty old rafters and elaborate roofs of Chinatown's temples, but is still extremely popular; all along the pavement outside, old ladies in floppy, wide-brimmed hats sell fresh flowers from baskets. Religious artefact shops on the ground floor of the apartment building opposite are well placed to catch worshippers on their way out – one shop specializes in small **shrines** for the house: the deluxe model boasts flashing lights and an extractor fan to expel unwanted incense smoke. **Fortune-tellers** and street traders operate along this stretch of the road too, and look out for the cage containing turtles and a sleepy old snake: make a donation, touch one of the creatures inside, and it's said that good luck will come your way.

BUGIS VILLAGE

Map 4, E10. Bugis MRT; bus #12 or #33.

One block east of Waterloo Street's shops and temples, at the junction of Rochor Road and Victoria Street sits **Bugis Village**, a rather tame manifestation of infamous Bugis Street. Until it was demolished to make way for an MRT station, Bugis Street embodied old Singapore: after dark it was a chaotic place, crawling with rowdy sailors, preening transvestites and prostitutes – and as such it was anathema to the Singapore government, keen to clean up the country's reputation. Singaporean public opinion demanded a replacement, though when Bugis Village opened in 1991 it was revealed as a shadow of its former self. Beer gardens, seafood restaurants, pubs and street stalls line its streets, and while local reaction has been largely negative, a steady stream of tourists passes through nightly. The transvestites are noticeable only by their absence, the sole reminder of their heritage a weak cabaret show in the *Boom Boom Room* nightclub.

Details of the *Boom Boom Room* and other nightclubs are listed on pp.225–227.

THE SINGAPORE HISTORY MUSEUM

Map 3, F1. Tues & Thurs–Sun 9am–5.30pm, Wed 9am–9pm; $3 including free tour (Tues–Fri 11am & 2pm, Sat & Sun 11am, 2pm & 3.30pm); ☎ 3752510. Dhoby Ghaut MRT; bus #171 or #190.

Across Bras Basah Park from the Singapore Art Museum, an eye-catching dome of stained glass tops the entrance to the **Singapore History Museum** on Stamford Road. The museum's forerunner, the Raffles Museum and Library, was opened in 1887 and soon acquired a reputation for the excellence of its natural history collection. In 1969, the place was renamed the National Museum in recognition of Singapore's independence, and subsequently altered its bias towards local history and culture: it's a fairly low-key collection. Following a recent shake-up, the only permanent exhibitions are the **History of Singapore Gallery**, which features twenty dioramas depicting significant historical events, from the arrival of Raffles in 1819 to the first session of parliament in 1965; and the **Rumah Baba**, or **Peranakan** house, where the lifestyle and culture of the

Straits Chinese is brought to life. Recent visiting exhibitions have focused on the Hakka people, Chinese secret societies in Singapore, and nineteenth-century botanical prints; check the local press for details. The free film shows in the **AV Theatrette** (daily at 10am, noon, 2pm & 4pm), on subjects like old Chinatown and Little India, the Singapore River, and traditional kampung life, are worth catching.

FORT CANNING PARK AND AROUND

Map 3, F3 (entrance). City Hall MRT.

When Raffles first caught sight of Singapore, **Fort Canning Park** was known locally as Bukit Larangan (Forbidden Hill). Malay annals tell of the five ancient kings of Singapura, said to have ruled the island from this point six hundred years ago – and archeological digs have unearthed artefacts which prove it was inhabited as early as the fourteenth century. The last of the kings, Sultan Iskandar Shah, reputedly lies here, and a *keramat*, or auspicious place, on the eastern slope of the hill marks the supposed site of his grave. It was out of respect for and fear of his spirit that the Malays decreed the hill forbidden, and these days the *keramat* still attracts a trickle of Singaporean Muslims, as well as childless couples who offer prayers here for fertility.

In colonial times, the report of a 68-pound artillery gun fired from Fort Canning Hill marked the hours of 5am, noon and 7pm.

However, when the British arrived, Singapore's first British resident, William Farquhar, displayed typical colonial tact by promptly having the hill cleared and building a bungalow on the summit; named Government House, it stood on what was then called Government Hill. The bungalow was replaced in 1859 by a fort named after Viscount George Canning, governor-general of India, but of this only a gateway, guardhouse and adjoining wall remain. An early European **cemetery** survives, however, upon whose stones are engraved intriguing epitaphs to nineteenth-century sailors, traders and residents, among them the pioneering colonial architect, George Coleman.

History apart, Fort Canning Park is spacious and breezy, and offers respite from, as well as fine views of, Singapore's crowded streets. There's a "back entrance" to the park which involves climbing the exhausting flight of steps that runs between the Hill Street Building and Food Centre, on Hill Street. Once you reach the top, there's a brilliant view along High Street towards the Merlion. The hill, which houses two theatres, is ringed by two walks, signs along which illuminate aspects of the park's fourteenth- and nineteenth-century history. What's more, the underground operations complex from which the Allied war effort in Singapore was masterminded has recently been opened to the public. Known as the **Battle Box** (Tues–Sun 10am–6pm, adults $8, children $5), the complex uses audio and video effects and animatronics to bring to life the last hours before Japanese occupation in February 1942.

The Asian Civilization Museum

Map 3, F3. Tues, Thurs–Sun 9am–5.30pm, Wed 9am–9pm; $3 including free guided tours (Tues–Fri 11am & 2pm, Sat & Sun 11am, 2pm & 3.30pm); ⓣ 3323015. City Hall MRT.

Given its past, it seems appropriate that the spectacular colonial-era mansion, fronted by two black eagles, on Armenian Street should house so worthy a tenant as the **Asian Civilization Museum**. Dating from 1910, the building was once home to the Tao Nan School, the first Hokkien school in Singapore.

The museum features ten permanent galleries, which together provide a cultural and historical context to Singapore's Chinese population. (The second phase of the Asian Civilization Museum, due to open in Empress Place Building in the next year or two, will focus on the heritages of the state's Indian and Malay contingents.)

After kicking off with a breakdown of the Middle Kingdom's various imperial dynasties, the museum's galleries walk visitors through the architecture, religions, arts and crafts of the Chinese. There is much to be learnt here. The Symbolism Gallery, for instance, explains the bats, dragons and other auspicious motifs featured in Oriental art. There is also much of beauty – nowhere more so than in the Ceramics Gallery, which yields some exquisite cobalt-blue Ming pieces.

The Substation

Map 3, F2. City Hall MRT; bus #7, #14, #36, #124, #167 or #190.

At 45 Armenian Street, the **Substation**, a disused power station, has been converted into a multimedia arts centre. Even if you don't have the time to check out its classes, discussions and performances (see p.236 for more details), the coffee shop is a pleasant place to hang out for a while. A market takes place in the courtyard every Sunday afternoon, with stalls selling anything from local crafts to secondhand Russian watches.

The Armenian Church

Map 3, F3. City Hall MRT; bus #7, #14, #36, #124, #167 or #190.

The tiny **Armenian Church** of St Gregory the Illuminator next to the former American Embassy was

FORT CANNING PARK AND AROUND

67

designed by George Drumgould Coleman in 1835 (which makes it one of the oldest buildings in Singapore). Inside is a single, circular chamber, fronted by a marble altar and a painting of the Last Supper. Among the white gravestones and statues in the church's grounds is the tombstone of Agnes Joaquim, a nineteenth-century Armenian resident of Singapore, after whom the national flower, the delicate, purple Vanda Miss Joaquim Orchid, is named; she discovered the orchid in her garden, and had it registered at the Botanic Gardens.

The Chinese Chamber of Commerce

Map 3, G3. City Hall MRT; bus #7, #14, #36, #124, #167 or #190.
The **Singapore Chinese Chamber of Commerce**, at 47 Hill Street, along the eastern side of Fort Canning Park, is a brash, Chinese-style building from 1964 featuring a striking pagoda roof. Along its facade are two large panels, depicting nine intricately crafted porcelain dragons.

The Chettiar Hindu Temple

Map 3, C3. Daily 8am–noon & 5.30–8.30pm. Bus #32, #54 or #139.
The **Chettiar Hindu Temple**, to the west of Fort Canning Park, is the goal of every participant in Singapore's annual Thaipusam Festival (see p.239). This large temple, dwarfed by the pink shell of the erstwhile *Imperial Hotel*, is dedicated to Lord Subramaniam and boasts a wonderful *gopuram* or bank of sculpted gods and goddesses. Erected in 1984, it replaced a nineteenth-century temple built by Indian chettiars (moneylenders); inside, 48 glass panels etched with Hindu deities line the roof.

FORT CANNING PARK AND AROUND

Clarke Quay

Map 3, D5. Raffles Place MRT, then river taxi; bus #124, #174 or #190.

Clarke Quay, by the river below Fort Canning Park, is a chain of nineteenth-century *godowns* renovated into an attractive shopping and eating complex. Clarke Quay has never quite managed to muster the same appeal as Boat Quay (see p.91): whatever it does somehow seems gimmicky. That said, its street performers, souvenir stalls and arcades make it a reasonably buzzy place. A river taxi for Clarke Quay (daily 11am–11pm; $2 return) departs every five minutes from the quayside above the Standard Chartered Bank, two minutes' walk from Raffles Place MRT.

FORT CANNING PARK AND AROUND

Orchard Road

I t would be hard to conjure an image more opposed to the reality of modern-day **Orchard Road** than C.M. Turnbull's description of it during early colonial times as "a country lane lined with bamboo hedges and shrubbery, with trees meeting overhead for its whole length". One hundred years ago, a stroll down Orchard Road would have passed row upon row of nutmeg trees and would have been enjoyed in the company of strolling merchants taking their daily constitutionals, followed at a discreet distance by their trusty manservants. Today, Orchard Road is synonymous with **shopping** – indeed, tourist brochures refer to it as the "Fifth Avenue, the Regent Street, the Champs Elysées, the Via Veneto and the Ginza of Singapore". Huge malls, selling everything you can imagine, line the road, though don't expect shopping to be relaxing; hordes of dawdling tourists from the numerous hotels along the road make browsing difficult. The road runs northwest from Fort Canning Hill and is served by three MRT stations – Orchard, Somerset and Dhoby Ghaut – of which Orchard is the most convenient for shopping expeditions.

Orchard Road does have one or two other diversions if you get tired of staring at CDs, watches and clothes. Near its eastern extent, the president of Singapore's abode – the **Istana Negara Singapura** – is open to the public a few times a year, and rows of houses that hark back to old Singapore flank Cuppage Road and Emerald Hill Road. And, way up beyond the most westerly point of the road, the **Singapore Botanic Gardens** make for a relaxing stroll in beautiful surroundings. On the whole, though, you really only come to Orchard Road in the daytime to shop and at night for a whole host of clubs and bars (see pp.221–222 & 225–229 for details).

For a full rundown of shopping in Singapore, see pp.245–258.

DHOBY GHAUT

Map 5, I5. Dhoby Ghaut MRT; bus #7, #14, #124, #139, #171 or #190.

In the **Dhoby Ghaut** area, at the eastern tip of Orchard Road, Indian *dhobies*, or laundrymen, used to wash clothes in the Stamford Canal, which once ran along Orchard and Stamford roads. Those days are long gone, and today the area is ringed by shopping centres, though there is a remnant of old Singapore in the **Hotel Rendezvous**, on the corner of Selegie and Bras Basah roads, where the venerable *Rendezvous Restaurant* is once again cooking up its famous curries (see p.206).

The Istana Negara Singapura

Map 5, I5. Dhoby Ghaut MRT; bus #7, #14, #124, #139, #171 or #190.

Three minutes' walk west along Orchard Road from Dhoby Ghaut MRT takes you past Plaza Singapura, beyond which stern-looking soldiers guard the gate of the **Istana Negara Singapura.** Built in 1869, the istana, with its ornate cornices, elegant louvred shutters and high mansard roof, was originally the official residence of Singapore's British governors, though on independence it became the residence of the president of Singapore – currently S.R. Nathan, whose portrait you'll see in banks, post offices and shops across the state. The shuttered palace is only open to visitors on public holidays; the president goes walkabout at some point during every open day as thousands of Singaporeans flock to picnic on the well-landscaped lawns, and local brass bands belt out jaunty tunes.

The changing of the guard ceremony at the Istana Negara Singapura takes place at 5.45pm on the first Sunday of the month.

Tan Yeok Nee Mansion

Map 5, I6. Dhoby Ghaut MRT; bus #7, #14, #124, #139, #171 or #190.

The **Tan Yeok Nee Mansion**, across Orchard Road from the Istana Negara Singapura at 207 Clemenceau Ave, is currently closed and its future is unclear. Built in traditional South Chinese style for a wealthy Teochew pepper and gambier (a resin used in tanning) merchant, and featuring ornate roofs and massive granite pillars, the mid-1880s mansion served as headquarters to the Singapore Salvation Army from 1940 until 1991.

EMERALD HILL ROAD

Map 5, G5. Somerset MRT; bus #7, #14, #124, #139, #171 or #190.

In the **Emerald Hill** area of Orchard Road, most of Cuppage Road has been pedestrianized, making it a great place to sit out and have a beer or a meal. **Cuppage**

ORCHARD ROAD SHOPPING CENTRES

The main Orchard Road shopping centres are detailed below; they're all marked on Map 5 at the end of the guide.

Centrepoint (Map 5, G5). Dependable all-round complex, whose seven floors of shops include the second incarnation of Robinsons – Singapore's oldest department store.

C.K. Tang's (Map 5, E5). Singapore's most famous department store, whose pagoda-style construction gives Orchard Road one of its most recognizable landmarks.

Delfi Orchard (Map 5, C5). Good for crystalware, glassware and art galleries.

Forum the Shopping Mall (Map 5, C5). Kids' clothes, toyshops, modelling specialists and clothes stores.

Lucky Plaza (Map 5, E5). Chock-a-block with tailors and electronics; Orchard Road's classic venue for haggling.

Ngee Ann City (Map 5, F5). A brooding twin-towered complex – Singapore meets Gotham City – with a wealth of good clothes shops and Kinokuniya, the biggest bookstore on the island.

Orchard Plaza (Map 5, H5). Tailors, leather jackets and silks galore, as well as a glut of audio, video and camera stores where haggling is par for the course.

Palais Renaissance (Map 5, D5). One of Singapore's classiest complexes, featuring Prada, Versace, Christian Dior, Ralph Lauren, Gucci and other heavyweights.

Plaza Singapura (Map 5, I5). Sportswear and sports equipment, musical instruments, audio, video and general electrical equipment, plus the Yaohan department store.

Tanglin Shopping Centre (Map 5, C5). Unsurpassed for art, antiques and curios.

Wheelock Place (Map 5, D5). One of the newer shopping centres on the block, this impressive pyramid of a building boasts a Border's bookshop and a Marks and Spencer.

ORCHARD SHOPPING CENTRES

Terrace, halfway along Cuppage Road on the left, is an unusually (for Orchard Road) old row of shophouses, where a burgeoning restaurant and bar scene has recently developed. A number of even more architecturally notable houses have also survived the developers' bulldozers in Emerald Hill Road, parallel to Cuppage Road. Emerald Hill was granted to Englishman William Cuppage in 1845 and for some years afterwards was the site of a large nutmeg plantation. After Cuppage's death in 1872, the land was subdivided and sold off, much of it bought by members of the **Peranakan** community, which evolved in Malaya as a result of the intermarriage between early Chinese settlers and Malay women. A walk up Emerald Hill Road takes you past a number of exquisitely crafted houses dating from this period, built in a decorative architectural style known as Chinese Baroque, typified by highly coloured ceramic tiles, carved swing doors, shuttered windows and pastel-shaded walls with fine plaster mouldings.

- -

Restaurants serving Nonya food, the cuisine of the Peranakans, are listed on pp.211–213.

- -

THE SINGAPORE BOTANIC GARDENS

Map 5, A6. Daily 5am–midnight, free; ⊤ 4717361. Bus #7, #106 or #174.

After a few hours' shopping you'll be glad of the open space afforded by the **Singapore Botanic Gardens**, a short walk beyond the western end of Orchard Road on Cluny Road. Founded in 1859, it was here, in 1877, that the Brazilian seeds from which grew the great **rubber plantations** of Malaysia were first nurtured. No one had taken much notice of them by the time Henry Ridley was named director of the Botanic Gardens the following year, but he recognized their financial potential and spent the next twenty years of his life persuading Malayan plantation-owners to convert to this new crop, an occupation which earned him the nickname "Mad" Ridley. The fifty-odd hectares of land feature a mini-jungle rose garden, topiary, fernery, palm valley and lakes that are home to turtles and swans. There's also the **National Orchid Garden** (daily 8.30am–7pm; $2) with sixty thousand plants; orchid jewellery, made by plating real flowers with gold, is on sale here – pieces cost around $100. At dawn and dusk, joggers and students of Tai Chi haunt the lawns and paths of the gardens, while at the weekend, newlyweds bundle down from church for their photos to be taken – a ritual recalled in Lee Tzu Pheng's poem *Bridal Party at the Botanics*, whose bride's "two hundred dollar face/is melting in the sun", while beside her is her groom, "black-stuffed, oil-slicked, fainting/in his finery, by the shrubbery". You can pick up a free **map** of the grounds at the ranger's office, a little to the right of the main gate.

A couple of minutes north of Orchard Road along Scotts Road, the impressive *Goodwood Park Hotel* started life in 1900 as the *Teutonia Club* for German expats. With the start of war across Europe in 1914, the club was commandeered by the British Custodian of Enemy Property. After the war, the *Goodwood* served for several years as a function hall, and, in 1929, it was turned into a hotel. During World War II like *Raffles* the hotel lodged Japanese officers and, fittingly, it was later chosen as one of the venues for a war crimes court.

THE SINGAPORE BOTANIC GARDENS

Chinatown

The two square kilometres of **Chinatown** once constituted the focal point of Chinese life and culture in Singapore. Nowadays, the area is on its last traditional legs, scarred by demolition and dwarfed by the skyscrapers of the Financial District (see p.90), where the island's yuppies oversee the machinations of one of Asia's most dynamic money markets. Even so, a wander through the surviving nineteenth-century streets still unearths musty and atmospheric temples, old craft shops and restaurants unchanged in forty years. Provision stores crammed with bird's nests, dried cuttlefish, ginger, chillies, mushrooms and salted fish do a brisk trade, and you might hear the rattle of a game of mahjong being played. Chinatown is bounded by New Bridge Road to the west, Neil and Maxwell roads to the south and Cecil Street to the east, while to the north, the Singapore River snakes west and inland passing the last few surviving *godowns* from Singapore's original trade boom.

TELOK AYER STREET AND AMOY STREET

Map 3, E11–12. Tanjong Pagar or Raffles Place MRT; bus #125, #131, #167 or #186.

Telok Ayer Street's Malay name – meaning 'Watery Bay' – recalls a time when the street would have run along the

THE HISTORY OF CHINATOWN

The area now known as Chinatown was earmarked for settlement by the Chinese community by Sir Stamford Raffles himself, who decided in June 1819 that the ethnic communities should live separately. As increasing numbers of **immigrants** poured into Singapore, Chinatown became just that – a Chinese town, with temples, shops and, most importantly, clan associations (*kongsi*), which helped new arrivals to find food, lodgings and work, mainly as small traders and coolies. The prevalent architectural form was the **shophouse**, a shuttered building with a moulded facade fronting living rooms upstairs and a shop on the ground floor.

By the mid-twentieth century, the area southwest of the Singapore River was rich with the imported cultural heritage of China, but independence brought ambition. The government regarded the tumbledown slums of Chinatown as an eyesore and embarked upon a catastrophic **redevelopment** campaign that saw whole roads bulldozed to make way for new shopping centres, and street traders relocated into organized complexes. Only recently has public opinion finally convinced the Singaporean authorities to restore rather than redevelop Chinatown. There are some renovated buildings that remain faithful to the original designs, though there's a tendency to render once characterful shophouses improbably perfect. The latest problem to threaten the fabric of Chinatown is spiralling rents, which in time are likely to drive out the last few families and traditional businesses, leaving the area open for full exploitation by bistros, advertising agencies and souvenir shops.

shoreline of the Straits of Singapore. Nowadays, thanks to land reclamation, it's no closer to a beach than is Beach Road, but alongside the shops and stores there are still a number of temples and mosques that have survived from the time when immigrants and sailors stepping ashore wanted to thank the gods for their safe passage.

Running parallel to Telok Ayer Street is **Amoy Street**, which – together with China and Telok Ayer streets – was also designated as a Hokkien enclave in the colony's early days. Long terraces of shophouses flank the street, all featuring characteristic **five-foot ways**, or covered verandahs, so-called simply because they jut five feet out from the house. Some of the shophouses are in a ramshackle state, while others have been marvellously renovated, only to be bought by companies in need of some fancy office space.

The three-day Verandah Riots of 1888 erupted when colonial administrators ordered Chinatown's merchants to clear their five-foot ways of stalls to enable pedestrians to pass by.

Thian Hock Keng Temple

Map 3, E12. Tanjong Pagar or Raffles Place MRT; bus #125, #131, #167 or #186.

The enormous **Thian Hock Keng Temple** (Temple of Heavenly Happiness) between Telok Ayer and Amoy streets is a hugely impressive Hokkien building. Built on the site of a small joss house where immigrants made offerings to Ma Chu Por (or Tian Hou), the queen of heaven, the temple was started in 1839 using materials imported from China. By the time the temple was finished in 1842 a statue of the goddess had been shipped in from southern China, and this still stands in the centre of the temple's main hall, flanked by the god of war on the right and the protector of life on the left. From the street, the temple looks spectacular: dragons stalk its broad roofs, while the entrance to the temple compound bristles with ceramic flowers, foliage and figures. Two stone lions stand guard at the entrance, and door gods, painted on the front doors, prevent evil spirits from entering. Look out for the huge

SONGBIRDS

One of the most enduringly popular of Singaporean hobbies is the keeping and training of **songbirds**. Every Sunday morning scores of enthusiasts and their birds congregate at an unnamed nondescript coffee shop on the corner of Tiong Bahru and Seng Poh roads, just west of Chinatown. Songbird competitions are commonplace in Singapore, but this gathering is an informal affair with bird owners coming to show off their pets and admire those of fellow collectors. The **exquisite cages** that house the birds are hung on a metal frame that fronts the coffee shop. Birds are grouped according to their breed, lest they pick up the distinctive songs of other breeds. The various breeds of bird you'll see include the delicate green mata puteh, or "white eye bird", the jambul, with its showy black crest and red eye patches, and the sharma, with beautiful long tail feathers. You can have toast and coffee at the café while watching and listening to the proceedings, which start around 6am – a good early morning start to a tour around nearby Chinatown. Take bus #851 from North Bridge Road which passes along Tiong Bahru Road, or hop in a cab.

The other central Sunday songbird venue is Sturdee Road, off Petain Road, which lies between Serangoon Road and Jalan Besar in Little India.

ovens, always lit, in which offerings to gods and ancestors are burnt.

Far East Square and the Fuk Tak Ch'i Street Museum

Map 3, F10. Daily 10am–10pm; free. Tanjong Pagar or Raffles Place MRT; bus #125, #131, #167 or #186.

Along Telok Ayer Street just north of Cross Street is **Far East Square**, a new shopping-cum-dining centre which taps Chinatown's heritage for its inspiration, and which

SONGBIRDS

boasts the **Fuk Tak Ch'i Street Museum** as its party-piece. It's the surest sign yet of the gentrification of Chinatown that one of its oldest temples has had to suffer the ignominy of being turned into a tourist attraction – and a fairly dull one at that. The Fuk Tak Ch'i Temple was established by Singapore's Hakka and Cantonese communities in 1824. The temple has scrubbed up nicely – too nicely, in fact: none of the musty ambience that once made it such an interesting and atmospheric place has survived its $200,000 renovation.

A model junk of the kind that would have brought across Singapore's earliest Chinese settlers sits on what used to be the temple's main altar. Elsewhere, you'll see odds and sods – opium pillows and pipes, Peranakan jewellery, an instrument once used by food hawkers to drum up trade – from old Singapore, though the most arresting exhibit is a diorama depicting how Telok Ayer would have appeared when it was still a waterfront street in the nineteenth century.

LAU PA SAT FESTIVAL MARKET

Map 3, G12. Daily 24hr. Raffles Place MRT; bus #97, #107, #125, #167 or #186.

To the east of Telok Ayer Street near Raffles Quay is Telok Ayer Market, recently renamed **Lau Pa Sat Festival Market**. Built in 1894 on land reclaimed from the sea, its octagonal cast-iron frame has been turned into Singapore's most tasteful food centre, which offers a range of Southeast Asian cuisines, as well as laying on free entertainment such as local bands and Chinese opera. After 7pm, the portion of Boon Tat Street between Robinson Road and Shenton Way is closed to traffic, and traditional hawker stalls take over the street.

CHINA STREET

Map 3, E10–F9. Raffles Place MRT; bus #51, #103, #124, #166, #174 or #190.

Around **China Street** and its offshoots, Chinatown is more residential. The old ways still survive in this part of Singapore: in the upper windows of tumbledown shophouses, wizened old men in white T-shirts and striped pyjama trousers stare out from behind wooden gates, flanked by songbird cages and laundry poles hung with washing. Down at street level, **trishaws** are still a recognized form of transport. But the traditional trades and industries – medicine shops, bakers, *popiah* skin-makers – which operated here as recently as the mid-1990s are now a thing of the past, their shophouses converted into architects' studios, marketing agencies and the like. At the southern end of China Street is steep Club Street, once noted for its temple-carving shops, though these too have now fallen to the demolition ball and been replaced by swish apartment blocks and swanky bars and restaurants. An impromptu **flea market** often takes place on the far side of the car park opposite, where traders squat on their haunches surrounded by catalogues, old coins, sleeveless records and phone cards.

Even the **clan associations** and **guilds** that gave Club Street its name are fast disappearing, though there are still a few to be seen, higher up the hill. These are easy to spot; black-and-white photos of old members cover the walls, and behind the screens which almost invariably span the doorway, old men sit and chat. From upstairs, the clacking sound of mahjong tiles reaches the street.

Wak Hai Cheng Bio Temple

Map 3, F9. Raffles Place MRT; bus #51, #103, #124, #166, #174 or #190.

The Wak Hai Cheng Bio Temple on Philip Street is fronted by an ugly concrete courtyard crisscrossed by a web of ropes supporting numerous spiralled incense sticks. Its name means "Temple of the Calm Sea", which made it a logical choice for early worshippers who had arrived safely in Singapore; an effigy of Tian Hou, the queen of heaven and protector of seafarers, is housed in the temple's right-hand chamber. This temple, too, has an incredibly ornate roof, crammed with tiny models of Chinese village scenes. The temple cat meanders across here sometimes, dwarfing the tableaux like a creature from a Godzilla movie

TANJONG PAGAR

Map 3, B12–C13. Tanjong Pagar MRT; bus #103, #124, #145 or #166.

The district of **Tanjong Pagar** at the southern tip of South Bridge Road, between Neil and Tanjong Pagar roads, has changed beyond recognition in recent years. Once a veritable sewer of brothels and opium dens, it was earmarked as a conservation area, following which over two hundred shophouses were painstakingly restored, painted in sickly pastel hues and converted into bars catering to the Financial District crowd, or restaurants and shops which prey on passing tourists.

See p.224 for details of bars around the Tanjong Pagar area.

While touring Tanjong Pagar, it's worth making time for a stop at one of the traditional **teahouses** along Neil Road. At *Tea Chapter* at no. 9a–11a (daily 11am–11pm), you can have tea in the very chair in which Queen Elizabeth sat when she visited in 1989; the shop is plastered with photographs of the occasion. The Chinese take tea-drinking very seriously. Buy a bag of tea here and one of the staff

TAKING CHINESE TEA

If you're in need of a quick, thirst-quenching drink, avoid **Chinese teahouses**: the art of tea-making is heavily bound up with **ritual**, and unhurried preparation time is crucial to the production of a pleasing brew. What's more, when you do get a cup, it's barely more than a mouthful and then the whole process kicks off again.

Tea-drinking in China traces its origins back thousands of years. Legend has it that the first cuppa was drunk by Emperor Shen Nong, who was pleasantly surprised by the aroma produced by some dried tea leaves falling into the water he was boiling. He was even more pleased when he tasted the brew. By the eighth century, the art form was so complex that Chinese scholar Lu Yu produced a three-volume tome on the processes involved.

Teashops normally have conventional tables and chairs but the authentic experience involves kneeling at a much lower traditional table. The basic procedure is as follows: the server places a towel in front of himself and his guest, with the folded edge facing the guest, and stuffs leaves into the pot with a bamboo scoop. Water, boiled over a flame, has to reach an optimum temperature, depending on which type of tea is being made; experts can tell its heat by the size of the bubbles rising, which are described, rather confusingly, as "sand eyes", "prawn eyes" and "fish eyes". Once the pot has been warmed inside and out, the first pot of tea is made, transferred into the pouring jar and then, frustratingly, poured back *over* the pot – the thinking being that over a period of time, the porous clay of the pot becomes infused with the fragrance of the tea. Once a second pot is ready, a draught is poured into the **sniffing cup**, from which the aroma of the brew is savoured. Only now is it time to actually drink the tea and, if you want a second cup, the whole procedure has to start again.

will teach you all the attached rituals (see box); 100g bags cost from $5 to over $65 and tea sets are also on sale, though they don't come cheap.

EU YAN SANG MEDICAL HALL

Map 3, D11. Open Mon–Sat 8.30am–6pm. Bus #51, #103, #124, #166, #174 or #190.

Amongst the numerous dingy shops that line South Bridge Road, and which look as if they've seen no custom since the war, is found the beautifully renovated **Eu Yan Sang Medical Hall**, at nos. 267–271. First opened in 1910, the shop is partially geared to the tourist trade – some of the staff speak good English. It smells a little like a compost heap on a hot day and there is a weird assortment of ingredients on the shelves, which to the uninitiated look more likely to kill than cure. Besides the usual herbs and roots favoured by the Chinese are various dubious remedies derived from exotic and **endangered species**. Blood circulation problems and external injuries are eased with centipedes and insects crushed into a "rubbing liquor", the ground-up gall bladders of snakes or bears apparently work wonders on pimples, monkey's gallstones aid asthmatics, and deer penis is supposed to provide a lift to any sexual problem. Antlers, sea horses, scorpions and turtle shells also feature regularly in Chinese prescriptions, though the greatest cure-all of Oriental medicine is said to be **ginseng**, a clever little root that will combat anything from weakness of the heart to acne and jet lag. If you need a pick-me-up, or are just curious, the shop administers free cups of ginseng tea.

- -
Try the Pearl's Centre (see box on p.88) if you want a
consultation with a herbal doctor.
- -

SRI MARIAMMAN HINDU TEMPLE

Map 3, D10. Bus #51, #103, #124, #166, #174 or #190.

Opposite the Eu Yan Sang Medical Hall on South Bridge

Road, the compound of the **Sri Mariamman Hindu Temple** bursts with primary-coloured, wild-looking statues of deities and animals. There's always some ritual or other being attended to by one of the temple's priests, drafted in from the subcontinent and dressed in simple loincloths. A wood-and-atap hut was erected on this site in 1827, on land belonging to Naraina Pillay – a government clerk who arrived in Singapore on the same ship as Stamford Raffles. The present temple was completed in 1843 and boasts a superb *gopuram* over the front entrance. Once inside the temple, look up at the roof and you'll see splendidly vivid friezes depicting a host of Hindu deities, including the three manifestations of the supreme being: Brahma the Creator (with three of his four heads showing), Vishnu the Preserver, and Shiva the Destroyer (holding one of his sons). The main sanctum, facing you as you walk inside, is devoted to Goddess Mariamman, who's worshipped for her power to cure disease. Smaller sanctums dotted about the open walkway which runs round the temple honour a host of other deities. In that dedicated to Goddess Periachi Amman, a sculpture portrays her with a queen lying on her lap, whose evil child she has ripped from her womb. Odd, then, that the Periachi Amman should be the protector of children, to whom one-month-old babies are brought. Sri Aravan, with his bushy moustache and big ears, is far less intimidating. His sanctum is at the back on the right-hand side of the complex.

During the Japanese occupation, roadblocks were set up at the point where South Bridge Road meets Cross Street, and Singaporeans were vetted at an interrogation post for signs of anti-Japanese feeling. Those whose answers failed to satisfy the guards either ended up as POWs or were never seen again.

SRI MARIAMMAN HINDU TEMPLE

To the left of the main sanctum there's a patch of sand which, once a year during the festival of **Thimithi** (see p.243), is covered in red-hot coals, across which male Hindus run to prove the strength of their faith. The participants, who line up all the way along South Bridge Road waiting their turn, are supposedly protected from the heat of the coals by the power of prayer, though the ambulance parked round the back of the temple suggests that some aren't praying quite hard enough.

SAGO STREET

Map 3, C11. Bus #51, #103, #124, #166, #174 or #190.
Compared to crumbling Telok Ayer and China streets, much of Chinatown west of **South Bridge Road** seems far less authentic. This is tour-bus Chinatown, heaving with gangs of holidaymakers plundering souvenir shops. However, until as recently as the 1950s, **Sago Street** was home to several death houses – rudimentary hospices where skeletal citizens saw out their final hours on rattan camp beds. These houses were finally deemed indecent and have all now gone, replaced by lifeless restaurants and shops stacked to the rafters with cheap Chinese vases, teapots, cups and saucers. Sago, Smith, Temple and Pagoda streets only really recapture their youth around the time of Chinese New Year, when they're crammed to bursting with stalls selling festive branches of blossom, oranges, sausages and waxed chickens – which look as if they have melted to reveal a handful of bones inside.

Sago Street skirts to the right of the Chinatown Complex, and its name changes to **Trengganu Street**. Despite the hordes of tourists, and the shops selling Singapore Airlines uniforms, presentation chopstick sets and silk hats with false pigtails, there are occasional glimpses of Chinatown's old trades and industries, such as Nam's

Supplies at no. 22, which offers shirts, watches, mobile phones, money and passports – all made out of paper – which the Chinese burn to ensure their ancestors don't want for creature comforts in the next life. They even have "Otherworld Bank" credit cards and "Hell Airlines" air tickets. Nam Cheong and Co, off nearby Kreta Ayer Street, takes this industry to its logical conclusion, producing huge paper houses and near life-size paper safes, servants and Mercedes for the self-respecting ghost about town; the shop is at 01-04 Block, 334 Keong Saik Rd, between Chinatown Complex and New Bridge Road.

The Chinatown Complex

Map 3, C11. Bus #51, #103, #124, #166, #174 or #190.

The hideous concrete exterior of the **Chinatown Complex**, at the end of Sago Street, belies the charm of the teeming market it houses. Walk up the front steps, past the garlic, fruit and nut hawkers, and once inside, the market's many twists and turns reveal stalls selling silk, kimonos, rattan, leather and clothes. There are no fixed prices, so you'll need to haggle. Deep in the market's belly is Yun Shi Services Agency (shop 01-K3) – where a **calligrapher** can quickly draw an Oriental ink sign for you – while the Capitol Plastics stall (01-16) specializes in **mahjong sets**. There's a food centre on the second floor, while the wet market within the complex gets pretty packed early in the morning, when locals come to buy fresh fish or meat. Here, abacuses are still used to tally bills, and sugar canes lean like spears against the wall.

NEW BRIDGE ROAD AND EU TONG SEN STREET

Chinatown's main shopping drag comprises southbound **New Bridge Road** and northbound **Eu Tong Sen**

SHOPPING IN CHINATOWN

As well as the markets and stores covered in the text, look out for the following, all either on or near to New Bridge Road and Eu Tong Sen Street. Opening hours are generally 10am–9.30pm.

Chinatown Point, 133 New Bridge Rd (Map 3, D8). One of its two buildings houses bright, fashionable, Orchard Road-style shop units; the other is a handicraft centre, with scores of tourist-orientated businesses.

Hong Lim Complex, 531–531a Upper Cross St (Map 3, D9). Several Chinese provisions stores, fronted by sackfuls of dried mushrooms, cuttlefish, chillies, garlic cloves, onions, fritters and crackers. Other shops sell products ranging from acupuncture accessories to birds' nests.

Lucky Chinatown Complex, 11 New Bridge Rd (Map 3, C10). Fairly upmarket place with lots of jewellery shops, and even an Oriental-style *McDonald's*.

New Bridge Centre, 336 Smith St (Map 3, B10). The Da You Department Store (second floor) sells Chinese religious arte-facts, tea sets and crockery.

Pearl's Centre, 100 Eu Tong Sen St (Map 3, A11). A centre for Chinese medicine. The Chinese Patent Medicines and Medicated Liquors Centre at 03-19 and TCM Chinese Medicines at 02-21 both have a Chinese clinic, where a con-sultation will cost you $5.

People's Park Centre, 101 Upper Cross St (Map 3, C8). Stall-like shop units selling cheap shoes, cassettes, electronics and gold. Look into Nison Department Store, on the first and sec-ond floors, which has some beautiful statues and rosewood screens.

People's Park Complex, 1 Park Rd (Map 3, B9). The Overseas Emporium is at 02-70 and sells Chinese instruments, calligra-phy pens, lacquerwork and jade. Cobblers set up stall in the courtyard beside the complex, behind which is a market and food centre.

Street, along which are found a handful of large malls (see below). Try to pop into one of the barbecue pork vendors around the intersection of Smith, Temple and Pagoda streets with New Bridge Road — the squares of red, fatty, delicious meat that they cook on wire meshes over fires produce an odour that is pure Chinatown.

The **Thong Chai Medical Institute** (Map 3, D8) has been sited at the top of Eu Tong Sen Street since 1892, when it first opened its doors with the avowed intention of dispensing free medical help regardless of race, colour or creed. Listed as a national monument, this beautiful southern Chinese-style building has recently been turned into a bar-disco (see p.224) — a criminal waste of its wonderful serpentine gables and wooden inscribed pillars.

NEW BRIDGE ROAD AND EU TONG SEN STREET

The Financial District

U ntil an early exercise in land reclamation in the mid-1820s rendered the zone fit for building, the patch of land south of the river where **Raffles Place** now stands was a swampland. However, within just a few years Commercial Square (later renamed Raffles Place) was the colony's busiest business address, boasting the banks, ship's chandlers and warehouses of a burgeoning trading port. Raffles Place was Singapore's central shopping area until Orchard Road superseded it in the late 1960s. Two department stores, Robinsons and John Little, dominated the area then, but subsequent development has turned it into the centre of Singapore's **Financial District**, ringed by buildings so tall that pedestrians crossing the square feel like ants in a canyon. Cutting through the district is **Battery Road**, whose name recalls the days when Fort Fullerton (named after Robert Fullerton, first governor of the Straits Settlements) and its attendant battery of guns used to stand on the site of the Fullerton Building.

RAFFLES PLACE

Map 3, G9. Raffles Place MRT.

The most striking way to experience the giddy heights of the Financial District is by surfacing from Raffles Place MRT, following the signs for Raffles Place itself out of the station, and looking up to gleaming towers, blue skies and racing clouds. To your left is the soaring metallic triangle of the **OUB Centre** (Overseas Union Bank), and to its right, the rocket-shaped **UOB Plaza 2** (United Overseas Bank); in front of you are the rich brown walls of the **Standard Chartered Bank**, and to your right rise sturdy **Singapore Land Tower** and the almost Art Deco **Caltex House**. A smallish statue, entitled *Progress and Advancement*, stands at the northern end of Raffles Place. Erected in 1988, it's a miniature version of what was then the skyline of central Singapore. Inevitably, the very progress and advancement it celebrates has already rendered it out of date – not featured is the **UOB Plaza**, a vast monolith of a building only recently built beside its twin, the UOB Plaza 2. The three roads that run southwest from Raffles Place – Cecil Street, Robinson Road and Shenton Way – are all chock-a-block with more high-rise banks and financial houses; to the west is Chinatown.

BOAT QUAY

Map 3, F7–H8. Raffles Place MRT; bus #51, #124, #145, #166, #174 or #190.

Just north of Raffles Place, and beneath the "elephant's trunk" curve of the Singapore River, the pedestrianized row of shophouses known as **Boat Quay** is presently enjoying a renaissance. Derelict until a few years ago, it's currently Singapore's most fashionable hangout, sporting a

THE BARINGS BANK SCANDAL

Singapore hit the international headlines early in 1995, when the City of London's oldest merchant bank, **Barings**, collapsed as a result of what the London *Evening Standard* called "massive unauthorised dealings" in derivatives on the Japanese stock market. The supposed culprit – "the man who broke the bank", as the press dubbed him – was named as Nick Leeson, an Englishman dealing out of the bank's offices in the Financial District of Singapore. Leeson, it was alleged, had gambled huge funds in the hope of recouping losses made through ill-judged trading, only calling it a day when the bank's losses were approaching one billion pounds. One of his colleagues claimed that Leeson made "other fraudsters look like Walt Disney", although many have questioned the quality of Barings' management and financial controls, which allowed such a catastrophe to happen.

By the time the scandal broke, Leeson was missing, and a pan-Southeast Asian search was in full swing when he finally turned up – and was promptly arrested – six days later in Frankfurt. News of his capture was greeted with cheers from dealers in the Singapore Stock Exchange when it flashed across their screens. In the weeks that followed, Dutch bank ING bought out Barings for one pound sterling, while Nick Leeson languished in a Frankfurt jail. In time, Singapore's application for extradition was duly granted, and less than two weeks after being passed into Singaporean custody, on December 2, 1995, the rogue trader pleaded guilty to two charges of deceit, and received a six-and-a-half-year sentence, three and a half years of which he served out in Tamah Merah Prison. While inside, Leeson was divorced from his wife, and diagnosed with cancer of the colon. In 1999, the movie *Rogue Trader* was released with Ewan McGregor playing the part of Leeson.

huge collection of thriving restaurants and bars, and is an excellent spot for an alfresco meal or drink. There are those around the Singapore restaurant scene who think that the authorities aren't vetting tenants of Boat Quay's units rigorously enough, and that the area's charm is becoming diluted as a result. Certainly, some stretches of the quay are noisier than others, so it's worth taking a stroll before you pick a spot for dinner.

See p.219 for reviews of the bars along Boat Quay. See Chapter 13 for restaurant reviews.

CHANGE ALLEY AERIAL PLAZA AND CLIFFORD PIER

Map 3, H10. Raffles Place MRT.

Branching off the second floor of the Clifford Centre, on the eastern side of Raffles Place, is **Change Alley Aerial Plaza**. The original Change Alley was a cheap, bustling street-level bazaar, which redevelopment wiped off the face of Singapore; all that remains is a sanitized, modern-day version, housed on a covered footbridge across Collyer Quay. The tailors here have a persuasive line in patter – you'll have to be very determined not to waste half an hour being convinced that you need a new suit. But if you want to have a suit made, there are better places to make for (see p.256).

Walking through Change Alley Aerial Plaza deposits you at **Clifford Pier**, long the departure point for trips on the Singapore River and to the southern islands (see p.51). There are still a few bumboats tied up here, though these days they're rented out as cruise boats rather than earning a living as cargo boats.

THE FULLERTON BUILDING AND MERLION PARK

Map 3, H8. Raffles Place MRT.

To the north of the Financial District is the elegant **Fullerton Building**, fronted by sturdy pillars. Built in 1928 as the headquarters for the General Post Office – a role it fulfilled until the mid-1990s – remarkably, this was once one of Singapore's tallest buildings. Old photographs of Singapore depict Japanese soldiers marching past the building after the surrender of the Allied forces during World War II. The Fullerton Building is set to be transformed into a luxury hotel.

Opposite the Fullerton Building is **Merlion Park**, in which Singapore's national symbol, the statue of the mythical Merlion, presides. Half-lion, half-fish, and wholly ugly, the creature reflects Singapore's name (*Singapura* means "Lion City" in Sanskrit) and its historical links with the sea. There are good views of Singapore's colonial buildings from the park, while beside the park entrance is a tacky souvenir shop selling Merlion T-shirts and paperweights to passing tourists.

MARINA SOUTH AND THE PORT OF SINGAPORE

Map 2, J8. Marina South MRT; bus #400.

One of Singapore's most ambitious land reclamation projects, **Marina South**, is plainly visible from Raffles Quay and Shenton Way to the south of the Financial District. This has all the makings of a splendid folly – the entertainment and recreation park which was built on it during the 1980s has already gone bankrupt, and the large patch of land now seems to serve no other purpose than to carry the East Coast Parkway on its journey west. Marina South is a ghost town, its only real asset an imaginative children's playground within a pleasant park.

Below Marina South, Singapore's **port** begins its sprawl westwards. Singapore is the world's busiest container port (the second busiest port overall after Rotterdam), and hundreds of ships are at anchor south of the island at any one time, waiting for permission from the Port of Singapore Authority to enter one of the state's seven terminals.

MARINA SOUTH AND THE PORT OF SINGAPORE

Little India

Faces, temples and sights suddenly change from Oriental to Indian when you head north of the Colonial District to Serangoon Road and **Little India**. A tour around Singapore's answer to Bombay amounts to an all-out assault on the senses. Indian pop music blares out from gargantuan speakers outside cassette shops, the air is perfumed with incense, spices and jasmine garlands, Hindu women promenade in bright sarees, and a wealth of "hole-in-the-wall" restaurants serve up superior curries.

Indians did not always dominate this convenient central niche of Singapore; its original occupants were Europeans and Eurasians who established country houses here, and for whom a racecourse was built (on the site of modern-day Farrer Park) in the 1840s. Only when Indian-run **brick kilns** began to operate here did a pronouncedly Indian community start to evolve. The enclave grew when a number of **cattle** and **buffalo yards** opened in the area in the latter half of the nineteenth century, and more Hindus were drawn in in search of work. Street names hark back to this trade: side by side off the western reach of Serangoon Road are Buffalo Road and Kerbau ("buffalo" in Malay, confusingly) Road, along both of which cattle were kept in slaughter pens. Singapore's largest maternity hospital, nearby on Bukit Timah Road, is called Kandang Kerbau

(Buffalo Pen) Hospital. Indians featured prominently in the development of Singapore, though not always out of choice: from 1825 onwards, convicts were transported from the subcontinent and by the 1840s there were over a thousand Indian prisoners labouring on buildings such as St Andrew's Cathedral and the istana.

Little India's remaining shophouses are fast being touched up from the same pastel paintbox which has "restored" Chinatown to its present doll's house tweeness, but fortunately the colours work far better in an Indian context. The district's backbone is the north–south **Serangoon Road**, whose southern end is alive with shops, restaurants and fortune tellers; to the east, stretching as far as Jalan Besar, is a tight knot of roads that's good for exploration.

THE ZHU JIAO CENTRE

Map 4, B8. Bus #65, #66, #81, #97, #103, #139 or #147.
At the southwestern end of Serangoon Road, the **Zhu Jiao Centre** combines many of Little India's ventures under one roof. Beyond its ground-floor food centre is a wet market that's not for the faint-hearted – traders push around trolleys piled high with goats' heads, while the halal butchers go to work in full view of the customers. Elsewhere, live crabs shuffle busily in buckets, their claws tied together, and there's a mouthwatering range of fruits on sale, including mangoes and whole branches of bananas. Upstairs, on the second floor, you'll find Indian fabrics, leatherware, footwear, watches, and cheap electronic goods. On Sunday, the forecourt of the centre becomes an ad hoc social club for immigrant labourers working in Singapore, most of whom are Bangladeshi. Along the northern side of the Zhu Jiao Centre, **Buffalo Road** has a cluster of provisions stores with sacks of spices and fresh coconut, ground using a primitive machine out on the road.

LITTLE INDIA CONSERVATION AREA

Map 4, B8. Bus #65, #66, #81, #97, #103, #139 or #147.

Bounded by Serangoon Road to the west, Campbell Lane to the north, and Hastings Road to the south, the lovingly restored block of shophouses comprising the **Little India Conservation Area** was opened recently as a sort of Little India in microcosm: behind its cream walls and green shutters you'll find the Hastings Road Food Court and the Little India Arcade, where you can purchase textiles and tapestries, bangles, religious statuary, Indian tapes and CDs, and even traditional Ayurvedic medicines. At the time of Deepavali, the arcade's narrow ways are choked with locals hastening to buy decorations, garlands, traditional confectionery and fine clothes.

The roads nearby are also worth exploring. Campbell Lane is a good place for buying Indian sandals, while walking along Clive Street towards Upper Dickson Road you'll find on your right a batch of junk dealers patiently tinkering with ancient cookers, air-con units and TVs. Left along Upper Dickson Road – past an old barber's shop where a short back and sides is followed by a crunching head yank to "relieve tension" – are the *Madras New Woodlands Restaurant*, at no. 12–14 and, around the corner, *Komala Vilas*, 76 Serangoon Rd, two of Little India's best southern Indian restaurants (see p.203 for full details). Dunlop Street's **Abdul Gaffoor Mosque** (at no. 41) is a little-known, crumbling beauty, bristling with small spires.

THE VEERAMAKALIAMMAN TEMPLE AND PINK STREET

Map 4, B6. Bus #65, #66, #81, #97, #103, #139 or #147.

In the heart of Little India on Serangoon Road, opposite

the turning to Veerasamy Road, the **Veeramakaliamman Temple** – dedicated to the ferocious Hindu goddess, Kali – features a fanciful *gopuram* that's flanked by majestic lions on the temple walls. Each year during Deepavali (p.244), a pulsating market takes place on the open land just above the temple.

North from the temple, and off to the right lies **Pink Street**, one of the most incongruous and sordid spots in the whole of clean, shiny Singapore – but you won't find it on any city map. The entire length of the "street" (in fact it's merely an alley between the backs of Rowell and Desker roads) is punctuated by open doorways, inside which gaggles of bored-looking prostitutes sit knitting or watching TV, oblivious to the gawping local men who accumulate outside. Stalls along the alley sell distinctly un-Singaporean merchandise such as sex toys, blue videos and potency pills, while con men work the "three cups and a ball" routine on unwary passers-by.

Running parallel to Serangoon Road, Race Course Road boasts a clutch of fine restaurants (for details of Indian restaurants, see pp.200–205) and some temples.

THE SRI SRINIVASA PERUMAL TEMPLE

Map 4, A2. Bus #65, #66, #81, #97, #103, #139 or #147.
Each year, on the day of the Thaipusam festival (see p.239), the courtyard of the **Sri Srinivasa Perumal Temple**, at 397 Serangoon Rd, witnesses a gruesome melee of activity, as Hindu devotees don huge metal frames (*kavadis*) topped with peacock feathers, which are fastened to their flesh with hooks and prongs. The devotees then leave the temple, stopping only while a coconut is smashed at their feet for good luck, and parade all the way to the Chettiar

Temple on Tank Road, off Orchard Road (see p.68). Even if you miss the festival, it's worth a trip to see the five-tiered *gopuram* with its sculptures of the various manifestations of Lord Vishnu the Preserver. On the wall to the right of the front gate is a sculpted elephant, its leg caught in a crocodile's mouth.

THE SAKAYA MUNI BUDDHA GAYA TEMPLE

Map 4, A1. Bus #65, #66, #81, #97, #103, #139 or #147.

The **Sakaya Muni Buddha Gaya Temple** (or Temple of the Thousand Lights) at no. 366 Race Course Rd is a slightly kitsch building that betrays a strong Thai influence – not surprising, since it was built entirely by a Thai monk, Vutthisasala. On the left of the temple as you enter is a huge replica of the Buddha's footprint, inlaid with mother-of-pearl, and beyond is a great Buddha ringed by the thousand electric lights from which the temple takes its alternative name. Twenty-five scenes from the Buddha's life decorate the pedestal on which he sits. It is possible to walk inside the statue, through a door in its back; inside is a smaller representation of the Buddha, this time reclining. The left wall of the temple features a sort of wheel of fortune – spin it (for 30c) and take the numbered sheet of paper that corresponds to the number at which the wheel stops, to discover your fortune. Further along the left wall, a small donation entitles you to a shake of a tin full of numbered sticks, after which, again, you get a corresponding sheet of forecasts.

The Arab Quarter

Before the arrival of Raffles, the area of Singapore west of the Rochor River housed a Malay village known as Kampong Glam, after the *Gelam* tribe of sea gypsies who lived there. After signing a dubious treaty with the newly installed "Sultan" Hussein Mohammed Shah, Raffles allotted the area to the sultan and designated the land around it as a Muslim settlement, and soon the zone was attracting Arab traders, as the road names in today's **Arab Quarter** – Baghdad Street, Muscat Street and Haji Lane – suggest. Even now, descendants of Sultan Hussein live in the grounds of the Istana Kampong Glam, a palace right in the centre of the district, bounded by Arab Street, Beach Road, Jalan Sultan and Rochor Canal Road. Just outside the quarter, **Beach Road** still maintains shops which betray its former proximity to the sea – ships' chandlers and fishing tackle specialists – and you should also take the time to walk southwest from Arab Street to see the two logic-defying office buildings that together comprise **The Gateway**. Designed by I.M. Pei, they rise magnificently into the air like vast razor blades and appear two-dimensional when viewed from certain angles.

ARAB STREET

Map 4, F7–H8. Bugis MRT; bus #7, #107, #130, #145 or #197.
Arab Street boasts the highest concentration of shops in the Arab Quarter; its pavements are an obstacle course of carpets, cloths, baskets and bags. Most of the shops have been renovated, though one or two (like Shivlal & Sons at no. 77, and Aik Bee at no. 73) still retain their original dark wood and glass cabinets, and wide wooden benches where the shopkeepers sit. Textile stores are most prominent, their walls, ceilings and doorways draped with cloths and batiks. Elsewhere you'll see leather, basketware, gold, gemstones and jewellery for sale, while the most impressive range of basketware and rattan work – fans, hats and walking sticks – is found at Rishi Handicrafts, at no. 58. It's easy to spend a couple of hours weaving in and out of the stores, but don't expect a quiet window-shopping session – the traders here are masters of the forced sale, and will have you loaded with sarongs, baskets and leather bags before you know it.

AROUND NORTH BRIDGE ROAD

Map 4, G6–10. Bugis MRT; bus #7, #107, #130, #145 or #197.
The Arab quarter's most evocative patch is the stretch of **North Bridge Road** between Arab Street and Jalan Sultan. Here, the men sport long sarongs and Abe Lincoln beards, while the women fantastically colourful shawls and robes, while the shops and restaurants are geared more towards locals than tourists: Jamal Kazura Aromatics, at 728 North Bridge Rd, for instance, sells alcohol-free perfumes, while neighbouring shops stock rosaries, prayer mats and the *songkok* hats worn by Muslim males in mosques, and *miswak* sticks – twigs the width of a finger used by some locals to clean their teeth.

A gaggle of Muslim Indian restaurants operates along this
stretch of North Bridge Road: see pp.201–205 for details.

Several roads run off the western side of North Bridge
Road, including Jalan Pisang (Banana Street), on which a
street barber works under a tarpaulin. A walk up Jalan
Kubor (Grave Street) and across Victoria Street takes you
to an unkempt Muslim **cemetery** where, it is said, Malay
royalty are buried. On Sundays, Victoria Street throngs
with children in full Muslim garb on their way to study
scripture at the Arabic school, **Madrasah Al Junied Al-
Islamiah**.

Istana Kampong Glam

Map 4, H6–7. Bugis MRT; bus #7, #107, #130, #145 or #197.
Squatting between Kandahar and Aliwal streets, the **Istana
Kampong Glam** was built as the royal palace of Sultan Ali
Iskandar Shah, son of Sultan Hussein who negotiated with
Raffles to hand over Singapore to the British; the sultan's
descendants live here to this day, and continue to share an
annual government allowance. Despite its royal provenance,
the istana is a modest, colonial-style building, run-down
and dingy, its grounds dotted with huts. This could change,
though, if plans to turn the property into a Malay heritage
museum come to fruition. Until this happens, tourists have
to make do with glimpsing the building from outside the
front gates.

Approaching the palace, there's a **stonemason's** shop on
the corner of Baghdad Street and Sultan Gate, which chips
out the lions that stand outside Chinese temples, and
Muslim gravestones – uniformly shaped stones that look
remarkably like chess pawns.

THE SULTAN MOSQUE

Map 4, G7. Daily 9am–1pm. Bugis MRT; bus #7, #107, #130, #145 or #197.

Looking down pedestrianized Bussorah Street from Baghdad Street, you get the best initial views of the golden domes of the **Sultan Mosque** or Masjid Sultan, the beating heart of the Muslim faith in Singapore. An earlier mosque stood on this site, finished in 1825 and constructed with the help of a $3000 donation from the East India Company. The present building was completed a century later, according to a design by colonial architects Swan and MacLaren: if you look carefully at the glistening necks of the domes, you can see that the effect is created by the bases of thousands of ordinary glass bottles, an incongruity which sets the tone for the rest of the building. Steps at the top of Bussorah Street lead into a wide lobby, where a digital display lists current prayer times. Beyond, and out of bounds to non-Muslims, is the main prayer hall, a large, bare chamber that's fronted by two more digital clocks. An exhaustive set of rules applies to visitors wishing to enter the lobby: shoes must be taken off and shoulders and legs covered, no video cameras are allowed inside the mosque, and entry is not permitted during the Friday mass congregation (11.30am–2.30pm). The best time to come is in the Muslim fasting month of Ramadan – the faithful can only eat after dusk, and Muskat Street and Kandahar Street are awash with stalls selling *biriyani*, barbecued chicken and cakes.

Northern
Singapore

W hile land reclamation has radically altered the east coast, and industrialization the west, the **northern** expanses of the island up to the Straits of Johor still retain pockets of the **rainforest** and mangrove swamp which blanketed Singapore on Raffles' arrival in 1819. These are interspersed today with sprawling **new towns** like Toa Payoh, maze-like Bishan and Ang Mo Kio, built in the 1970s. The name of the last, meaning "red-haired devil's bridge", refers to the nineteenth-century British surveyor, John Turnbull Thomson, under whose supervision the transport network of Singapore began to penetrate the interior of the island. Man-eating tigers roamed these parts well into the twentieth century, and it was here that Allied forces confronted the invading Japanese army in 1942, a period of Singaporean history movingly recalled by the **Kranji War Memorial** on Woodlands Road. Still visible at the far northern sweep of the island are the remnants of Singapore's agricultural past: you'll see prawn and poultry farms, orchards and vegetable gardens when travelling in these parts.

Dominating the central northern region are two nature reserves, divided by the main road route to Malaysia, the Bukit Timah Expressway. West of the expressway is **Bukit Timah Nature Reserve**, an accessible slice of primary rainforest, while to the east, the four reservoirs of the Central Catchment Area are one of Singapore's main sources of water. North of here, the principal tourist attraction is the excellent **Singapore Zoological Gardens**, sited on a finger of land pointing into the Seletar Reservoir. To the east are two of Singapore's most eye-catching Buddhist temples – **Siong Lim Temple** and the **Kong Meng San Phor Kark See** temple complex – as well as tiny Tai Gin Road, where the occasional residence of Chinese nationalist leader Dr Sun Yat Sen and Singapore's Burmese temple are found.

- -

Travel between the attractions in northern Singapore is decidedly tricky unless you are driving, or in a cab, so don't expect to take in everything in a day. However, Siong Lim Temple, Sun Yat Sen Villa and the Burmese Temple all nestle around the outskirts of Toa Payoh new town and could be incorporated into a single expedition; as could the zoo, Mandai Orchid Gardens and the Kranji Cemetery and Memorial. The Kong Meng San Phor Kark See temple complex really requires a separate journey.

- -

BUKIT TIMAH NATURE RESERVE

Map 6, D6. Daily 7am–7pm; free. Bus #170, #171, or #181.

Bukit Timah Road runs northwest from the junction of Selegie and Serangoon roads, to the faceless town of **Bukit Timah**, 8km further on. Bukit Timah boasts Singapore's last remaining pocket of primary rainforest, which now comprises **Bukit Timah Nature Reserve**. Visiting this area of Singapore in the mid-eighteenth century, natural historian Alfred Russel Wallace reported seeing "tiger pits, carefully covered with sticks and leaves and so well concealed, that in several cases I had a narrow escape from falling into them . . . Formerly a sharp stake was stuck erect in the bottom," he continued, "but after an unfortunate traveller had been killed by falling into one, its use was forbidden."

Today the reserve, established in 1883 by Nathaniel Cantley who was superintendent of the Botanic Gardens, yields no such hazards and is a refuge for the dwindling numbers of species still extant in Singapore – only 25 types of mammal now inhabit the island. Creatures you're most likely to see in Bukit Timah are long-tailed macaques, butterflies and other insects, and birds like the dark-necked tailorbird, which builds its nest by sewing together leaves. Scorpions, snakes, flying lemurs and pangolins (anteaters, whose name is derived from the Malay word *peng-goling*, meaning "roller", a reference to the animal's habit of rolling into a ball when threatened) still roam here too.

Buses drop you beside a row of shops where you can pick up light snacks and bottled water to take into the reserve.

Recent alterations have vastly improved the reserve, which now has an informative **visitor centre** (daily 8.30am–6pm) full of displays, specimens and photos relating to the wildlife beyond. Four main paths from the centre twist and turn through the forest around and to the top of **Bukit Timah Hill**, which, at a paltry 162.5m, is actually Singapore's highest hill. The paths are all well signposted, colour-coded and dotted with rest points, and they're clearly mapped on the free leaflet handed out to all visitors. You'd do best to visit in the cool of early morning and midweek, when there are fewer visitors.

BUKIT TIMAH NATURE RESERVE

Dramatic **Hindhede Quarry** (five minutes' walk up the slope to the left of the visitor centre) is a fine place to head for once you've explored the forest – its deep green waters are ideal for a cooling swim.

Bukit Batok

Map 6, C6.

Across Bukit Timah Road from the reserve, another forested hill, **Bukit Batok**, is where British and Australian POWs were forced to erect a fifteen-metre-high wooden shrine, the Syonan Tyureito, for their Japanese captors. Only the steps at its base now remain. Legend has it that the shrine itself was destroyed by termites, which the prisoners secretly introduced to the structure. Gone, too, is the wooden cross erected by the POWs to honour their dead. The hill is located at the end of the next left turning, Lorong Sesuai, which was laid by the same prisoners who built the shrine.

SINGAPORE ZOOLOGICAL GARDENS

Map 6, D4. Daily 8.30am–6pm; $10.30, children $4.60. Bus #171 to Mandai Road, then #138, or Ang Mo Kio MRT and then bus #138.

The **Singapore Zoological Gardens** on Mandai Lake Road are spread over a promontory jutting into peaceful Seletar Reservoir. The gardens attract over one million visitors a year – a fact perhaps explained by their status as one of the world's few open zoos, where moats are preferred to cages. Spacious exhibits manage to approximate the natural habitats of the animals, and though leopards, pumas and jaguars still have to be kept behind bars, this is a thoughtful, humane environment, described as "one of the really beautiful zoos" by no less an authority than conservationist Sir Peter Scott.

SINGAPORE ZOOLOGICAL GARDENS

There are over two thousand animals here, representing more than 240 species, so it's best to allow a whole day for your visit. A **tram** ($2) circles the grounds on a one-way circuit, but be prepared for a lot of footwork. Highlights include the Komodo dragons, the polar bears, which you view underwater from a gallery, and the primate kingdom. Also worth checking out is the **special loan enclosure** that has recently played host to a giant panda, an Indian white tiger and a golden monkey. Two **animal shows** are featured daily – a primate and reptile show (10.30am & 2.30pm) and an elephant and sea lion show (11.30am & 3.30pm). The **Children's World** area offers kids the chance to ride a camel, hold young chicks and watch a milking demonstration; at 9am and 4pm daily they can even share a **meal with an orang-utan** (see p.166).

The $1 *Guide to S'pore Zoo* gives details of riding and feeding times and a helpful map, and suggests itineraries which take in all the major shows and attractions. At the other end of your trip, you might care to drop by the **gift shop** next to the exit, which stocks cuddly toys and rather less tempting bags of "zoo poo" compost. Several food and drink kiosks are dotted around the zoo, or you can head for the reasonable *Makan Terrace*, bang in the centre of the grounds, where there are one or two hawker stalls.

The Night Safari

Daily 7.30pm–midnight; $15.45, children $10.30.

The opening of the **Night Safari** a few years back substantially increased the grounds of the zoo. Here, over a hundred species of animals – elephants, rhinos, giraffes and leopards, hyenas, otters and incredibly cute fishing cats – play out their nocturnal routines under a forest of standard lamps. Only five of the safari's eight zones are walkable – to see the rest you'll need to take a fifty-minute *Jurassic Park-*

style tram ride ($3), and tolerate the intrusive chattering of its taped guide. A meal at one of two restaurants outside the entrance will pass the time between the zoo's closing and the safari's opening.

MANDAI ORCHID GARDENS

Map 6, D4. Daily 8.30am–5.30pm; $2. Ang Mo Kio MRT, then bus #138.

It's only a ten-minute walk from the Singapore Zoological Gardens down Mandai Lake Road to the **Mandai Orchid Gardens**. Orchids are big business in Singapore: in 1991 alone, over $20 million of cut orchid flowers were exported from 56 farms across the state. Here, the flowers are cultivated on a gentle slope, tended by old ladies in wide-brimmed hats. Unless you are a keen horticulturist, the place will be of limited interest as little effort has been taken to make it instructive. Still, if you've been to the zoo, the gardens make a colourful detour on the way home, and the price of a gift box of orchids (under $70) compares favourably with more central flower shops.

THE SUN YAT SEN VILLA AND AROUND

Map 6, F7. Mon–Fri 9am–4pm, Sat 9am–3pm; free. Bus #139.

Between Jalan Toa Payoh to the north, and Balestier Road to the south is the **Sun Yat Sen Villa**, on tiny Tai Gin Road. Built to house the mistress of a wealthy Chinese businessman, this attractive bungalow changed hands in 1905, when one Teo Eng Hock bought it for his mother. Chinese nationalist leader Dr Sun Yat Sen paid his first of eight visits to Singapore the following year, and was invited by Teo to stay at Tai Gin Road, where he quickly established a Singapore branch of the Tong Meng Hui – a society dedicated to replacing the Manchu dynasty in China with a modern republic. After serving as a communications camp for the Japanese during World War II, the villa fell into disrepair until 1966, when it was opened to the public. Sadly, the collection of photographs inside is fairly dull unless you are familiar with that period of Chinese history; of more interest are the second-floor photos of Singapore during World War II, and a collection of combs, keys, pipes, glasses and other personal effects that once belonged to victims of the Japanese occupation.

Sasanaramsi Burmese Buddhist Temple

Map 6, F7. Daily 6am–10pm. Bus #139.

Next door to the Sun Yat Sen Villa is the **Sasanaramsi Burmese Buddhist Temple**, reconstructed in just two years after being forced to move from its previous site at Kinta Road because of redevelopment. Decorated by craftsmen from Burma, the temple's ground floor is dominated by a large, white marble statue of the Buddha brought over from Burma in 1932; upstairs is another Buddha statue, this time standing, and ringed by blue skies painted on the wall behind. Tiny Buddha images are presently being "bought" by worshippers at $1000 a throw in order to raise funds; when they're all sold they'll be mounted on the painted sky.

The Siong Lim Temple

Map 6, G7. Toa Payoh MRT, then bus #8.

The name of the popular **Siong Lim Temple**, at 184e Jalan Toa Payoh, means "Twin Groves of the Lotus Mountain" – a reference to the Buddha's birth in a grove of trees and his death under a Bodhi tree. The Chinese abbot Sek Hean Wei established the temple at the turn of the century when, passing through Singapore on his way home after a pilgrimage to Sri Lanka, he was waylaid by wealthy

THE SUN YAT SEN VILLA AND AROUND

Hokkien merchant and philanthropist Low Kim Pong, who supplied both land and finances for the venture. Several renovations have failed to rob the temple of its grandeur: set behind a rock garden that combines a water cascade, ponds, streams and bridges, it is guarded by statues of the **Four Kings of Heaven**, each posted to repel evil, symbolized by the demons on which they are treading. The highly regarded collection of carved and sculpted gods inside the temple's several halls includes a **Laughing Buddha**, believed to grant good luck if you rub his stomach, a shrine to Kuan Yin, goddess of mercy (in the rear hall), and a number of Thai-style Buddha figures.

Bidadari Cemetery

Map 6, H7. Bus #97 or #106.

One of Singapore's more offbeat attractions, **Bidadari Cemetery**, lies some 10km northeast of the city on Upper Serangoon Road. It's a Christian graveyard and the majority of its aged gravestones are in typical Western style, but there are Chinese graves here too, their semicircular design affording a natural kneeling place at which to pray for the wellbeing of one's ancestors. Buried somewhere in the area is A.P. Williams, a British sailor upon whose life Joseph Conrad based his novel *Lord Jim*. In his travelogue *In Search of Conrad*, Gavin Young describes how he tracked down Williams' burial plot in the depths of Singapore's public records offices – but seeking out the number he quotes (2559) yields no sign of the grave. Many species of birds flourish in the long grass of the grounds, making this a good spot for ornithologists – indeed, the Nature Society of Singapore periodically visits the cemetery. A word of warning, though: don't go wading into tall grass unless you are wearing ankle-high boots, as snakes also inhabit the cemetery.

PHOR KARK SEE TEMPLE

Map 6, F6. Bus #130.

The largest temple complex in Singapore – and one of the largest in Southeast Asia – lies north of MacRitchie Reservoir, right in the middle of the island. **Phor Kark See Temple** (known in full as the Kong Meng San Phor Kark See Temple Complex) at 88 Bright Hill Drive, spreads over nineteen acres and combines temples, pagodas, pavilions, a Buddhist library and a vast crematorium so impressively that it has been used several times as a backdrop to Chinese kung fu movies. More modern than Siong Lim, Phor Kark See boasts none of the faded charm of Singapore's older temples, but relies instead on its sheer magnitude and exuberant decor for effect. Multi-tiered roofs bristle with ceramic dragons, phoenixes, birds and human figures, while around the complex are statues of various deities, including a nine-metre-high marble statue of Kuan Yin, goddess of mercy. A soaring pagoda capped by a golden *chedi* (a reliquary tower) renders the complex even more striking. Even the **crematorium** – conveniently placed for the nearby Evergreen Home for the elderly – doesn't do things by half. Housed below a Thai-style facade of elaborately carved gilt wood, it can cope with five ceremonies at a time.

Below the crematorium is a pair of ponds, where thousands of turtles sunbathe precariously on wooden planks that slant into the waters. A nearby sign prohibits worshippers from putting new turtles into the ponds, a practice supposed to bring good luck. Old ladies beside the viewing gallery sell bunches of vegetables for "one dolla, one dolla", which purchasers then throw to the lucky turtles.

KRANJI WAR CEMETERY AND MEMORIAL

Map 6, C3. Bus #170, #181, or #182.

The **Kranji War Cemetery and Memorial** on Woodlands Road, where only the sound of birds and insects breaks the silence in the immaculately kept grounds, is the resting place of the many Allied troops who died in the defence of Singapore. As you enter, row upon row of graves slope up the landscaped hill in front of you, some identified only as "known unto God". The graves are bare: flowers are banned, as still water encourages mosquitoes to breed. A simple stone cross stands over the cemetery and above is the **memorial**, around which are recorded all the names of more than twenty thousand soldiers (from Britain, Canada, Sri Lanka, India, Malaysia, the Netherlands, New Zealand and Singapore) who died in this region during World War II. Two unassuming **tombs** stand on the wide lawns below the cemetery, belonging to Yusof Bin Ishak and Dr Benjamin Henry Sheares, independent Singapore's first two presidents.

SINGAPORE TURF CLUB

Map 6, C3. Day tickets from $5 to $20. For current race details, call ⓣ 8791000. Bus #170.

Singapore's only racecourse is at **Singapore Turf Club**, and as legal gambling in Singapore outside the course is restricted, the annual racing calendar here is very popular. The most prestigious events include the Lion City Cup, the Singapore Gold Cup and the Singapore Derby. Race dates change from year to year, so it's worth calling the information hotline (above) if you want to time your visit to coincide with a big race day. An evening's racing viewed from the enclosure can be booked in advance, but you'd do far better to just turn up, eat at the course's decent food centre and soak up the atmosphere in the stands. There's a fairly strict dress code – sandals, jeans, shorts and T-shirts are out – and foreign visitors have to take their passports with them. When there's no racing in Singapore, a giant video screen links the racecourse to various courses across the causeway in Malaysia.

SUNGEI BULOH NATURE PARK

Map 6, B2; daily 7am–7pm; $1; ☎ 7941401. Woodlands or Kranji MRT, then bus #925.

Sungei Buloh Nature Park on the north coast of Singapore is the island's newest wildlife sanctuary. Beyond its visitor centre, café and video theatre (shows daily 9am, 11am, 1pm & 3pm) stretches a vast expanse of mangrove, mud flats, orchards and grassland, home to kingfishers, mudskippers, herons and sea eagles. Visit between September and March and you're likely to catch sight of migratory birds from around Asia roosting and feeding.

Eastern Singapore

Thirty years ago, **eastern Singapore** was largely rural, dotted with Malay kampung villages which perched on stilts over the shoreline, harbouring the odd weekend retreat owned by Europeans or monied locals. Massive **land reclamation** and development programmes have altered the region beyond recognition, wiping out all traces of the kampungs and throwing up huge housing projects in their place. Today, former seafront suburbs like Bedok are separated from the Straits of Singapore by a broad crescent of man-made land, much of which constitutes the **East Coast Park**, whose five kilometres have leisure and watersports facilities, imported sand beaches and seafood restaurants. Despite the massive upheavals that have ruptured the communities of the east coast, parts of it, including the suburbs of **Geylang** and **Katong**, have managed to retain a strong Malay identity. **Geylang Road** runs east from the Kallang River; off the road are 42 lorongs, or lanes, down which clusters of brothels are decked out with fairy lights. At its far eastern end, Geylang Road meets **Joo Chiat Road**, which – after the restrictions of downtown Singapore – has a refreshingly laid-back and shambolic air.

Dominating the eastern tip of the island is Changi airport, and beyond that **Changi Village**, where the Japanese interned Allied troops and civilians during World War II. From Changi Point, it's possible to take a boat to **Pulau Ubin**, a small island which has echoes of pre-development Singapore.

East coast hotels are listed on p.160.

GEYLANG AND KATONG

Malay culture has held sway in and around the adjoining suburbs of **Geylang** and **Katong** since the mid-nineteenth century, when Malays and Indonesians first arrived to work in the local *copra* (coconut husk) processing factory and later on its *serai* (lemon grass) farms. Many of its shophouses, restaurants and food centres are Malay-influenced, less so the thriving trade in prostitution that carries on here, unchecked by the local authorities.

The Malay Village

Map 7, C3. Daily 10am–10pm; $10 (children $7) for attractions, otherwise free. Paya Lebar MRT; bus #2, #7, #51 or #67.

Opened in 1990, and conceived as a celebration of the cuisine, music, dance, arts and crafts of the Malay people, the **Malay Village** on Changi Road conspicuously failed either to woo tourists or to rent out its replica wooden kampung-style shops to locals, and seemed to be dying a slow death until a Hong Kong-based company took it over. Sadly, the three new tourist lures unveiled at the recent relaunch pack very little punch: the **Lagenda Fantasi**, an audiovisual presentation of Islamic and Malay legends such as Aladdin, Ali Baba and Nile Sang Utama, is aimed squarely at kids, but probably wouldn't impress them; the **Cultural Museum** features a humdrum array of household instruments, cloths, kites and *kris*, and a mock-up of a Malay wedding scene; and the dismal **Kampung Days** exhibition reproduces a traditional Malay kampung homestead, complete with fishing and rice-pounding scenes, a *wayang kulit* stage, an open-air cinema, and another (seemingly obligatory) wedding scene. If you give these attractions a miss, you're left with the village's **shops**, selling batik, kites, spinning tops, bird cages and textiles, and the evening **food court** with free cultural performances on Saturday and Sunday nights.

Just along Changi Road to the east of the road named Geylang Serai, a hawker centre and wet market provide a more authentic Malay atmosphere, from the smell of clove cigarettes to the line of sarong sellers beyond the food stalls.

Joo Chiat Road

Map 7, C4. Paya Lebar MRT or bus #16.

As you walk south down Joo Chiat Road you'll have to negotiate piles of merchandise that spill out of shophouses and onto the pavement. In particular, there's cane and wood furniture in the Phoon Fang Cheong shop at no. 175, while the store at no. 86 specializes in Chinese religious paraphernalia. Of the buildings, none are as magnificent as the immaculate **Peranakan shophouses** on Koon Seng Road (on your left about halfway down Joo Chiat Road), where painstaking work has restored the multicoloured facades, eaves and mouldings. In the **Joo Chiat Complex** at the northern end of the road, textile merchants drape their wares on any available floor and wall space, transforming the drab interior. More market than shopping centre, it's a prime destination for anyone interested in buying cheap silk, batik, rugs or muslin.

CHANGI PRISON

Map 7, G3. Museum Mon–Sat 10am–5pm, Sun open for 5.30pm religious service only; free. Bus #2.

Infamous **Changi Prison** was the site of a World War II POW camp in which Allied prisoners were subjected to the harshest of treatment by their Japanese jailers. The prison itself is still in use (drug offenders are periodically executed here), and on its north side, through the outer gates, is the hugely moving **museum**. The museum displays sketches and photographs that plot the Japanese invasion of Singapore and the fate of the soldiers and civilians subsequently incarcerated here and in nearby camps. Predominant are photos by George Aspinall, which record the appalling living conditions and illnesses suffered by POWs in Malaya and Thailand during the occupation. Aspinall, then a young Australian trooper, took his photographs using a folding Kodak 2 camera, later developing them with a stock of processing materials which he found while working on a labour gang in Singapore's docks. Novelist James Clavell was a young British artillery officer in Singapore at the time of the Japanese invasion; later he drew on his own experience of the "obscene forbidding prison" at Changi in writing *King Rat*, never forgetting that in the cells of the prison camp ". . . the stench was nauseating. Stench from rotting bodies. Stench from a generation of confined human bodies." Elsewhere in the museum, sketches drawn by W.R.M. Haxworth of prisoners playing bridge, amongst other things, betray a dry sense of humour and some stiff upper lips in the face of adversity.

Beyond the museum is a replica of a simple wooden chapel, typical of those erected in Singapore's wartime prisons; its brass cross was crafted from spent ammunition casings, while the north wall carries poignant messages, penned by visiting former POWs and relatives.

On a lighter note, among the war-related books stocked in the souvenir shop is *The Happiness Box*, the first copy of which was written, illustrated and bound by POWs in Changi in 1942 as a Christmas present for children in the prison. The Japanese became suspicious of the POWs' motives when they noticed one of the book's central characters was called Winston, but it was buried in the prison grounds before it could be confiscated, and only recovered after the war had ended.

CHANGI VILLAGE

Map 7, I1. Bus #2.

There's little to bring you out to **Changi Village**, ten minutes further on from the prison, save to catch a boat from **Changi Point**, behind the bus terminal, for Pulau Ubin (see opposite) or for the coast of Johor in Malaysia (see "Departure", p.42). The left-hand jetty is for Ubin, the right-hand one for bumboats to Johor.

A stroll over the footbridge to the right of the two jetties takes you to **Changi Beach**, the execution site of many thousands of Singaporean civilians by Japanese soldiers during World War II. As a beach it wins few prizes and its most pleasant aspect is its view: to your left as you look out to sea is Pulau Ubin; slightly to the right is the island of Tekong (a military zone), behind which you can see a hill on mainland Malaysia. In the water you'll see *kelongs* (large fish traps), and boats galore, from bumboats to supertankers. Changi Village Road, the village's main drag, has a smattering of good restaurants, or try the hawker centre near the bus terminal.

PULAU UBIN

Map 1, H3. Bus #2, then boat from Changi Point.

Pulau Ubin, 2km offshore, gives visitors a pretty good idea of what Singapore would have been like fifty years ago. A lazy backwater tucked into the Straits of Johor, it's a great place to come if you're tired of shops, high-rises and traffic. It's almost worth coming for the boat trip alone, made in an old oil-stained bumboat which chugs noisily across Serangoon Harbour, belching fumes all the way. Boats depart from Changi Point throughout the day from 6am onwards, leaving whenever they're full. The last boat back to Changi leaves as late as 10pm, if there's a demand, but plan to be at the jetty by 8.30pm at the latest, just in case. The trip takes ten minutes and costs $1.50 each way.

The boats dock at a rickety old pier in **Ubin Village**, where Malay stilt houses teeter over the sludgy mangrove beach. The main road is lined with scores of battered old mopeds, locals sit around, watching the day take its course, and chickens run free in the dirt. The best, and most enjoyable, way to explore the dirt tracks of Ubin is by **mountain bike**: at *Universal Adventure*, on the left-hand side of the road leading west from the jetty, you'll pay $5–15 for a day's rental, depending on the bike and the season (it's most expensive during school holidays). You'll be given a baffling map of the island's labyrinthine network of tracks, though it's more fun to strike off and see where you end up – Ubin is only a small island (just 7km by 2km) so you won't get lost.

Ride through the village until you come to a basketball court, where a right turn takes you past raised kampung houses and rubber trees to the eastern side of the island. Turning left instead takes you to the centre of the island; after about five minutes you'll come to an impressively deep quarry, from which granite was taken to build the causeway linking Singapore to Malaysia – Ubin is the Malay word for granite. Further north along this track is a rather incongruous **Thai Buddhist Temple**, complete with portraits of the king and queen of Thailand, and a bookcase full of Thai books. Pictures telling the story of the life of Buddha ring the inner walls of the temple, along with images of various Buddhist hells – most disturbing of which depicts demons pouring boiling liquid down the mouths of "those who always drink liquor". If you follow the left track out of Ubin Village for twenty or thirty minutes, you'll come to a steep slope: a right turn at the top takes you straight to the temple, just beyond which is another quarry where you can take a swim and cool off.

Ignoring the right turn to the temple at the top of the steep slope and continuing straight ahead takes you towards the island's best eating place, the *Ubin Seafood Restaurant* (see p.187). It's a bit tricky to find though – look out for taxis taking Singaporean diners there to discover which track to turn down.

Western Singapore

Since the government's industrialization programme began in the late 1960s, far **western Singapore** has become the manufacturing heart of the state, and today thousands of companies occupy units within the towns of Jurong and Tuas. Manufacturing is the backbone of Singapore's economic success – the state presently produces more than half the world's hard disk drives, for example. Despite this saturation, much of the western region – developed from former swampland and wasteland – remains remarkably verdant. Surprisingly, given the industrial surroundings, several major tourist attractions are located here, including **Haw Par Villa**, as garish a theme park as you'll ever set eyes on, and – the pick of the bunch – fascinating **Jurong BirdPark**. Slightly further east, the **Singapore Science Centre** is packed with imaginative and informative exhibitions, and is not to be missed if you've got kids to entertain, while further west – and not to be missed if you've got adults to entertain – is the **Tiger Brewery**. Just west of Chinatown is the district of **Telok Blangah**, once the seat of Singapore's *temenggong* or chieftain, and still dominated by Mount Faber, as well as the **World Trade Centre**, from where cable cars, boats and buses make for Sentosa (see p.133). All of these places are easily reached from the city centre, using either buses or the MRT.

THE WORLD TRADE CENTRE AND MOUNT FABER

Map 8, I5–6. Bus #97, #143, or #166.

A twenty-minute walk west of Chinatown is the area known as **Telok Blangah** in which stands Singapore's **World Trade Centre**, itself a splendid shopping centre-cum-marine terminal, from where boats depart for Indonesia's Riau Archipelago. You'll know when to get off the bus, because you'll see cable cars rocking across the skyline in front of you, on their way to and from **Mount Faber** and across to Sentosa Island (see p.131). This "mount" (hillock would be a better word), lying 600m north of the WTC, commands fine views of Keppel Harbour and central Singapore to the northeast, which are even more impressive at night when the city is lit up. Originally called Telok Blangah, the mount was renamed in 1845 after government engineer Captain Charles Edward Faber. It's a long, steep walk from Telok Blangah Road up to the top of Mount Faber, and it's better to take the **cable car** from the World Trade Centre complex (daily 8.30am–9pm; $6.90 return, children $3.90). An accident in 1983, when a ship's mast clipped the cables on which the cars are suspended, cost seven passengers their lives, but today laser eyes ensure that history won't repeat itself. There's a strong souvenir shop presence at the top, though you can escape this by moving away from the area immediately around the cable car station and up into the park.

In the early days of colonial rule, Temenggong Abdul Rahman played prime minister to Sultan Hussein Shah's president, and his signature graced the treaty authorizing the East India Company to operate out of Singapore. All that's left of his settlement on the southern slopes of Mount Faber is its pillared mosque – the **State of Johor Mosque** – and, behind that, a small Malay cemetery and a portion of the brickwork that once housed the *temenggong*'s baths.

HAW PAR VILLA

Map 8, F5. Daily 9am–6pm; $5, children $2.50. Buona Vista MRT, then bus #200; or bus #51 or #143.

As an entertaining exercise in bad taste, **Haw Par Villa** has few equals. Located 7km from the downtown area at 262 Pasir Panjang Rd, it describes itself as a "historical theme park founded on Chinese legends and values", for which read a gaudy, gory parade of over a thousand grotesque statues. Previously known as Tiger Balm Gardens, the park now takes its name from its original owners, the Aw brothers, Boon Haw and Boon Par, who made a fortune early this century selling **Tiger Balm** – a cure-all unction created by their father. When the British government introduced licensing requirements for the possession of large animals, the private zoo which the brothers maintained on their estate here was closed down and replaced by statues.

The rides, theatre shows and multimedia attractions which were added a few years back to broaden the appeal of the place actually did no such thing. All have now been closed, leaving only the hundreds of **statues** for which the park is famous.

HOLLAND VILLAGE

Map 8, F3. Buona Vista MRT; bus #7 or #105.

Holland Village was previously home to some of the British soldiers based in Singapore and has now developed into an expat stronghold, with a whole row of Western restaurants and shops. The **Holland Road Shopping Centre** at 211 Holland Ave is the place to head for if you want to buy Asian art, crafts or textiles: there are shops on two levels where you can buy anything from an Indian pram to a Chinese opium pipe, while outside there are cobblers, key-cutters and newsagents. The small road alongside the shopping centre is called **Lorong Liput**, and off it is Lorong Mambong, home to a thriving restaurant scene and to **craft shops** that specialize in ceramic elephants, dragon pots, porcelain, rattan and bamboo products. **Pasar Holland**, opposite the shops, is a small, tumbledown market selling fruit, flowers, fish and meat, as well as housing a handful of hawker stalls.

Details of arts and crafts outlets are given on pp.247–251.

SINGAPORE SCIENCE CENTRE

Map 8, C4. Tues–Sun 10am–6pm; $3, children $1.50. Jurong East MRT, then bus #66 or #335.

At the **Singapore Science Centre**, situated southwest of tranquil **Jurong Lake**, seven exhibition galleries hold over six hundred hands-on exhibits designed to inject interest into even the most impenetrable scientific principles. The majority of the centre's visitors are local schoolchildren, who sweep around the galleries in vast, deafening waves, frantically trying out each interactive display. The exhibits allow you to experience sight through an insect's eyes, to write in Braille, and to see a thermal heat reflection of yourself. The **Omnimax-Theatre** (planetarium show $6, movie $10; call ☏5603316 for details of current movie), within the centre's grounds, has entertaining features about science, space and history shown on a huge dome screen.

THE CHINESE AND JAPANESE GARDENS

Map 8, B4. Daily 9am–6pm; $4.50, children $2. Chinese Garden MRT.

The Chinese and Japanese gardens by Jurong Lake defy categorization – too expensive and too far out to visit for just

SINGAPORE SCIENCE CENTRE • THE CHINESE AND JAPANESE GARDENS

a sit down in the park and too dull to be a fully fledged tourist attraction. In the **Chinese Garden** (or Yu Hwa Yuan), pagodas, pavilions, bridges, arches and weeping willows attempt to capture the style of Beijing's Summer Palace – and fail. If you visit at the weekend, be prepared to be confronted by hordes of newlyweds scouring the garden for a decent photo opportunity. The Chinese Garden is best explored on the day of the annual Moon Cake Festival (see p.242), when it stays open late so that children can parade with their lanterns after dark.

Walking across the impressive, 65-metre Bridge of Double Beauty takes you to the **Japanese Garden** (or Seiwaen, meaning "Garden of Tranquillity"), whose wooden bridges, carp ponds, pebble footpaths and stone lanterns do much to help you forget the awful formica chairs and tables in the central pavilion.

JURONG BIRDPARK

Map 8, A6. Mon–Fri 9am–6pm, Sat & Sun 8am–6pm; $10.30, children $4.12. Boon Lay MRT, then bus #194 or #251.

The **Jurong BirdPark** on Jalan Ahmad Ibrahim contains more than eight thousand birds from over six hundred species, ranging from Antarctic penguins to New Zealand kiwis. This makes this one of the world's largest bird collections, and the biggest in Southeast Asia. A ride on the **Panorail** ($2.50) is a good way to get your bearings; the bullet-shaped monorail skims over, past or through all the main exhibits, with a running commentary pointing out the attractions.

Be sure at least to catch the **Waterfall Walk-in Aviary**, which allows visitors to walk amongst 1500 free-flying birds in a specially created tropical rainforest, dominated by a thirty-metre-high waterfall. Other exhibits to seek out are the colourful **Southeast Asian Birds** (a tropical thunderstorm

JURONG BIRDPARK

is simulated daily at noon), featuring the Luzon Bleeding Heart Pigeon, which looks like it's just walked off the set of *Reservoir Dogs*; the **Penguin Parade** (feeding times 10.30am & 3.30pm); and the **World of Darkness**, a fascinating exhibit which swaps day for night with the aid of a system of reversed lighting, in order that its cute collection of nocturnal residents doesn't snooze throughout the park's opening hours. The best of the **bird shows** is undoubtedly the "Kings of the Skies" show (4pm) – a *tour de force* of speed flying by trained eagles, hawks and falcons. Entrance to this, and to the similar "World of Hawks" show (10am) and "All Star Bird Show" (11am & 3pm), is free. Back at the entrance complex you'll find snacks and drinks for sale.

Jurong Reptile Park

Map 8, A6. Daily 9am–6pm; $7, children $3.50. Boon Lay MRT, then bus #194 or #251.

Across the car park in front of the Birdpark, **Jurong Reptile Park** houses the biggest gathering of crocodiles in Singapore among its fifty-plus species of reptile. The park has wisely jettisoned its previous name, the Crocodile Paradise. Certainly, it's no paradise for the poor beasts forced to feature in the daily shows, in which crocs are pushed, pulled and sat on in the name of entertainment by a character swathed in crocodile hide and dripping with crocodile teeth. Given the scant respect shown by the park for its reptilian inmates, it comes as no surprise to find the *Seafood Paradise Restaurant* serving up crocs on plates in the main entrance building.

THE SINGAPORE DISCOVERY CENTRE

Map 1, B5. Tues–Fri 9am–7pm, Sat & Sun 9am–8pm; $9, children $5. Boon Lay MRT, then bus #192 or #193.

THE SINGAPORE DISCOVERY CENTRE

The hands-on **Singapore Discovery Centre** at 510 Upper Jurong Road is mainly geared towards local school parties. The emphasis is on Singapore's technological achievements, but there are exhibits with broader appeal, such as a computer-simulated **Shooting Gallery** ($3), a **motion simulator** ($4) and a clutch of virtual reality games. In the grounds outside the centre are a cluster of military vehicles of varying vintages, and an imaginative playground complete with its own maze.

TIGER BREWERY

Map 1, A5. For tour details, call ☎ 8606483. Boon Lay MRT, then bus #193.

Tiger Beer, now the flagship brew of the Asia Pacific Breweries Limited, has been brewed in Singapore since 1931, though back then its home was the Malayan Breweries on Alexandra Road, where it was developed with help from Heineken. A few years later, the establishment of Archipelago Brewery by German giants Beck's seemed to set the scene for a Singaporean **beer war**, especially when Tiger's new rival, Anchor Beer, was priced slightly lower. But in 1941, Archipelago was bought out by Malayan Breweries, since when the organization has gone from strength to strength, moving in May 1990 into new holdings in Tuas, and changing its name to reflect "the new international role the company has assumed", although it's still commonly known as the Tiger Brewery.

Today, the tiger beneath a palm tree that adorns the label on every bottle of Tiger Beer can be seen in ads across the state. The original slogan for the beer was used by Anthony Burgess as the title for his debut novel, *Time for a Tiger*. As the embattled, debt-ridden police-lieutenant, Nabby Adams, gulps down another beer, ". . . fresh blood flowed

TIGER BREWERY

through his arteries, the electric light seemed brighter, what were a few bills anyway?"

A **tour** of the brewery is made up of three component parts, arranged in rising order of appeal: first comes a film show which fills visitors in on the history of the setup; next a walk through the space-age brewing, bottling and canning halls; and finally an hour or two's free drinking in the company's own bar – Nabby would have approved. You need at least ten people in the party, though all is not lost if you are travelling alone – phone up, and if there's a tour already arranged, ask to tag along.

Sentosa and the southern isles

Rampant development over the past two decades has transformed **Sentosa** and it's ironic that its name means "tranquillity" in Malay. Sentosa has come a long way since World War II, when it was a British military base known as Pulau Blakang Mati, or the "Island of Death Behind". Today, promoted for its beaches, sports facilities, hotels and attractions, and ringed by a speeding monorail, it's a contrived but enjoyable experience. The island is linked to the mainland by a brand-new five-hundred-metre causeway and a necklace of cable cars.

Sentosa is big business: millions of visitors descend upon this tiny island, which measures just 3km by 1km, every year. Nevertheless you'll hear mixed reports of the place around Singapore. Ultimately, it's as enjoyable as you make it; there's certainly plenty to do (though few of the attractions would make the grade at Disneyland), so much so that it's a good idea to arrive early, with a clear plan of action. Taking a round trip on the trans-island monorail on arrival helps you get your bearings. **Admission** to several attractions is included in the Sentosa entry ticket (see

SENTOSA ISLAND

"Practicalities" below), though for the more popular attractions a further charge is levied. It's wise to avoid coming at the weekend, or on public holidays.

Many other little **islands** stud the waters immediately south of Singapore. Some, like Pulau Bukom, are owned by petrochemical companies and are off-limits to tourists. **St John's** and **Kusu** are the only two, apart from Sentosa, that are served by ferries and they can be visited without difficulty, though their accessibility has geared them very much to tourism. If you crave a more secluded spot, you'll have to charter a bumboat to one of the more remote islands from the World Trade Centre or Clifford Pier (see p.93 for details) or head for Pulau Ubin, off Singapore's east coast (p.121).

SENTOSA PRACTICALITIES

Basic **admission** to Sentosa costs $5 (children $3), though this doesn't include the cost of actually reaching the island. From the **World Trade Centre** at 1 Maritime Square (buses #65, #97, #143 and #166), **ferries** depart every twenty minutes (9.30am–9pm; $2.30 return). However, the most spectacular route is by the **cable cars** (daily 8.30am–9pm) which travel on a loop between mainland Mount Faber (see p.124) and Sentosa. For the round trip from the WTC up to Mount Faber, across to Sentosa and back to the WTC, you'll pay $6.90 (children $3.90), not including the basic $5 admission fee.

Crossing the **bridge** to Sentosa costs nothing if you walk, though you still have to pay the admission fee to the island. Bus A operates out of the WTC bus terminal, from where it runs across the bridge every ten to fifteen minutes (7am–12.30am; $6, children $3 – ticket includes entry to island). Service C, meanwhile, shuttles between Tiong Bahru MRT station and the ferry terminal on Sentosa

(7am–12.30am; $6, children $3 – ticket includes entry to island), while bus E runs from Orchard Road to Sentosa's Gateway station (10am–10.45pm; $7, children $5 – ticket includes entry to island).

Sentosa's basic admission fee gives unlimited rides on the **monorail** and **bus systems** – bus #2 circles the island between 9am and 7pm and services A, C and M are often handy too, while the monorail runs from 9am until 10pm. But the best way to get about is to **rent a bike** for the day ($4–8 an hour depending on the machine) from the kiosk beside the ferry terminal; tandems are also available.

The *Rasa Sentosa Food Centre* beside the ferry terminal is the cheapest **eating** option; otherwise, try the nearby *Sentosa Riverboat* for fast food, or monorail station #5's *Sweetimes Café*. There's a *Burger King* and a coffee house as well as a beer garden at the ferry terminal. Sentosa has two international-class **hotels**, one budget hotel and limited camping possibilities (see p.161 for more details).

SENTOSA'S MAIN ATTRACTIONS

Sentosa is no Disneyland: with one or two exceptions, its attractions are resoundingly B-list. Nevertheless, you'll find it easy to fill a day here – there are enough sights to make the place appealing, and when you've visited all the parks and exhibitions you can stomach, there's always the beach.

Underwater World

Daily 9am–9pm; $13, children $7. Monorail station #2.

At the **Underwater World**, a moving walkway carries you the length of a hundred-metre acrylic tunnel that snakes through two large tanks: sharks lurk menacingly on all sides, huge stingrays drape themselves languidly above you, and immense shoals of gaily coloured fish dart to and fro. This may not sound all that exciting, but the sensation of being engulfed by sea life is a breathtaking one, and the nearest you'll get to the ocean floor without a wet suit. Of particular interest is the Deadly Corridor, which is home to electric eels, piranha and stonefish. A **touchpool** beside the entrance allows you to pick up starfish and sea cucumbers – the latter rather like socks filled with wet sand – while beyond that is the **Marine Theatre** which screens educational films throughout the day.

Images of Singapore Exhibition

Daily 9am–9pm; $5, children $3. Monorail station #2.

At the **Images of Singapore Exhibition** the history and heritage of Singapore from the fourteenth century through to the surrender of the Japanese in 1945 are presented through life-sized dioramas. Though some of the wax dummies look like they've been pinched from clothes shop windows, the effect is fascinating. The highlight of the exhibition is the Surrender Chambers, where audiovisuals, videos, dioramas and artefacts combine to recount the events of World War II in Singapore. There are more wax dummies in the new Festivals of Singapore gallery, this time dolled up in festive costumes to represent Singapore's various ethnic celebrations.

Fort Siloso

Daily 9am–7pm; $3, children $2. Monorail station #3.

A trip up to the new improved **Fort Siloso**, at the far western tip of the island, ties in nicely with a visit to the Surrender Chambers. The fort – actually a cluster of buildings and gun emplacements above a series of tunnels bored into the island – guarded Singapore's western approaches from the 1880s until 1956, but was rendered obsolete in 1942, when the Japanese moved down into Singapore from Malaysia. Today, the recorded voice of Battery Sergeant Major (BSM) Cooper talks you through a mock-up of a nineteenth-century barracks, complete with living quarters, laundry and assault course. After that, you can explore the complex's hefty gun emplacements and tunnels, and sit in on the Battle for Singapore, when British soldiers were forced to surrender to the Japanese.

Asian Village

Daily 10am–9pm; free. Ferry terminal and monorail station #1 or #4.

The Asian Village showcases Asian life by way of restaurants, craft shops and street performances, and is little more than a vehicle for selling overpriced arts, crafts and food. Within the village are the fairground rides of "Adventure Asia" ($10) and the **Thai Pavilion Theatre**, in which the "Colours of Asia" (10.15am & 4pm; $5) and "Fascinating Asia" (6.30pm & 7.15pm; $18 including dinner) cultural shows are staged daily.

OTHER ATTRACTIONS ON SENTOSA

The rest of Sentosa has lots of less interesting options. You might consider one of Sentosa's three latest attractions: **Volcanoland** (daily 10am–7pm; $12, children $6) with a simulated eruption and trip to the earth's core; **Fantasy Island** (daily 10am–6.30pm; $16, children $10) with hi-tech water rides – "Flashflood", "Blackhole" and "Pygmy Puddle" – for small children; or **Wondergolf** (daily 9am–9pm; $8, children $4), with 45 crazy holes. There isn't much to recommend the **Maritime Museum** (daily 10am–7pm; free); you'd do better strolling in the elegant

grounds of the **Sentosa Orchid Gardens** (daily
9.30am–6.30pm; $3.50, children $2), near monorail station
#1. For something slightly more exciting head for the
Butterfly Park and Insect Kingdom Museum (daily
9am–6.30pm; $6, children $3), near monorail station #5,
which is stuffed with all sorts of creepy-crawlies, of which
only the butterflies are alive; the beetles, bugs and scorpions
are all mounted in display cases.

Musical Fountain

Shows at 5pm, 5.30pm, 7.30pm, 8.30pm & 9.30pm. Ferry terminal
and monorail station #1.

By 7pm, many of Sentosa's attractions are closed, but not so
the **Musical Fountain**, which is either cute or appalling,
depending on your point of view. The fountain dances
along to such classics as the *1812 Overture*, with colourful
lights and lasers adding to the effect. Recently, the display
has been overlooked by a new, 37-metre-high statue of
Singapore's tourism totem, the **Merlion**, which itself takes
centre-stage in the laser-illuminated "Rise of the Merlion"
portions of the shows.

BEACHES ON SENTOSA

Monorail stations #2 or #5, or bus A or M.

Probably the best option on Sentosa, after a trip on the
monorail and a visit to one or two attractions, is to head for
the three beaches, **Siloso**, **Central** and **Tanjong** on the
southwestern coast. Created with thousands of cubic metres
of imported white sand and scores of coconut palms, they
offer canoes, surfboards and aqua-bikes for rent, as well as
plain old deckchairs. The water here is great for swimming
and Singapore does not demand the same modesty on its
beaches as Malaysia, although topless and nude bathing are

out. In recent years, Singapore's annual Dragon Boat Festival (p.241) has been held off Siloso Beach. Food and drinks are available at the **Food Village**, situated on the patch of land that divides Siloso Beach from Central Beach.

KUSU AND ST JOHN'S ISLANDS

Well kept and clean as they are, Sentosa's beaches do tend to get overcrowded and you may do better to head for either **St John's** or **Kusu** islands, which are 6km south of Singapore and connected to the mainland by a **ferry** from the WTC. Both islands have decent sand beaches, though the most interesting of the two is Kusu, also known as **Turtle Island**. Singaporean legend tells of a Chinese and a Malay sailor who were saved from drowning by a turtle which transformed itself into an island; a pool of turtles is still kept on Kusu. Another legend describes how an epidemic afflicting a ship moored off Kusu was banished by the god Tua Pek Kong. Whatever the truth in these tales, once a year during the ninth lunar month (usually in October or November), tens of thousands of Singaporean pilgrims descend upon the **Chinese temple** and **Malay shrine** a few minutes' walk from the jetty on Kusu, to pray for prosperity. The island is impossibly crowded during this time, but the rest of the year it offers a tranquil escape from the mainland. There is a modest cafeteria on St John's, but if you're going to Kusu it's wise to take a picnic.

The ferry ($9, children $6) from the WTC reaches Kusu in thirty minutes and then continues on to St John's, arriving shortly afterwards. On weekdays and Saturdays there are only two departures from the WTC. On Sundays and public holidays the number of services rises to six. Call ☏ 8628322 for current ferry times.

OTHER ISLANDS

Since no regular ferries run to any of Singapore's other southern islands, you'll have to **charter** a bumboat from Jardine Steps (beside the World Trade Centre) or from Clifford Pier. Boats take up to twelve passengers, and cost at least $30–40 an hour. Unless you rent a boat for the whole day, you must arrange to be picked up again. **Lazarus Island** and the attractive **Sister's Island**, which lie in the same cluster of isles as St John's and Kusu, are popular snorkelling and fishing haunts, as is **Pulau Hantu** ("Ghost Island" in Malay), 12km further west and under the shadow of Shell-owned Pulau Bukum. Most interesting of all, though, is **Pulau Seking**, three or four kilometres east of Hantu; here a handful of Malays continue to live in traditional stilt houses that teeter over the sea, their lifestyle almost untouched by the progress that has transformed the mainland. These islands are all very basic, so take a picnic and a day's supply of bottled water with you.

LISTINGS

LISTINGS

Accommodation

Accommodation in Singapore needn't take too big a bite out of your holiday budget; good deals abound if your expectations aren't too lofty or – at the budget end of the scale – if you don't mind sharing. Singapore's status as one of the main gateways to Southeast Asia means that occupancy rates at all levels of accommodation are permanently high. Even so, you shouldn't encounter too many difficulties in finding a room, and advance booking isn't really necessary unless your visit coincides with Chinese New Year (usually Jan/Feb) or Hari Raya (usually March/April).

The **Singapore Hotel Association** has a booking counter at each of Changi airport's two terminals (both terminals open daily 7am–2am, except Fri 7am–11.30pm) which will find you a room in the city free of charge, though they only represent Singapore's official hotels, all of which are listed in two free STB booklets, *Hotels Singapore* and *Budget Hotels Singapore*. Touts at the airport also hand out flyers advertising rooms in guesthouses and hostels. If you prefer to book ahead, you might wish to book online through the Singapore Tourism Board (Ⓦ*www.newasia-singapore.com*) or at Ⓦ*singapore-hotel.com.sg*

The cheapest beds are in the communal **dormitories** of many of Singapore's resthouses, where you'll pay $10 or less a night. The next best deals are at **guesthouses**, most of which are situated along Beach Road and Bencoolen Street, with an increasing number in nearby Little India and some also south of the river, in Chinatown. Singapore's classic guesthouse address is Peony Mansion, where a cluster of establishments is shoehorned into several floors of a decrepit apartment building, though the Bencoolen area is becoming less fashionable with every passing year. Guesthouses aren't nearly as cosy as their name suggests; at the $20–30 mark, rooms are tiny, bare, and divided by paper-thin partitions, toilets are shared and showers are cold. However, paying another $10–20 secures a bigger, air-con room, and often TV, laundry and cooking facilities, lockers and breakfast are included. Always check that everything works before you hand over any money. It's always worth asking for a discount, too, especially if you are staying a few days.

The appeal of Singapore's **Chinese-owned hotels**, similar in price to guesthouses, is their air of faded grandeur – some haven't changed in forty years. Sadly, faded grandeur is something the government frowns upon, with the result that there are very few left. In more modern, **mid-range hotels**, a room for two with air-con, private bathroom and TV will set you back around $60–90 a night. From there, prices rise steadily, and at the top end of the scale Singapore boasts some extraordinarily opulent hotels, ranging from the colonial splendour of *Raffles* to the awesome spectacle of the *Westin Stamford* – until very recently the world's tallest hotel. Though you'll find the greatest concentration of **upmarket hotels** around Orchard Road, most of the new breed of **boutique hotels** – which use antique furniture and fittings to create an air of Oriental nostalgia – are based in Chinatown.

Most mid-range and upmarket hotels in Singapore make no charge for children under 12 years old if they are

ACCOMMODATION

ACCOMMODATION PRICE CODES

We've used the following **price codes** to denote the cheapest available room for two people. Single occupancy should cost less than double, though this is not always the case. Some guesthouses provide dormitory beds, for which the dollar price is given.

- **1** under $25
- **2** $25–40
- **3** $40–60
- **4** $60–100
- **5** $100–150
- **6** $150–200
- **7** $200–300
- **8** $300–400
- **9** $400 and over

occupying existing spare beds in rooms. However, if you require an extra bed to be put in your room, 10 to 15 percent of the room rate is usually charged. Cots are provided free.

BENCOOLEN STREET AND AROUND

Bencoolen Street has long been the mainstay of Singapore's backpacker industry – so long, in fact, that its buildings are beginning to show their age, while others have already fallen to the demolition ball. Still, the location is handy for all parts of central Singapore, and the proliferation of guesthouses makes it a great place for meeting people. Several of Bencoolen Street's backpacker haunts are to be found off the scurfy stairways of Peony Mansion.

To get to Bencoolen Street, take the MRT to Dhoby Ghaut station and walk, or bus #7, #14, #36, #97, #124, #166, #174 or #190.

Bencoolen Hotel
Map 4, D13. 47 Bencoolen St Ⓣ 3360822.
Recently refurbished, the Bencoolen now represents better value than ever, with business facilities, laundry service, air-ticketing facilities, roof-top spa pool and smart rooms with all mod cons. ❹

City Bayview
Map 4, D13. 30 Bencoolen St Ⓣ 3372882; Ⓕ 3382880.
One of Bencoolen Street's posher hotels, with very comfortable rooms, a compact roof-top swimming pool and a friendly, modern café. ❻

Goh's Homestay
Map 4, D11. 4th floor, 169d Bencoolen St Ⓣ 3396561; Ⓕ 3398606.
The smartest guesthouse in town, with fresh and inviting (if slightly cell-like) rooms, pricier dorm beds than usual, laundry service, and a bright, comfortable lounge/canteen area serving great breakfasts. Recommended unless you are allergic to cats – the place is teeming with them. Dorms $14. ❸

Hawaii Hostel
Map 4, D10. 2nd floor, 171b Bencoolen St Ⓣ 3384187.
Small, tidy, air-con rooms with breakfast included, as well as dorm beds for $10. ❷

Latin House Home Stay
Map 4, D13. 03-46 Peony Mansion, 46–52 Bencoolen St Ⓣ 3396308.
The budget-priced dorms are adequate, but the rooms are inevitably a little run-down, given the price of them. Dorms $7. ❶

Lee Boarding House
Map 4, D13. 07-52 Peony Mansion, 46–52 Bencoolen St Ⓣ 3383149.
The brightest place in Peony Mansion: clean, simple rooms and dorms (a dollar more for air-con), a pleasant breakfast area and laundry facilities. There's another *Lee*'s on Beach Road (see below). Dorms $9. ❶

Peony Mansion Green Curtains
Map 4, D13. 04-46 Peony Mansion, 46–52 Bencoolen St Ⓣ 3385638.

A travel consultant's desk, noticeboard and Internet access ($5 per hour) make this a handy place to stay. The dorms are cramped, while rooms range from basic to more comfortable with TV, air-con and toilet. Dorms $8. ❷

Peony Mansion Travellers' Lodge

Map 4, D11. 2nd floor, 131a Bencoolen St ⓣ 3348697.
Actually a couple of hundred metres down the road from its parent guesthouse, *Green Curtains* (see above), this branch has lots of clean featureless rooms (the cheapest share common showers) and an air-con dorm ($10); the Airpower travel agency operates right beside the lodge's friendly reception area. ❷

San Wah Hotel

Map 4, D13. 36 Bencoolen St ⓣ 3362428.
Shambling but spotless and rather charming old Chinese hotel which benefits from being set back slightly from the road, and from being run by a friendly family. $5 surcharge for air-con. ❸

South East Asia Hotel

Map 4, D10. 190 Waterloo St ⓣ 3382394.
Spotless doubles with air-con, TV and phone for those yearning for a few creature comforts. Downstairs is a vegetarian restaurant (see p.195) serving Western breakfasts, and right next door is Singapore's liveliest Buddhist temple. ❹

Strand Hotel

Map 4, D13. 25 Bencoolen St ⓣ 3381866; ⓕ 3363149.
Excellent-value hotel with clean, welcoming rooms, a café serving Western and local dishes, and a variety of services. ❹

Summer View Hotel

Map 4, D10. 173 Bencoolen St ⓣ 3381122; ⓕ 3366346.
The future face of Bencoolen Street: a smart but unpretentious hundred-room hotel with all the facilities the budget-minded business traveller or tourist might need – café, car-rental facilities, valet services, currency exchange and tour desk – but none of the

BENCOOLEN STREET AND AROUND

needless frills that push up prices. **⑤**

the wonderful *L.E. Cafe & Confectionery*. **③**

Sun Sun Hotel

Map 4, C11. 260–262 Middle Rd ⊤ 3384911.

Housed in a splendid 1928 building, the *Sun Sun* isn't overpriced – decent rooms and plenty of communal bathrooms. Ask for one of the rooms with a balcony. Air-con rooms are also available for an extra $5, while downstairs is

Waterloo Hostel

Map 4, D12. 4th Floor, Catholic Centre Building, 55 Waterloo St ⊤ 3366555; Ⓕ 3362160; Ⓔ *waterhtl@mbox2.singnet.com .sg*

Catholic-run hostel, centrally located, spick and span, and boasting rooms with air-con, TV and phone. **③**

BEACH ROAD TO VICTORIA STREET

A few blocks east of Bencoolen Street, **Beach Road** boasts a mixture of charismatic old Chinese hotels and smart new guesthouses. What's more, you can brag about having stayed down the road from *Raffles Hotel* (or even in it – see below) when you get home.

> To get to hotels in the Beach Road/Victoria Street area, take the MRT to City Hall station, or bus #7, #14, #36, #97, #124, #166, #171 or #190

Ah Chew Hotel

Map 4, G11. 496 North Bridge Rd ⊤ 8370356.

Simple but charismatic rooms with "Wild West" swing doors, crammed with period furniture, and run by T-shirted

old men lounging on antique opium couches. There are also air-con dorms, with beds at $12. Try and get a room at the front of the building – despite its address, the *Ah Chew* is just around the corner from North

Bridge Road, on buzzing Liang Seah Street. ②

Allson Hotel
Map 4, F12. 101 Victoria St ⓣ3360811; ⓕ3397019; ⓔ allson.sales@pacific.net.sg
Reasonable 450-room hotel with shopping arcade, health and business centres and a clutch of restaurants. Some effort has been made to cater for visitors in wheelchairs: there are low counters and phones and adapted toilets, but you'll need to book well ahead for the hotel's one specifically designed bedroom. ⑥

Beach Hotel
Map 4, H11. 95 Beach Rd ⓣ3367712; ⓔ mstay@mbox2.singnet.com.sg
The Lee empire's latest addition: professionally run and very tidy, though you'd expect a few more amenities for the price. ④

Intercontinental
Map 4, F11. 80 Middle Rd ⓣ3387600; ⓕ3387366; ⓦ www.interconti.com
Smashing hotel within the thriving Bugis Junction development, convenient and sumptuously furnished, with business centre, swimming pool, health club and an array of excellent restaurants including *Pimai Thai* (see p.215) and *Olive Tree* (see p.208). ⑦

Landmark Mercure Hotel
Map 4, F8. 390 Victoria St ⓣ2972828; ⓕ2982038; ⓔ lanmak@mbox3.singnet.com.sg
Very pleasant, once you get past the dated shopping centre downstairs, and handy for Bugis MRT station and Arab Street. ⑤

Metropole Hotel
Map 4, G12. 41 Seah St ⓣ3363611; ⓕ3393610; ⓦ www.metrohotel.com
Friendly, great-value establishment, just across the road from *Raffles Hotel* and home to the recommended *Imperial Herbal Restaurant* (see p.193). ⑤

New 7th Storey Hotel
Map 4, G10. 229 Rochor Rd ⓣ3370251; ⓕ3343550; ⓔ nsshmail@mbox2.singnet .com.sg
Despite its rather old-

BEACH ROAD TO VICTORIA STREET

fashioned exterior, this is a clean hotel with perfectly respectable rooms, all with TV. Rooms with bathrooms en suite are available, though the communal ones are fine. ❸

Plaza Hotel

Map 4, I8. Beach Road Ⓣ 2980011; Ⓕ 2963600; Ⓦ www.hpl.com.sg/plaza

Luxurious, eye-catching hotel whose amenities include restaurants, and a business centre. Slightly off the beaten track, though there is a free shuttle service into town. ❼

Raffles Hotel

Map 4, G13. 1 Beach Rd Ⓣ 3371886; Ⓕ 3397650; Ⓦ www.raffles.com

The flagship of Singapore's tourism industry, *Raffles* takes shameless advantage of its reputation: $25 buys you a Singapore Sling and a glass to take home, while the souvenir shop stocks *Raffles* golf balls, socks and cuddly tigers. Still, it's a beautiful place, dotted with frangipani trees and palms, and the suites (there are

no rooms) are as tasteful as you would expect at these prices. See p.58 for more details. ❾

Season Homestay

Map 4, G11. 26a Liang Seah St Ⓣ 3372400.

Occupying one of the last few shophouses along Liang Seah not to have been turned into a trendy café, the *Season* has dorm beds for $9, and a modest range of private rooms, all sharing only two common bathrooms. Breakfast is free. ❷

Shang Onn Hotel

Map 4, H12. 37 Beach Rd Ⓣ 3384153.

Set in a quaint old building with attractive green shutters, the *Shang Onn* has clean rooms and communal toilets, and a friendly manager-owner. ❷

Waffles Home Stay

Map 4, G11. 3rd Floor, 490 North Bridge Rd Ⓣ 3341608.

Pleasantly tiled and painted crashpad, where prices include breakfast and a free flow of hot drinks. There are discounts if you introduce new guests, and oodles of advice are pinned up on noticeboards. To enter, walk through to the back of the curry house below, and up the stairs to your left. Recommended. Dorms $8–9. **②**

THE COLONIAL DISTRICT

There are a handful of expensive hotels at the edges of the **Padang**, just north of the Singapore River. The *Marina Mandarin* and *Oriental* stand on the reclaimed land which robbed Beach Road of its beach.

Carlton Hotel

Map 4, F13. 76 Bras Basah Rd. City Hall MRT; bus #56 or #171. ☏ 3388333; Ⓕax 3396866; Ⓦ *www.carlton.com.sg*
Swish high-rise hotel overlooking Bras Basah Park, bang in the centre of town. **⑥**

Excelsior Hotel

Map 3, G4. 5 Coleman St. City Hall MRT; bus #124 or #166. ☏ 3387733; Ⓕax 3393847; Ⓔ *pen_exc@ytchotels.com.sg*
Sister to the nearby *Peninsula* (whose gym can be used by guests), the *Excelsior*'s 271 rooms enjoy 24-hour room service, TV, safe and secretarial service, and are as handy for the Financial District as for Orchard Road's shopping

centres. There are a swimming pool and several food outlets, the best of which is the excellent *Annalakshmi* Indian vegetarian restaurant. **⑥**

Marina Mandarin Hotel

Map 2, K6. 6 Raffles Blvd. Bus #36 or #171. ☏ 3383388; Ⓕax 3394977; Ⓦ *www .marina-mandarin.com.sg*
Top-flight hotel, architecturally interesting and affording great harbour views; the atrium is particularly impressive. **⑦**

Oriental Singapore

Map 2, K6. 5 Raffles Ave. Bus #36 or #171. ☏ 3380066; Ⓕax 3399537; Ⓦ *www.mandarin-oriental.com*
Housed, like the *Marina*

Mandarin in Marina Square (claimed to be Southeast Asia's largest shopping centre and hotel complex), the *Oriental* is one of Singapore's priciest hotels, but with very good reason. The rooms are exquisitely furnished, views out over Marina Bay are breathtaking, and all the luxuries you could want are on hand. For a real treat, try their *Oriental Club* ($60 extra), whose two floors of luxury rooms have complimentary breakfast, evening cocktails and laundry service. Recommended. ⑨

Ritz-Carlton Millenia Singapore

Map 2, K6. 7 Raffles Ave. Bus #36 or #171. Ⓣ 3378888; Ⓕ 3380001; ⓦ www.ritzcarlton.com

This recent arrival has elbowed its way into the very top ranks of the island's hotels; all imaginable comfort can be found within its monolithic structure. ⑧

Westin Stamford

Map 3, I3. 2 Stamford Rd. City Hall MRT. Ⓣ 3388585; Ⓕ 3365117; ⓦ www.westinsingapore.com

Upper-floor rooms aren't for those with vertigo, though the views are as splendid as you'd expect from the second tallest hotel in the world. There are 1253 classy rooms here, sixteen restaurants and an MRT station downstairs. ⑦

ORCHARD ROAD AND AROUND

Sumptuous hotels abound in and around **Orchard Road** – at all except a handful be prepared to spend at least $80 a double. You can multiply that figure by four or five, though, if you decide to treat yourself.

Cavenagh Garden

Map 5, G4. 03-376, Block 73 Cavenagh Rd. Somerset MRT. Ⓣ 7374600.

At the end of Cuppage Road, cross the Expressway bridge

and walk to the left for 300m. A home stay in a literal sense: various rooms are dotted around a family home. It's a steep $20 extra for a private shower. ❸

The Elizabeth

Map 5, F4. 24 Mount Elizabeth. Orchard or Somerset MRT. ☏ 7381188; ℻ 7324173; ✉ elizabpra@pacific.net.sg
Within its toytown exterior, this boutique hotel oozes panache; delightful and well-appointed rooms. ❻

Garden Hotel

Map 5, D2. 14 Balmoral Rd. Newton MRT. ☏ 2353344; ℻ 2359730; ✉ garden@pacific.net.sg
A standard hotel with attractive rooms, a ten-minute walk north of Orchard Road. ❻

Goodwood Park Hotel

Map 5, E3. 22 Scotts Rd. Newton or Orchard MRT. ☏ 7377411; ℻ 7328558; ⓦ www.goodwoodparkhotel .com.sg
This opulent hotel may remind you of *Raffles* – both were designed by the same architect. The building has a long history (see p.75), but it's still a study in elegance, its arching facades fronting exquisitely appointed rooms. ❾

Hilton International Singapore

Map 5, D5. 581 Orchard Rd. Orchard MRT; bus #36. ☏ 7372233; ℻ 7322917; ⓦ www.hilton.com
Situated in the middle of Orchard Road, a gargantuan slab of a hotel with every conceivable facility. ❼

Holiday Inn Park View

Map 5, H5. 11 Cavenagh Rd. Somerset MRT; bus #36. ☏ 7338333; ℻ 7344593; ⓦ www.harilela.com/hipv
Guests of this smart hotel with all the trimmings are next-door neighbours of Singapore's president for the duration of their stay – the palace is just across the road. ❼

Lloyd's Inn

Map 5, H6. 2 Lloyd Rd. Somerset MRT; #bus 36. ☏ 7377309; ℻ 7377847.

ORCHARD ROAD AND AROUND

Motel–style building boasting attractive rooms and a fine location, just five minutes from Orchard Road. ❹

Mandarin Hotel

Map 5, F5. 333 Orchard Rd. Orchard MRT; bus #36. ⓣ 7374411; ⓕ 7322361; Ⓦ *www.mandarin-hotel.com.sg* Every luxury you could hope for; even if you don't stay, take a trip up to the top for the magnificent view of central Singapore. ❽

Metro-Y Lodge

Map 5, B2. 60 Stevens Rd. Bus #105 or #190. ⓣ 7377755; ⓕ 2355528; Ⓦ *www.singnet.com.sg/mynca* Not as central as the Y on Orchard Road, but perfectly adequate, and suitable for travellers in wheelchairs. ❹

Mitre Hotel

Map 5, G7. 145 Killiney Rd. Somerset MRT; bus #36. ⓣ 7373811. Reasonable old Chinese hotel, set amid overgrown grounds, and with an endearingly shabby air about

it; there's a great lobby bar downstairs. ❷

The Regent Singapore

Map 5, B6. 1 Cuscaden Rd. Bus #105, #123 or #174. ⓣ 7338888; ⓕ 7328838; Ⓦ *www.rih.com* At the western end of Orchard Road, the elegant rooms of this sumptuous hotel are a short stroll from the Botanic Gardens. ❼

Sandy's Place

Map 5, E2. 3c Sarkies Rd. Newton MRT. ⓣ 7341431. Rooms are all very tidy, if a touch overpriced, in this friendly, laid-back place, set across a field from Newton MRT. Expect to pay $15 above the basic rate for air-con. Prices include a fruit breakfast. It's best to phone ahead. ❷

Shangri-La Hotel

Map 5, B4. 22 Orange Grove Rd. Bus #36. ⓣ 7373644; ⓕ 7337220; Ⓦ *www.shangri-la .com* Top-flight hotel whose 750 rooms are set in six hectares of landscaped greenery, only five minutes from Orchard Road. Recent refurbishments have rendered the Shangri-La more stunning than ever. ❾

Sheraton Towers
Map 5, E2. 39 Scotts Rd. Newton MRT. ☏ 7376888; Ⓕ 7371072; Ⓦ www.sheraton.com Faultless hotel voted one of the top ten in the world by *Business Traveller* magazine; the lobby area is dazzling and there's even a waterfall out the back. ❾

Singapore Marriott Hotel
Map 5, E5. 320 Orchard Rd. Orchard MRT; bus #36. ☏ 7355800; Ⓕ 7359800; Ⓔ marriott@singnet.com.sg A superior hotel and a Singapore landmark, housed in a 33-storey pagoda-style building next door to C.K. Tangs Department Store. ❽

Sloane Court Hotel
Map 5, C1. 17 Balmoral Rd. Newton MRT. ☏ 2353311; Ⓕ 7339041; Ⓔ sloane@singnet.com.sg

As close to a Tudor house as you get in Singapore, the *Sloane Court* is tucked away in a prime residential area, near Newton MRT. ❹

Hotel Supreme
Map 5, H5. 15 Kramat Rd. Somerset or Dhoby Ghaut MRT; bus #36. ☏ 7378333; Ⓕ 7337404. A budget hotel, well placed at the eastern end of Orchard Road, which levies a hefty $200 deposit at check-in. ❹

Hotel VIP
Map 5, D1. Balmoral Crescent. Newton MRT. ☏ 2354277; Ⓕ 2352824. A quiet, affordable hotel with swimming pool within walking distance of Orchard Road. ❺

YMCA International House
Map 4, C14. 1 Orchard Rd. Dhoby Ghaut MRT; bus #36. ☏ 3366000; Ⓕ 3373140; Ⓦ www.ymcasin.org .sg/hostel_r.htm Plush but overpriced rooms, excellent sports facilities

(including roof-top pool) and free room service from the *McDonald's* downstairs. Dorm beds are the most expensive in town, though, and there's a first-day charge of $5 for non-members. Bus #36 from the airport stops right outside. Dorms $25. ❹

LITTLE INDIA

Buses along Jalan Besar connect **Little India** with the rest of central Singapore. Little India's hotels and guesthouses used not to attract many Western visitors, though many backpackers have been holing up here of late.

To get to the hotels in Little India, take bus #65, #66, #81, #97, #103, #139 or #147.

Albert Court Hotel
Map 4, B9. 180 Albert St
ⓣ 3393939; ⓕ 3393252;
ⓔ *sales.mktg@albertcourt.com.sg*
This charmingly conceived boutique hotel, designed around the restaurants of lively Albert Court Mall, is just a short walk from both Bugis Village and Little India; rooms have all the standard embellishments. ❼

Boon Wah Hotel
Map 4, D7. 43a Jalan Besar
ⓣ 2991466; ⓕ 2942176.
This decent Chinese hotel offers clean, if slightly cramped rooms with TV, air-con and shower. The entrance is around the corner, on Upper Dickson Road. ❹

Broadway Hotel
Map 4, B5. 195 Serangoon Rd
ⓣ 2924661; ⓕ 2916414.
Ugly-looking hotel in the heart of Little India, boasting pleasant enough rooms with air-con, bathroom and TV. ❹

Dickson Court
Map 4, D7. 3 Dickson Rd
ⓣ 2977811; ⓕ 2977833.

With smart, well-furnished rooms off light courtyard corridors, the *Dickson Court* is pretty good value; most corners of central Singapore are accessible from the bus stop across the road on Jalan Besar. ❹

Fortuna Hotel

Map 4, B3. 2 Owen Rd
Ⓣ 2953577.
Mid-range hotel offering brilliant value for money; facilities include a health centre and secretarial services.
❹–❺

Kerbau Hotel

Map 4, A7. 54–62 Kerbau Rd
Ⓣ 2976668.
Friendly place, if somewhat vault-like, with spruce and welcoming rooms; discounts for stays of three days or more. ❹

Little India Guest House

Map 4, B6. 3 Veerasamy Rd
Ⓣ 2942866; Ⓕ 2984866.
A smart guesthouse with excellent, fresh-looking rooms and spotless communal toilets. ❸

Mount Emily Hotel

Map 4, A11. 10a Upper Wilkie Rd, Mount Emily Park
Ⓣ 3389151; Ⓕ 3396008;
Ⓔ *emilyhtl@sthgroup.com*
Rooms here are pricey and starting to show their age, but the hotel's location, beside a lovely park above the city, makes it a relaxing option. ❺

Perak Lodge

Map 4, C8. 12 Perak Rd
Ⓣ 2969072; Ⓕ 3920919;
Ⓔ *perlodge@singnet.com.sg*
One of the new breed of upper-bracket guesthouses, set within a smashing blue-and-white shophouse in a back street behind the Little India arcade, and run by friendly staff. The rooms are secure, well appointed and welcoming, and the price includes a continental breakfast. Downstairs there's an airy, residents-only living area. Recommended. ❹–❺

LITTLE INDIA

CHINATOWN AND AROUND

Despite being such a big tourist draw, **Chinatown** isn't very well furnished with budget accommodation. On the other hand, the area does have a mass of upmarket hotels which benefit from their proximity to the business district.

Chinatown Guest House

Map 3, A11. 5th Floor, 325d New Bridge Rd. Bus #51, #103, #124, #166, #174 or #190. Ⓣ 2200671.

Friendly, no-frills place and a popular choice, offering varied rooms, free breakfast and luggage storage. However, the cheapest rooms are tiny, the dorms pretty cramped and there are just three bathrooms. Dorms $12. ❷

Chinatown Hotel

Map 3, B12. 12–16 Teck Lim Rd. Bus #51, #103, #124, #166, #174 or #190. Ⓣ 2200671 or 2255166; Ⓕ 2253912.
Decent boutique hotel with very smart rooms and a well-stocked business centre. ❺

Damenlou Hotel

Map 3, D11. 12 Ann Siang Rd. Bus #51, #103, #124, #166, #174 or #190. Ⓣ 2200671 or 2211900; Ⓕ 2258500.
Given its lovingly restored 1925 facade, the twelve compact but well-appointed rooms in this friendly hotel are surprisingly modern. After a pre-dinner drink on the roof-top garden overlooking Chinatown head down to the excellent *Swee Kee* restaurant (p.186). ❹

Dragon Inn

Map 3, C10. 18 Mosque St. Bus #51, #103, #124, #166, #174 or #190. Ⓣ 200671 or 2227227.
Sizeable and comfortable double rooms in the middle of Chinatown, all with air-con, TV, fridge and bathroom, and set in attractive shophouses. Try to avoid rooms backing onto the central air shaft, which houses many noisy air-con units. ❺

The Duxton

Map 3, B13. 83 Duxton Rd.
Tanjong Pagar MRT; bus #103,
#124, #145 or #166.
Ⓣ 2277678; Ⓕ 2271232;
Ⓦ www.duxtonhotels.com.sg
Tremendously elegant rooms
in a row of renovated
shophouses in the Tanjong
Pagar redevelopment zone.
Downstairs is the excellent
L'Aigle d'Or French
restaurant. ❼

Grand Copthorne Waterfront

Map 2, F6. 392 Havelock Rd
Ⓣ 7330880; Ⓕ 7378880.
Equidistant from the Orchard
and Chinatown districts, and a
short stroll along the river
from the nightspots of Clarke
Quay, the Grand Copthorne
demands consideration. Its
500-plus rooms are piled up
above a selection of riverfront
restaurants. Recommended. ❼

The Inn at Temple Street

Map 3, C10. 36 Temple St. Bus
#51, #103, #124, #166, #174 or
#190. Ⓣ 2200671 or 2215333;
Ⓕ 2255391.
Glossy and grand inside, this
boutique hotel has been
sculpted out of a row of
Chinatown shophouses. Its
owners have filled it to
bursting with furnishings and
curios from old Singapore.
Recommended. ❹

Majestic Hotel

Map 3, A12. 31–37 Bukit
Pasoh Rd. Bus #51, #103, #124,
#166, #174 or #190.
Ⓣ 2223377; Ⓕ 2230907.
Scrupulously clean, and
enormously friendly hotel
within strolling distance of the
sights of Chinatown.
Following recent renovations,
all rooms have air-con and
private bathroom, while those
at the front boast little
balconies. Try and secure a
room on the top floor – the
noise from the KTV lounge
next door carries
maddeningly at night. ❹

Royal Peacock Hotel

Map 3, B12. 55 Keong Saik
Rd. Bus #51, #103, #124, #166,
#174 or #190. Ⓣ 2233522;
Ⓕ 2211770.
Keong Saik Road was once a
notorious red-light district,

CHINATOWN AND AROUND

and the silky, sassy elegance of the *Royal Peacock* recalls those days. Sculpted from ten shophouses, it's a superb boutique hotel, with great rooms, a bar, café and business services. **6**

THE EAST COAST: GEYLANG AND KATONG

Geylang and **Katong**, along Singapore's southeastern coast, have traditionally both been Malay-dominated areas. If you can't face the noise and the bustle of central Singapore, this region might appeal – certainly its cool sea breezes and Malay markets are an advantage. MRT and buses connect you quickly with downtown Singapore.

Amber Hotel

Map 7, B4. 42 Amber Rd. Paya Lebar MRT, then bus #135; bus #36 from airport; or bus #197. ⊤ 3442323.
Comfortable rooms with TV, air-con and bathroom just a short walk from the coast. **4**

Hotel 81

Map 7, C4. 305 Joo Chiat Rd. Bus #16 or #33. ⊤ 3488181; Ⓦ www.hotel81.com.sg
Housed in a beautifully restored cream and burgundy Peranakan building, *Hotel 81* offers rooms pleasant enough for any self-respecting business person, but at a fraction of the prices of the downtown heavyweights. Great place. **4**

Kim Sun Hotel

Map 7, B4. 40 Amber Rd. Paya Lebar MRT, then bus #135; bus #36 from airport; or bus #197. ⊤ 3457502.
Right behind the *Amber,* housed in a traditional colonial-style building, rooms here are well past their heyday; TV and private bathroom set you back $10. **3**

Sing Hoe Hotel

Map 7, B4. 759 Mountbatten Rd. Bus #32 or #197. ⊤ 4400602.
Beautifully kept colonial house, with attractive reliefs on its external walls, but overpriced for its unmemorable, air-con rooms. **3**

Soon Teck Hotel

Map 7, C4. 57a Koon Seng Rd.
Bus #16 or #33. Ⓣ 3440240.
A peaceful Chinese hotel
with just five air-con rooms.

Communal facilities are
clean, and downstairs there's
a sleepy coffee shop.
Recommended. ❷

SENTOSA ISLAND

- -

Three luxury hotels on the island of **Sentosa** allow you to
bypass the bustle of downtown Singapore. If you aren't too
keen to negotiate any of the more long-winded means of
transport to the island, it's possible to get a taxi direct from
the airport to Sentosa (though note that from 7am to 10pm
a $6 surcharge is levied). All the hotels in this section are
keyed on the map on p.132.

The Beaufort

Ⓣ 2750331; Ⓕ 2750228;
Ⓦ www.travelweb.com/thisco
/beau/sing_b.html
A swanky hotel, fitted out in
varnished wood, bounded by
two 18-hole golf courses and
a beach. There is a $40 price
increase on Friday and
Saturday. ❽

Shangri-La's Rasa Sentosa Beach Resort

Ⓣ 2750100; Ⓕ 2750355;
Ⓦ www.shangri-la.com
Opened in 1993, the *Rasa
Sentosa* is the first hotel in
Singapore to have its own
beach front, and its situation
on Sentosa island makes it a
good option if you've got kids
to amuse. A $40 price rise
applies on Friday and
Saturday, and rooms with a sea
view cost an extra $40. ❽

Sijori Resort Sentosa

Ⓣ 2712002; Ⓕ 2740220.
Sentosa's latest
accommodation option, the
Sijori is slap-bang in the
middle of the island, making
it an ideal base for
exploring. ❼

SENTOSA ISLAND

Eating

Along with shopping, **eating** ranks as the Singaporean national pastime, and an enormous number of food outlets cater for this obsession. However, eating out is not afforded the same reverence that it receives in the West; as often as not, you'll find yourself eating off plastic plates in bare, unpretentious restaurants that ring to the sound of agitated conversation (invariably about food). In Singapore, it's the food, and not the surroundings, that's important. Singapore offers new arrivals in Asia the chance to sample the whole spectrum of the region's dishes. What's more, strict government regulations ensure that food outlets are consistently hygienic – you don't need to worry about food cooked at even the cheapest stall. Dining out in Southeast Asia is a family affair, so unless you're going really upmarket don't be shy of taking the kids with you. If they're not culinary adventurers, there are always the burger bars or pizza joints.

The mass of establishments serving **Chinese** cuisine reflects the fact that Chinese residents account for around three-quarters of the population. Singapore's development into a thriving seaport in the nineteenth century attracted labourers from many different regions of China, and the cuisines they brought with them still dominate the restaurant scene. You're most likely to come across Cantonese, Beijing and Szechuan restaurants, though there's not a region of China whose specialities you can't sample. **North** and **south Indian** cuisines give a good account of themselves too, as do restaurants serving **Malay**, **Indonesian**, **Korean**, **Japanese** and **Vietnamese** food. One thing you won't find, however, is a Singaporean restaurant: the closest Singapore comes to an indigenous cuisine is **Nonya**, a hybrid of Chinese and Malay food that developed following the intermarrying of nineteenth-century Chinese immigrants with Malay women. Of course, if you insist, you can eat **Western food** in Singapore – venture beyond the ubiquitous burger chains and pizza parlours, and you'll find a host of excellent restaurants cooking anything from haggis to jambalaya. These and other dishes may be enjoyed at places geared to the dishes of a particular nation, or at **international restaurants**, whose confused menus are a patchwork of Western cuisines. A more informal alternative is to opt for a plate of **British** food – fish and chips, say – at a pub or bar.

Several specialist Chinese restaurants and a number of Indian restaurants serve **vegetarian food**, but otherwise, tread very carefully: chicken and seafood will appear in a whole host of dishes unless you make it perfectly clear that you don't want them. **Halal food** is predictably easy to find, given the number of Muslims in Singapore; the Arab Street end of North Bridge Road, and Serangoon Road's Zhu Jiao Centre both have proliferations of restaurants and stalls. There are no **kosher** restaurants, but you could try the food store at the Maghain Aboth Synagogue opposite the Church of St Peter and Paul on Waterloo Street.

By far the cheapest and most fun place to dine in Singapore is in a **hawker centre** or **food court**, where

EATING

BUYING YOUR OWN FOOD: WET MARKETS AND SUPERMARKETS

Some guesthouses do have cooking facilities, and if you want to buy your own food or fancy a bag of fresh fruit, you're most likely to go to a **wet market** – so called because of the pools of water perpetually covering the floor. If you don't know a mango from a mangosteen, vendors are usually very helpful (see also pp.170–175). Singapore also has plenty of **supermarkets**, most of which have a delicatessen counter and bakery – some offer familiar beers from back home, too.

Wet markets

Little India is served by the large wet market in the Zhu Jiao Centre (Map 4, A8; bus #65, #66, #81, #97, #103, #139 or #147; see p.97), at the southern end of Serangoon Rd; the Chinatown Complex (Map 3, C11; bus #51, #103, #124, #166, #174 or #190; see p.87) market in

Chinatown rewards a visit, too; and you'll find other wet markets out of the city centre, in Singapore's new towns.

Supermarkets

Cold Storage, branches at Centrepoint, Orchard Rd (Map 5, G5; Somerset MRT); 293 Holland Rd (Map 8, F3; Buona Vista

scores of stalls let you mix and match good Asian dishes at really low prices. For a few extra dollars you graduate into the realm of proper **restaurants**, ranging from no-frills, open-fronted eating houses and coffee shops to sumptuously decorated establishments – often, though not always, located in swanky hotels. Restaurant **opening hours**, on average, are 11.30am–2.30pm and 6–10.30pm daily; hawker stall owners tend to operate to their own schedules, but are almost always open at peak eating times.

EATING

MRT; bus #7 or #105); 31 Amber Rd, Katong (Map 7, C4; Paya Lebar MRT, then bus #135; or bus #197). Local chain that stocks a wide range of Western products.

Diamaru, Liang Court Shopping Complex, 177 River Valley Rd (Map 3, D5; Raffles Place MRT; bus #124, #174 or #190). Japanese department store containing a large food hall with takeaway counters.

Good Gifts Emporium, Golden Mile Complex, 5001 Beach Rd (Map 2, M3; bus #82 or #100). A smallish supermarket with a leaning towards Thai produce.

NTUC Fairprice, Rochor Centre, 1 Rochor Rd (Map 4, E9; bus #7, #14, #36, #97, #124, #166, #174 or #190). Basic supermarket that's handy for Bencoolen Street.

Sogo, Raffles City Shopping Centre, 252 North Bridge Rd (Map 3, H3; City Hall MRT). Japanese department store where you can buy either groceries or take-away snacks.

Yaohan, Plaza Singapura, 68 Orchard Rd (Map 5, I5; Dhoby Ghaut MRT). Japanese department store and supermarket similar to Diamaru and Sogo.

BREAKFAST

Guesthouses sometimes include coffee or tea and toast in the price of the room but the chances are you'll want to head off elsewhere for breakfast. **Western breakfasts** are available, at a price, at all bigger hotels, most famously at the *Hilton* or *Raffles*; otherwise, there are a number of cafés serving continental breakfasts, while *McDonald's*, *KFC* and *Burger King* all rustle up breakfasts before reverting to chicken and burgers after 11am. For a really cheap **fry-up** you can't beat a Western food stall in a hawker centre: here, $8 will buy you enough steak, chops and sausage to challenge even the most starving carnivore. Many visitors to Singapore find the **local breakfasts** a little hard to stomach, but if you shelve your preconceptions, there are some tasty possibilities. The classic Chinese breakfast is *congee*, a watery rice porridge augmented with chopped spring onion, crispy fried onion and strips of meat, though the titbits that comprise *dim sum* (see "Chinese: Cantonese", p.183) tend to be more palatable to occidental tastebuds. An abiding favourite among Malays is *nasi lemak*, rice cooked in coconut milk and served with *sambal ikan bilis* (tiny crispfried anchovies in hot chilli paste), fried peanuts and slices of fried or hard-boiled egg. Otherwise, try investigating one of the scores of Indian establishments that serve up curry and bread breakfasts.

Breakfast With An Orang-utan

Map 6, D4. Singapore Zoo, 80 Mandai Lake Rd. Bus #171 to Mandai Road, then #138, or Ang Mo Kio MRT and then bus #138. ⊤ 3608509.

Daily 9–10am.

A bumper American-style spread with seasonal tropical fruits, shared with whichever orang is on duty; $15.45 (children $11.30).

Breakfast With The Birds

Map 8, A6. Jurong BirdPark, Jalan Ahmad Ibrahim. Boon Lay

MRT, then bus #194 or #251. ⊤ 2650022.

Daily 8am–11am.

A buffet of local and Western breakfast favourites, eaten to the accompaniment of the caged songbirds hanging above you; $12 (children $10).

Brooklyn Bagels

Map 3, B3. 235 River Valley Rd. Bus #32, #54 or #139. ⊤ 7320056.

Mon–Thurs 7am–8pm, Fri & Sat 7am–midnight, Sun 7am–6pm.

Tiny takeaway joint where you choose from plain, egg,

BREAKFAST

onion, garlic, sesame or pumpernickel bagels, filled with pastrami, salmon or roast beef, or make do with a plain old muffin. All produce is baked in-house daily.

Champagne Brunch At The Hilton

Map 5, D5. *Hilton Hotel*, 581 Orchard Rd. Orchard MRT; bus #36. ⊤ 7372233.
Sun 11.30am–2.30pm only.
For around $60 you get a superb free flow of delicacies – oysters, salmon, curry and cakes – washed down with litres of champagne and orange juice. Reservations are essential.

De Boa (HK) Restaurant

Map 3, C10. 42 Smith St. Bus #51, #103, #124, #166, #174 or #190.
Daily 7.30am–5pm.
Set right opposite the Chinatown Complex, a smashing little café offering *dim sum*, *pau* (Chinese dumplings) and Chinese tea.

Delifrance

Map 5, G5. 01-03 Peranakan Place, 180 Orchard Rd.

Somerset MRT.
Daily 7.30am–10pm.
This stylish café is one of a chain of French delis specializing in filled croissants and pastries. Recommended.

Dôme

Map 3, G9. Ground floor, UOB Plaza. Raffles Place MRT. ⊤ 5333266. Branch at Singapore Art Museum (Map 3, G9; City Hall MRT; bus #171, #190 or #197).
Daily 7.30am–10pm.
Slick café – one of a global chain – boasting an impressive range of coffees and teas and a superb view over the Singapore River. Muffins, toast and croissants are reasonable, and a selection of international papers are on hand for the full breakfast effect.

Famous Amos

Map 5, H5. 01-05 Specialists' Shopping Centre, 277 Orchard Rd. Somerset MRT.
Daily 10am–9pm.
Sublime, handmade cookies to take away.

Mr Bean's Café

Map 4, C12. 30 Selegie Rd.

BREAKFAST

Dhoby Ghaut MRT.
Open 24hr.
Based in the same wedge-shaped colonial building as the *Selegie Arts Centre*, *Mr Bean's* draws an interesting crowd, who breakfast on muffins, croissants, toast and coffee. American/English and continental breakfasts are available (around $6) until 11am, after which the menu turns to pizzas, sandwiches and finger food.

Mr Cucumber
Map 3, H10. 02-02 Clifford Centre, 24 Raffles Place. Raffles Place MRT. ☎ 5340363.
Mon–Fri 10am–6pm, Sat 11am–3pm.
Sandwich bar with a wide variety of fillings, catering for the business district crowd. Sandwiches from $3 upwards, or try one of the bagels supplied by *Brooklyn Bagels*.

Red Lantern Beer Garden
Map 3, H10. Basement, 60a Change Alley Aerial Plaza, Collyer Quay. Raffles Place MRT.
Daily 7–10.30am.

The continental set breakfast in this enclosed beer garden is great value, at under $5.

Spinelli Coffee Company
Map 4, F11. 01-15 Bugis Junction, 230 Victoria St. Bugis MRT.
Daily 10am–10pm.
San Francisco–based outfit that's riding on the crest of Singapore's current mania for fresh coffee; the narrow bar is ideal for a quick espresso.

Starbucks Coffee
Map 3, H3. 01-46 Raffles City Shopping Centre, 252 North Bridge Rd. City Hall MRT. ☎ 3333083.
Mon–Fri 7.30am–10.30pm, Sat & Sun 8am–midnight.
Central branch of the American coffee chain that's spreading like wildfire across the island.

Tan Hock Seng Cake Shop
Map 3, F10. 88 Telok Ayer St. Raffles Place MRT; bus #125, #131, #167 or #186.
Daily 10am–8pm.
They've been baking cakes and biscuits on site for more

than fifty years at this famous Hokkien shop, just next door to the Fuk Tak Chi Street Museum.

Tiffin Room

Map 3, I2. *Raffles Hotel*, 1 Beach Rd. City Hall MRT; bus #56 or #171. ☎3371886.
Daily 7.30–10am.
Have your buffet breakfast here and you won't need to eat until dinner; $25 per person.

Yasinn Restaurant

Map 4, D11. 127 Bencoolen St. Bus #7, #14, #36, #97, #124, #166, #174 or #190.
Open 24 hours daily.
Does a roaring trade in *roti prata* (fried bread) and curry sauce each morning.

HAWKER CENTRES AND FOOD COURTS

To eat inexpensively in Singapore, you go to the hawker stalls, traditionally simple wooden stalls on the roadside, with a few stools to sit at. Today, tighter regulations have swept the hawkers off the streets, and corralled them in custom-made **hawker centres**, where scores of permanent stalls line wide corridors, bristling with fixed stools and chairs. Though hygienic, hawker centres are often housed in functional buildings which tend to get extremely hot and, if you're sat next to a stall cooking fried rice or noodles, extremely smoky. As a result, an increasing number of smaller, air-conditioned **food courts** are popping up; brighter and more civilized than hawker centres, these suffer from a lack of atmosphere. In both hawker stalls and food courts, it's possible to pick up different dishes from a variety of stalls.

The standard of cooking is also very high at most stalls, and politicians and pop stars crowd in with the locals to eat at a cramped hawker's table. Hawker stalls serve a range of cuisines reflecting Singapore's ethnic make-up. Standard

A FOOD AND DRINK GLOSSARY

Many menus in Singapore are written in English, but it's worth noting that transliterated spellings are not standardized – you may well see some of the following dishes written in a variety of ways; we've used the most widely accepted spellings.

General terms

Assam	Sour	*Istimewa*	Special (as in "today's special")
Garam	Salt	*Kari*	Curry
Goreng	Fried	*Makan*	Food
Gula	Sugar	*Manis*	Sweet

Meat, fish and basics

Ayam	Chicken	*Sayur*	Vegetable
Babi	Pork	*Sotong*	Squid
Daging	Beef	*Sup*	Soup
Ikan	Fish	*Tahu*	Bean curd
Kambing	Mutton	*Telor*	Egg
Kepiting	Crab	*Udang*	Prawn

Noodles (mee) and noodle dishes

Bee hoon	Thin rice noodles, like vermicelli; *mee fun* is similar.
Char kuey teow	Flat noodles with any combination of prawns, Chinese sausage, fishcake, egg, vegetables and chilli.
Foochow noodles	Steamed and served in soy and oyster sauce with spring onions and dried fish.
Hokkien fried mee	Yellow noodles fried with pieces of pork, prawn and vegetables.
Kuey teow	Flat noodles, comparable to Italian tagliatelle; *hor fun* is similar.

La mien	"Pulled noodles", made by spinning dough skipping-rope-style in the air.
Laksa	Noodles, beansprouts, fishcakes and prawns in a spicy coconut soup.
Mee	Standard round yellow noodles made from wheat flour that looks like spaghetti.
Mee goreng	Indian fried noodles.
Mee suah	Noodles served dry and crispy.
Sar hor fun	Flat rice noodles served in a chicken stock soup, to which prawns, fried shallots and beansprouts are added: a Malaysian speciality.
Wan ton mee	Roast pork, noodles and vegetables in a light soup containing dumplings.

Rice (nasi) dishes

Biriyani	Saffron-flavoured rice cooked with chicken, beef or fish; a north Indian speciality.
Claypot	Rice topped with meat (as diverse as chicken and turtle), cooked in an earthenware pot over a fire to create a smoky taste.
Daun pisang	Malay term for banana-leaf curry, a south Indian meal with chutneys and curries, served on a mound of rice, and presented on a banana leaf with *poppadoms*.
Hainan chicken rice	Singapore's unofficial national dish: steamed or boiled chicken slices on rice cooked in chicken stock, served with chicken broth and chilli and ginger sauce.
Kunyit	Rice cooked in tumeric; a side dish.
Nasi campur	Rice served with an array of meat, fish and vegetable dishes.
Nasi goreng	Fried rice with diced meat and vegetables.

| *Nasi lemak* | A Malay classic: fried anchovies, cucumber, peanuts and fried or hard-boiled egg slices served on coconut rice. |
| *Nasi puteh* | Plain boiled rice. |

Other specialities

Ayam goreng	Malay-style fried chicken.
Bak kut teh	Literally "pork bone tea", a Chinese dish of pork ribs in soy sauce, herbs and spices.
Char siew pow	Cantonese steamed bun stuffed with roast pork in a sweet sauce.
Chay tow kueh	Also known as "carrot cake", this is actually an omelette made with white radish and spring onions.
Congee	Rice porridge, cooked in lots of water and eaten with slices of meat and fish.
Dim sum	Chinese titbits – dumplings, rolls, chicken's feet – steamed or fried and served in bamboo baskets.
Dosai	South Indian pancake, made from ground rice and lentils, and served with *daal* (lentils) and spicy dips.
Fish-head curry	The head of a red snapper (usually), cooked in a spicy curry sauce with tomatoes and okra; one of Singapore's most famous dishes.
Gado gado	Malay/Indonesian salad of lightly cooked vegetables, boiled egg, slices of rice cake and a crunchy peanut sauce.
Ikan bilis	Deep-fried anchovies.
Kai pow	Similar to *char siew pow*, but contains chicken and boiled egg.
Kerupuk	Crackers.

Murtabak	Thick Indian pancake, stuffed with onion, egg and chicken or mutton.
Otak-otak	Fish mashed with coconut milk and chilli paste and steamed in a banana leaf; a Nonya dish.
Popiah	Chinese spring rolls, filled with peanuts, egg, beansprouts, vegetables and a sweet sauce; sometimes known as *lumpia*.
Rendang	Dry, highly spiced coconut curry with beef, chicken or mutton.
Rojak	Indian fritters dipped in chilli and peanut sauce; the Chinese version is a salad of greens, beansprouts, pineapple and cucumber in a peanut-and-prawn paste sauce, similar to *gado gado*.
Roti canai	Light, layered Indian pancake served with a thin curry sauce or *daal*; sometimes called *roti pratha*.
Roti john	Simple Indian dish of egg, onion and tomato sauce spread on bread and heated.
Satay	Marinated pieces of meat, skewered on small sticks and cooked over charcoal; served with peanut sauce, cucumber and *ketupat* (rice cake).
Sop kambing	Spicy Indian mutton soup.
Steamboat	Chinese equivalent of the Swiss fondue: raw vegetables, meat or fish dunked into a steaming broth until cooked.

Desserts

Bubor cha cha	Sweetened coconut milk with pieces of sweet potato, yam and tapioca balls.

A FOOD AND DRINK GLOSSARY

●

Cendol	Coconut milk, palm sugar syrup and pea-flour noodles poured over shaved ice.
Es kachang	Shaved ice with red beans, cubes of jelly, sweetcorn, rose syrup and evaporated milk.
Pisang goreng	Fried banana fritters.

Tropical fruit

The more familiar fruits available in Singapore include coconut, watermelon, several types of banana, seven varieties of mango and three types of pineapple.

Ciku	Looks like an apple; varies from yellow to pinkish brown when ripe, with a soft, pulpy flesh.
Durian	Singapore's most popular fruit has a greeny-yellow, spiky exterior and grows to the size of a football. It has thick, yellow-white flesh and an incredibly pungent odour likened to a mixture of mature cheese and caramel.
Guava	A green, textured skin and flesh with five times the vitamin C content of oranges.
Jackfruit	This large, pear-shaped fruit grows up to 50cm long and has a greeny-yellow exterior with sweet flesh inside.
Langsat	Together with its sister fruit, the *duku*, this looks like a small, round potato, with juicy white flesh which can be anything from sweet to sour.
Longgan	Similar to the lychee, this has juicy white flesh and brown seeds.
Mangosteen	Available from June to August and November to January, it has a sweet though slightly acidic flavour. Its smooth rind deepens to a distinctive crimson colour when ripe.

Markisa	Known in the West as passion fruit, this has purple-brown dimpled skin with a rich flavour; frequently an ingredient in drinks.
Papaya	The milky orange-coloured flesh is a rich source of vitamins A and C.
Pomelo	The pomelo, or *limau bali*, is the largest of all the citrus fruits and looks rather like a grapefruit, though it is slightly drier and has less flavour.
Rambutan	The bright red rambutan's soft, spiny exterior has given it its name – *rambut* means "hair" in Malay. Usually about the size of a golf ball, it has a white, opaque fruit of delicate flavour, similar to a lychee.
Salak	Teardrop-shaped, the *salak* has a skin like a snake's and a bitter taste.
Star fruit	Waxy, pale-green star-shaped fruit said to be good for high blood pressure; the yellower the fruit, the sweeter its flesh.
Zirzat	Inside its bumpy, muddy green skin is smooth white flesh like blancmange, hence its other name, custard apple; also known as soursop.

Drinks

Kopi	Coffee.
Kopi-o	Black coffee.
Kopi susu	Coffee with milk.
Lassi	Sweet or sour yoghurt drink of Indian origin.
Teh	Tea.
Teh-o	Black tea.
Teh susu	Tea with milk.
Teh tarik	Sweet, milky tea, poured between two cups to produce a frothy drink.

A FOOD AND DRINK GLOSSARY

Indian and Malay noodle and rice dishes are widely available, but it's Chinese food which is prevalent. In certain venues, you'll also come across Western food like burgers, and steak and eggs; or Indonesian or Korean food.

Hawker stalls don't have menus, though most have signs in English detailing their specialities; otherwise point at anything you like the look of. When you order a dish, make it clear if you want a small, medium or large portion – or else you'll get the biggest and most expensive one. You don't have to sit close to the stall you're patronizing: find a free seat, and the vendor will track you down when your food is ready. Meals are paid for when they reach your table. A hearty meal – say, curry and rice, a fruit juice and a dessert – will cost you around $8, though if your budget doesn't run that far, you can eat well for half the price.

Hawker centres and food courts are open from lunchtime through to dinner and sometimes beyond, though individual stalls tend to open and shut as they please. Most close well before midnight, one notable exception being **Newton Circus**, where the **late-night** seafood is a constant tourist draw. There are always hot and cold drinks stalls on hand, and getting a bottle of beer is rarely difficult. If you avoid the peak lunching (12.30–1.30pm) and dining (6–7pm) periods, when hungry Singaporeans funnel into their nearest hawker centre, you should have no problems in finding a seat.

Chinatown Complex

Map 3, C10. Smith Street, at end of New Bridge Road. Bus #51, #103, #124, #166, #174 or #190.

A huge range of dishes with a predictably Chinese bias.

Food Junction

Map 4, F11. B1, Seiyu Department Store, Bugis Junction, 200 Victoria St. Bugis MRT.

Happening food court whose trendy piped music provides a

stirring soundtrack to your dinner. Culinary themes as diverse as Thai, Japanese, *nasi padang* and claypot are represented, and there's a choice of local desserts or Häagen Dazs ice creams.

Funan the IT Mall Food Court

Map 3, F5. 109 North Bridge Rd. City Hall MRT; bus #51, #124, #145, #166, #174 or #190.

Smart basement court whose stalls serve herbal soup, claypots, Hainanese chicken and local desserts.

Geylang Serai Food Centre

Map 7, B4. Geylang Serai. Payar Lebar MRT.

In the heart of Singapore's Malay quarter, with a corresponding range of stalls. Turn left out of Paya Lebar MRT and left again onto Sims Avenue; the centre is five minutes' walk along, on your right.

Hastings Road Food Court

Map 3, B8. Little India Arcade, Serangoon Road. Bus #65, #66, #81, #97, #103, #139 or #147. Diminutive food court whose handful of stalls are labelled by region – Keralan, Mughlai, Sri Lankan and so on.

Hill Street Centre

Map 3, F5. 64 Hill St. City Hall MRT; bus #7, #14, #36, #124, #167 or #190.

A number of fine Chinese and Indian stalls on two floors. On the far right-hand side as you enter is a stall serving excellent *popiah* (spring rolls stuffed with bamboo shoots, beansprouts, prawns, and hot chilli paste).

Lau Pa Sat Festival Market

Map 3, G12. 18 Raffles Quay. Raffles Place MRT; bus #97, #125, #167 or #196.

The smartest hawker stalls in Singapore, and now open round the clock. At lunchtime the place is full to bursting with suits from the city; at night the clubbers take over.

New Bugis Street

Map 4, F10. Bugis MRT.

A handful of evening hawkers

HAWKER CENTRES AND FOOD COURTS

177

dish up Asian specialities like satay, *laksa*, *kueh* and sushi.

Newton Circus Hawker Centre

Map 5, F2. North end of Scotts Road. Newton MRT.
Prices are a little higher than other centres because it's on the mainstream tourist trail, but it has the advantage of staying open until late. Noted for its seafood stalls.

Orchard Emerald Food Chain

Map 5, G5. Basement, Orchard Emerald, 218 Orchard Rd. Somerset MRT.
Smart food court, halfway along Orchard Road, where the Indonesian buffet is great value.

Picnic Food Court

Map 5, E5. Scotts Shopping Centre, 6 Scotts Rd. Orchard MRT.
Slap-bang in the middle of the Orchard Road district, squeaky clean, and with lots of choice.

Satay Club

Map 3, D5. Clarke Quay.

Raffles Place MRT; bus #124, #174, #190.
A Singapore institution, serving inexpensive chicken and mutton satay. Open evenings only, from around 7pm.

Sim Lim Square Food Court

Map 4, D9. 1 Rochor Canal Rd. Bus #7, #14, #36, #97, #124, #166, #174 or #190.
Convenient if you are staying on Bencoolen Street; it's even got its own jukebox.

Taman Serasi

Map 5, A6. Junction of Napier and Cluny roads. Bus #7, #106 or #174.
Opposite the main entrance to the Botanic Gardens, the speciality here is *roti john*.

Telok Blangah

Map 8, I5. Telok Blangah Rd. Bus #97, #143 or #166.
Opposite the World Trade Centre, and good for a snack before or after a trip to Sentosa.

Victoria Street Food Court

Map 4, E13. 83 Victoria St.

City Hall MRT; bus #171 or #190.
Open-fronted food court
with around ten stalls; handy
for Bencoolen Street.

Zhujiao Hawker Centre
Map 4, B8. Corner of Bukit

Timah and Serangoon roads,
Little India. Bus #65, #66, #81,
#97, #103, #139 or #147.
The bulk of its stalls,
naturally enough, serve
Indian food.

RESTAURANTS AND COFFEE SHOPS

Restaurants in Singapore rnge from simple coffee shops to
the most sumptuous establishments you could imagine.
Coffee shops, invariably Chinese- or Indian-run, and usually open throughout the day, serve basic noodle and rice
dishes, and sometimes feature a selection of cakes and
sweetmeats. The culinary standard is never spectacularly
high, but you're unlikely to spend more than $5 for a filling
meal. Indian coffee shops tend to be a bit livelier, and are
sometimes decidedly theatrical. Here you can watch the
Muslim *mamak* men at work, whose job it is to make the
frothy *teh tarik* (tea), by pouring liquid from a height from
one vessel into another, and pound and mould the *roti* into
an oily, bubble-filled shape; in some Indian coffee shops,
you'll also be treated to the sight of plate-sized *murtabaks*
being spun and griddle-fried.

On the whole, proper **restaurants** are places you go if
you want a bit of comfort, or to savour particular delicacies
found nowhere else, like fish-head curry, Chinese specialities
like shark's-fin dishes and bird's-nest soup, high-quality
seafood and fine international cuisine. Singapore also has a
tradition of **haute cuisine**, usually available in the top-
notch hotels. Many of the best hotel-restaurants in
Singapore boast reputable chefs, drawing in the punters with
well-received French, Thai, Italian and Japanese food as well

RESTAURANTS AND COFFEE SHOPS

as more local delicacies. That said, in many restaurants, the food is not necessarily superior to that served at a good café or hawker stall – you're just paying the (often considerable) extra for air-conditioning and tablecloths. One reason to splash out, though, is to experience a **cultural show** of music and dance, found in several of the large Chinese seafood restaurants, all of which are detailed below.

Unless you're in a Muslim restaurant, you'll be able to wash down your meal with a glass of cold **beer**; wine is less common, though smarter establishments will normally retain a modest choice. Few **desserts** feature on Southeast Asian restaurants' menus, but the region's bounty of tropical **fruit** more than compensates; the glossary on pp.170–175 lists some of the less familiar fruits you may come across.

Tipping is not expected in Singaporean restaurants, and bills arrive complete with service charge and government tax (presently fourteen percent). Making yourself understood is rarely a problem, nor is negotiating a menu, as nearly all are written in English.

If possible, try to book ahead at more upmarket restaurants, particularly on Saturday nights and Sunday lunchtimes, when they are at their busiest; moreover, bear in mind that many restaurants close over Chinese New Year, and those that don't are often bursting at the seams.

CHINESE

The majority of the **Chinese** restaurants in Singapore are **Cantonese**, that is, from the province of Canton (Guangdong) in southern China, though you'll also come across northern **Beijing** (or Peking) and western **Szechuan** cuisines, as well as the **Hokkien** specialities of the southeastern province of Fujian, and **Teochew** dishes from the area east of Canton. Whatever the region, it's undoubtedly the real thing – Chinese food as eaten by the Chinese – which means

EATING OUT – AN OVERVIEW

Eating in Singaporean restaurants is quite different to dining out, Western-style. Singaporeans – and particularly Singapore Chinese – tend to choose as many dishes as there are people at the table, and then order a couple more for good luck, a custom which bypasses the problem of choosing badly and then slavering after your neighbour's dish. When the food arrives, everyone dips in. English menus are available in most restaurants.

Depending on the cuisine you are eating, you have a choice of utensils at your command. **Chinese food** is traditionally eaten with **chopsticks**, which look nightmarishly difficult to use, but are actually quite easily mastered. One is laid between thumb and forefinger, and supported by your fourth and little fingers; the second chopstick is held between thumb, forefinger and second finger, and manipulated to form a pincer. To make your task slightly easier, eat, not from your plate, but from the bowl provided, holding it right up to your lips. Chinese eaters are able to feed rice from bowl to mouth with such speed that they seem to be sucking it up a tube; a china spoon is always provided in case you can't get the hang of chopsticks, but don't give up just because you're making a mess, as this isn't frowned upon in the least.

In upmarket **Indian restaurants** your placing will be set with spoon and fork, but in more basic establishments, food often arrives at table minus any utensils, and sometimes on a **banana leaf** instead of a plate. Traditionally, Indians eat by affecting a scooping action with their right hands, but if you don't fancy this, it's perfectly acceptable to ask for cutlery.

A Chinese meal is typically taken with plain steamed rice; be careful not to take too much, as leaving rice is considered rude by the Chinese. In an Indian restaurant, you can either eat your main course with rice, or scoop and mop it up with hunks of Indian bread.

it won't always sound particularly appealing to foreigners: the Chinese eat all parts of an animal, from its lips to its undercarriage, and it's important to retain a sense of adventure when exploring menus. Fish and seafood is nearly always outstanding in Chinese cuisine, with prawns, crab, squid and a variety of fish on offer. Noodles, too, are ubiquitous, and come in wonderful variations (see p.170–171). For something a little more unusual, try a **steamboat**, a Chinese-style fondue filled with boiling stock in which you cook meat, fish, shellfish, eggs and vegetables; or a **claypot** — meat, fish or shellfish cooked over a fire in an earthenware pot.

The other thing to note is that in many Cantonese restaurants (and in other regional restaurants, too), lunch consists of **dim sum** — steamed and fried dumplings served in little bamboo baskets.

BEIJING

Beijing was traditionally the seat of China's Imperial households, and the sumptuous presentation of its cuisine reflects its opulent past. Meat dominates, typically flavoured with garlic and spring onions, though the dish for which Beijing is most famous is roast duck, served in three courses: the skin is eaten in a pancake filled with spring onion and radish, and smeared with plum sauce; afterwards, the flesh is stir-fried with vegetables, and the carcass boiled to make a soup.

Jade Room

Map 5, E1. *Hotel Royal*, 36 Newton Rd. Newton MRT. ☎ 2548603. Daily 11.30am–2.30pm & 6.30–10.30pm. The full Imperial effect – red and gold decor, serenading musicians and waiters in traditional attire – is at work here. Play safe with standards like Peking duck and Peking-style mutton steamboat ($21 per person), or plump for a set meal (from $48 for two people).

Pine Court Restaurant
Map 5, F6. 35th floor, *Mandarin Hotel*, 333 Orchard Rd. Orchard MRT; bus #36. ⊤ 7374411. Daily noon–2.30pm & 6.30–10.30pm.

Three elegant pine trees dominate this beautiful restaurant, where the speciality is whole Peking duck ($70) – enough for three hungry people. Cheaper set meals are available, too. You'll need to reserve in advance.

CANTONESE

Cantonese cuisine is noted for its delicacy of flavour and memorable sauces. Cantonese dishes are stir-fried, steamed or roasted, and often taken with black bean, lemon, oyster or soy sauce. Fish and seafood weigh in heavily on a Cantonese menu, either fried or steamed, and other specialities include pigeon, roast meats and frogs' legs. **Dim sum** is also a classic Cantonese meal: literally translated as "to touch the heart", it's a blanket term for an array of dumplings, cakes and titbits steamed in bamboo baskets. Though you do occasionally see it on lunch menus, traditionally *dim sum* is eaten by the Chinese for breakfast, with one basket (of three or four pieces) costing as little as $3.

Bugis Village
Map 4, F10. Bugis MRT. Daily 5pm–3am.

Touts at the several seafood restaurants here hassle you incessantly to take a seat and a menu. The furious competition ensures prices are reasonable, despite the high proportion of tourists; all restaurants have similar, mainstream menus.

Capital Restaurant
Map 3, A14. 01-207, Block 2, Cantonment Rd. Bus #167 or #196. ⊤ 2213516. Daily noon–2.30pm & 6–10.30pm.

The friendly staff in this spotless

RESTAURANTS AND COFFEE SHOPS: CANTONESE

restaurant recommend fried deer meat with ginger; also worth a try are the fried prawns rolled in bean curd skin. A feast for two costs under $35.

Dragon Town Garden Seafood Restaurant

Map 3, C12. 1 Neil Rd. Tanjong Pagar MRT; bus #103, #124, #145 or #166. ⓣ 2251223.
Daily 11am–2.30pm & 6pm–11pm.
Once a rickshaw station – and with a sign outside to prove it – this distinguished building at the intersection of Neil and Tanjong Pagar roads offers seafood dishes of a high quality; a meal for two costs around $80.

Fatty's Wing Seong Restaurant

Map 4, D10. 01-31 Burlington Complex, 175 Bencoolen St. Bus #7, #14, #36, #97, #124, #166, #174 or #190.
ⓣ 3381087.
Daily noon–11pm.
A Singapore institution, where every dish on the wide Cantonese menu is well cooked and speedily delivered. Around $20 a head.

Grand City Chinese Restaurant

Map 4, B13. 07-04 Cathay Bldg, 11 Dhoby Ghaut. Dhoby Ghaut MRT. ⓣ 3383622.
Mon–Sat 11.30am–2.30pm & 6.30–10.30pm, Sun 10am–2.30pm & 6.30–10.30pm.
Sizeable, enduringly popular restaurant, whose tables have rotating glass tops which ensure you needn't miss out on any of the dishes ordered. Oddities like emu with black pepper and Teochew-style goose sit alongside better-known dishes on the menu here.

Hai Tien Lo

Map 2, K6. 37th floor, *Pan Pacific Hotel*, 7 Raffles Blvd, Marina Square. Bus #36 or #171. ⓣ 4348338.
Daily noon–2.30pm & 6.30–10.30pm.
If you have money enough for just one blowout, come here for exquisitely presented food and stunning views of downtown Singapore. Extravagant set meals are available, while Sunday lunchtimes (10.30am–2.30pm) are set aside for *dim sum*.

Hillman Restaurant

Map 3, A14. 01-159, Block 1, Cantonment Rd. Bus #167 or #196. ☎ 2215073.
Daily 11.30am–2.30pm & 5.30–10.30pm.

Extremely popular, thanks to its famous paper-wrapped chicken, and its rich-tasting earthen pot dishes of flavoursome stews featuring various meats and seafood in a rich sauce; small pots (around $10) fill two.

Li Bai

Map 5, E2. *Sheraton Towers Hotel*, 39 Scotts Rd. Newton MRT. ☎ 7376888.
Daily noon–2.30pm & 6.30–10.30pm.

Named after a poet of the Tang dynasty, a suitably sophisticated place in the bowels of the *Towers*, where your best bet is the five-course luncheon, weighing in at $50; you can opt for lighter *dim sum*.

If you want a table with a view, check these out these places:
Compass Rose Restaurant, see p.206.
Hai Tien Lo, see p.184.
Top of the M, see p.208.
Top of the Plaza, see p.187.

Mitzi's

Map 3, C12. 24–26 Murray Terr. Tanjong Pagar MRT; bus #103, #124, #145 or #166. ☎ 2220929.
Daily 11am–3pm & 6–10pm.

The cracking Cantonese food in this simple place, situated in a row of restaurants known as "Food Alley", draws crowds, so be prepared to queue. Two can eat for $30, drinks extra.

Mouth Restaurant

Map 3, D9. 02-01 Chinatown Point, 133 New Bridge Rd. Bus #33, #54, #124 or #190. ☎ 5344233.
Daily 11am–4am (*dim sum* 11.30am–5pm).

Beside a popular *dim sum* menu, this jam-packed restaurant offers classy Hong Kong new-wave Cantonese food, at under $20 a head.

RESTAURANTS AND COFFEE SHOPS: CANTONESE

Northern Palace

Map 4, F13. B1-01 Odeon
Towers, 331 North Bridge Rd,
Colonial District. City Hall MRT;
bus #56 or #171. ☎3384513.
Daily 11am–2.30pm & 6–10pm.
Dim sum dishes here all cost
under $3, and are served in
the traditional way from a
trolley – but only during the
lunchtime sitting.

Ponggol Hock Kee Seafood Restaurant

Map 8, I6. 01-124 World Trade
Centre, 1 Maritime Square. Bus
#97, #143 or #166. ☎2743500.
Daily 11.30am–2.30pm &
5.30–10.30pm.
Long since evicted from its
seaside location on the north
coast, but still turning out
superior seafood. $25 feeds
two; try the crab, either
steamed or cooked with chilli
or pepper.

Soup Restaurant

Map 3, C11. 25 Smith St. Bus
#51, #103, #124, #166, #174 or
#190. ☎2229923.
Daily 11.30am–10.30pm.
Traditional Cantonese
double-boiled and simmered
soups are the speciality at this
steam-heat-dependent soup
shop whose elegant tables and
low-hung lights recall old
Chinatown. The *samsui*
ginger chicken comes
recommended.

Swee Kee

Map 3, D11. *Damenlou Hotel*,
12 Ann Siang Rd. Bus #51,
#103, #124, #166, #174 or #190.
☎2211900.
Daily 11am–2.30pm &
5.30–11pm.
A Cantonese restaurant with
real pedigree: Tang Swee Kee
hawked the first bowl of his
trademark *ka shou* fish-head
noodles more than sixty years
ago, and now his son sells this
and other well-cooked dishes
from the attractive coffee shop
on the ground floor of his
Chinatown hotel.

Thye Choon Huan Restaurant and Bar

Map 3, C9. Corner of New
Bridge St and Upper Cross St.
Bus #33, #54, #124 or #190.
Daily 7am–5pm.
Old-style coffee shop whose
fittings ooze antiquity, from

its marble-topped tables to its huge, liver-spotted mirror; *wan ton* and noodle soups, chicken, and duck rice can all be whistled up in a trice.

Top of the Plaza

Map 3, G9. 60th floor, UOB Plaza, 80 Raffles Place. Raffles Place MRT. ☎ 5383232.
Mon–Sat 11.30am–2.30pm & 6–10.30pm.
With menu prices suitably sky-high in this elegant Cantonese restaurant, opting for the cut-price set lunches ($15 a head) is the best way to take in the great views.

Tung Lok Shark's Fin Restaurant

Map 3, D5. 04-07/9 Liang Court, 177 River Valley Rd. Raffles Place MRT; bus #124, #174 or #190. ☎ 3366022.
Daily 11am–2.30pm & 6.30–11pm.
The twelve types of shark's-fin dishes (from $20 per person) inevitably constitute the highlight of this lavish restaurant. Meals cost around $50 a head.

Ubin Seafood

Map 1, H3. 2161 Pulau Ubin. Boat from Changi Point. ☎ 5458202.
Daily 11.30am–9pm.
One of the finest seafood restaurants in Singapore – and with a great view of Johor. Take bus #2 from Victoria Street to Changi Village, and hop on a bumboat to Pulau Ubin. Then catch a taxi or rent a bike.

Union Farm Eating House

Map 8, E3. 435a Clementi Rd. From Clementi MRT take bus #154 and get off when you see Maju army camp. ☎ 4662776.
Daily 11.30am–8.30pm.
Until thirty years ago, this used to be a poultry farm, and palms and bamboos still surround the restaurant. The house special, *Chee Pow Kai* (marinated chicken wrapped in greaseproof paper and deep fried; $14 buys enough for two), is messy and wonderful.

Wang Jiang Lou

Map 3, D5. Blk A, Clarke Quay. Raffles Place MRT; bus #124,

RESTAURANTS AND COFFEE SHOPS: CANTONESE

187

#174 or #190. ☏ 3383001.
Daily 11.30am–2.30pm &
6.30–10.30pm.
Slick Cantonese-Teochew
restaurant where the
ingredients of a full seafood
menu eye you suspiciously
from tanks on the walls. Also
available is a medley of *dim
sum* (weekday lunchtime;
$14), and night-time
steamboat ($16).

HAINANESE

Hainanese cuisine is synonymous in Singapore with
chicken rice – the country's unofficial national dish.
Chicken rice is a simple but tasty dish featuring, predictably
enough, slices of chicken laid on rice that has been cooked
in chicken stock. A chilli and ginger sauce is always served
with the meal.

Mooi Chin Palace Restaurant
Map 3, F5. B1-03 Funan the IT
Mall, 109 North Bridge Rd. City
Hall MRT; bus #51, #124, #145,
#166, #174 or #190.
☏ 3397766.
Daily 11.30am–3pm & 6–10pm.
Open for *dim sum* daily
7.30–9am.
Hainanese immigrants often
worked as domestics to
colonial families, resulting in
crossover dishes like
Hainanese mutton soup and
Hainanese pork chop – both
cooked to perfection in this
sixty-year-old place, where
whole *pomfret sambal* ($24) is
a speciality, and set menus
start from around $30 for
two.

Yet Con Chicken Rice Restaurant
Map 4, G12. 25 Purvis St. City
Hall MRT; bus #171 or #190.
☏ 3376819.
Daily 10.30am–9.30pm.
Cheap and cheerful, old-time
restaurant: try "crunchy,
crispy" roast pork with
pickled cabbage and radish, or
chicken rice, washed down
with barley water; $12 for two
people.

HOKKIEN

The **Hokkien** chef relies heavily upon sauces and broths to cook his meat and (primarily) seafood. Without doubt, Hokkien fried *mee* is the most popular Hokkien dish in Singapore – you'll find it in nearly every hawker centre on the island.

Bee Heong

Map 3, F11. 4th floor, Pil Building, 140 Cecil St. Raffles Place MRT; bus #97, #107, #125, #167 or #186.
ⓣ 2229075.
Daily 11am–2.30pm.
Customers are pumped through at a rate of knots in this lunchtime-only, cafeteria-style place; there's no menu, but the beggar chicken and dried chilli prawn come recommended, or ask the friendly staff for advice.

Beng Hiang Restaurant

Map 3, F10. 115 Amoy St. Raffles Place MRT; bus #125, #131, #167 or #186.
ⓣ 2216695.
Daily 11.30am–2pm & 6–9pm.

The lack of a menu makes ordering distinctly tricky, but persistence is rewarded by well-cooked food at good-value prices – you can eat well for under $15.

Beng Thin Hoon Kee Restaurant

Map 3, G9. 05-02 OCBC Centre, 65 Chulia St. Raffles Place MRT. ⓣ 5332818.
Daily 11.30am–3pm & 6–10pm.
Hidden inside the OCBC car park, this minty green restaurant is very popular at lunchtime with city slickers from the nearby business district. Big portions make it a good and filling introduction to Hokkien cuisine.

SZECHUAN AND HUNANESE

Szechuan food is hot and spicy, with chilli, pepper, garlic and ginger conspiring to piquant effect in classic dishes such as camphor-and-tea-smoked duck, and chicken with dried chilli. The food of neighbouring Hunan province is similarly fiery; popular dishes include Hunanese honey-glazed ham and minced pigeon steamed in a bamboo tube.

Cherry Garden Restaurant

Map 2, K6. *The Oriental*, 5 Raffles Ave, Marina Square. Bus #36 or #171. ☎ 3380066 ext 3538.

Daily noon–2.30pm & 6.30–10.30pm.

Elegant restaurant, designed to resemble a Chinese courtyard, and serving tasty Szechuan and Hunanese dishes. Hunanese honey-glazed ham is delectable, as is the Szechuan house speciality, camphor-smoked duck and bean curd crust (both under $30); the set lunches cost $40–60 a head.

Long Jiang Restaurant

Map 5, F5. *Crown Prince Hotel*, 270 Orchard Rd. Orchard MRT. ☎ 7321111 ext 1700.

Daily 11.30am–2.30pm & 6.30–10.30pm.

The daily buffet lunch here is an excellent initiation into Szechuan cuisine ($22 a head, weekends $26).

Magic of Chongqing Hotpot

Map 5, C5. 04-0617 Tanglin Shopping Centre, 19 Tanglin Rd. Bus #105, #123 or #174. ☎ 7348135.

Daily noon–3pm & 6–11pm.

Established in 1995, this homely restaurant has got local pundits raving over its zesty Szechuan hotpots; two can dine well for $80.

Min Jiang Restaurant

Map 5, E3. *Goodwood Park Hotel*, 22 Scotts Rd. Newton or Orchard MRT. ☎ 7375337.

Daily noon–2.30pm & 6.30–10.30pm.

This restaurant's reputation for fine Szechuan classics makes reservations a good idea. The decor's red tones match the fieriness of the food on offer. The hot and sour soup is really challenging; or try the simpler steamed fish in black bean sauce. A meal for two costs around $60.

RESTAURANTS AND COFFEE SHOPS: SZECHUAN AND HUNANESE

Taikan-En Chinese Restaurant

Map 3, D5. *Hotel New Otani*, 177a River Valley Rd. Raffles Place MRT; bus #124, #174 or #190. ⊤ 3383333 ext 8690.

Daily 11.30am–2.30pm & 6.30–10.30pm.

A tiny replica of a Chinese teahouse is the centrepiece of the dining room; most dishes cost under $15.

TEOCHEW

Steaming is the most commonly used form of cooking in the **Teochew** kitchen, producing light but flavourful dishes such as fish steamed with sour plums. Other Teochew classics are braised goose, steamed crayfish and *oh nee* – a dessert made from creamed yam. Teochew meals are traditionally washed down with strong Chinese tea.

Ban Seng Restaurant

Map 3, F6. B1-44 The Riverwalk, 20 Upper Circular Rd. Raffles Place MRT; bus #51, #124, #145, #166, #174 or #190. ⊤ 5331471.

Daily 12–2pm & 6–10pm.

Road widening caused this venerable restaurant to decamp to just around the corner not long ago, and the traditional charcoal ovens didn't survive the move. The food is still top-notch, however: try the steamed crayfish, braised goose or stuffed sea cucumber; all moderately priced.

Liang Kee Restaurant

Map 3, C12. 16 Murray Terrace. Tanjong Pagar MRT; bus #103, #124, #145 or #166. ⊤ 5341029.

Noon–2.30pm & 6–9.30pm; closed Wed.

Recently uprooted from the Teochew enclave of Ellenborough St to make way for a new MRT line, this remains an unpretentious, popular local restaurant that thwarts tourists with its lack of menus. Good quality, though.

RESTAURANTS AND COFFEE SHOPS: TEOCHEW

191

Teochew City Seafood Restaurant

Map 5, G5. 05-16 Centrepoint, 176 Orchard Rd. Somerset MRT. ⓣ 7333338.

Daily 11.30am–2.30pm & 6.30–11pm.

Standard Teochew restaurant whose karaoke facilities are, mercifully, confined to two private rooms; $50 suffices for a meal for two, and set lunches start at around $90.

OTHER SPECIALITY CHINESE RESTAURANTS

Doc Cheng's

Map 3, I2. *Raffles Hotel*, 328 North Bridge Rd. City Hall MRT; bus #56 or #171. ⓣ 3311612.

Daily noon–10.30pm.

East meets West in the most recent addition to *Raffles*, an ice-cool joint themed around the global travels of imagined local *bon viveur* Doc Cheng. Though the menu betrays Alaskan, Japanese, Cajun and Spanish influences, Chinese culinary ideology provides the backbone to much of the food; decor presents a

similarly eclectic blend of Oriental, Art Deco and modernist influences. Two pay around $60.

Goldleaf Taiwan Restaurant

Map 3, C13. 24–24a Tanjong Pagar Rd. Tanjong Pagar MRT; bus #103, #124, #145 or #166. ⓣ 2256001.

Daily 11am–3pm & 6pm–4am.

Long-established but dowdy joint that's best avoided unless you've got a taste for congee: Taiwan porridge is the speciality, augmented by such fillings as century egg, oysters and abalone.

House of Mao

Map 3, F10. 03-02 China Square Food Centre, 51 Telok Ayer St. Raffles Place MRT; bus #125, #131, #167 or #186. ⓣ 5330660.

Daily 11.30am–2.30pm & 6–10pm.

Really rather a good restaurant, once you get over the shock of being served by waitresses in full Red Guard fatigues, and the eerie sense of being watched by the scores of images of Mao on the walls. The Hunan shredded pork comes recommended, but it seems churlish not to try Chairman Mao's favourite braised garlic pork.

Imperial Herbal Restaurant

Map 4, G12. 3rd floor, *Metropole Hotel*, 41 Seah St. City Hall MRT; bus #56 or # 171. ☎ 3370491 ext 212.
Daily 11.30am–2.30pm & 6.30–10.30pm.
The place to go if you are concerned about your Yin and Yang balance: after checking your pulse and tongue, a resident Chinese physician recommends either a cooling or a "heaty" dish from the menu. For migraine sufferers the drunken scorpions are, by all accounts, a must; rheumatics should opt for crispy black ants.

Moi Kong Hakka Restaurant

Map 3, C12. 22 Murray St. Tanjong Pagar MRT; bus #103, #124, #145 or #166. ☎ 2217758.
Daily 10.30am–2.30pm & 6–10pm.

Hakka food relies heavily on salted and preserved ingredients, and dishes here, in the best Hakka food outlet in Singapore, encompass abacus yam starch beads ($6) and stewed pork belly with preserved vegetables.

Mosque Street Taiwanese Style Steamboat House

Map 3, C9. 44 Mosque St. Bus #51, #103, #124, #166, #174 or #190. ☎ 2229560.
Daily 6pm–5am.
Take a seat at the food bar, on which sixty individual woks are set on built-in heaters, purchase your steamboat ingredients ($6 per person) – noodles, egg, prawns, pork, fish – and get cooking. Great late-night fun.

One More Shabu Shabu Mini Steamboat

Map 2, K5. 02-211/212 Marina Square, 6 Raffles Blvd. Bus #36 or #71. ☎ 3399496.
Daily 11.30am–10pm.
A vast buffet spread of meat, seafood and vegetables which you cook at your table.

RESTAURANTS AND COFFEE SHOPS: OTHER SPECIALITY CHINESE

Shanghai Palace Seafood Restaurant

Map 3, G4. *Excelsior Hotel*, 5 Coleman St. City Hall MRT; bus #124 or #166.
Ⓣ 3393428.

Daily noon–2.30pm & 6.30–10.30pm.

Authentic Shanghai dishes – drunken chicken, fried hot and sour chicken, bean curd claypot – and a smattering of Cantonese and Szechuan favourites served in unfussy surroundings; two people pay upwards of $50.

Snackworld

Map 5, H5. 01-12/13 Cuppage Plaza, 5 Koek Rd. Somerset MRT.

Daily 11am–midnight.

Hectic terrace restaurant where the Chinese menu is enlivened by hotplate crocodile meat ($25) and emu.

Superbowl

Map 3, F7. 80 Boat Quay. Raffles Place MRT; bus #51, #124, #145, #166, #174 or #190.
Ⓣ 5386066.

Daily 11am–11pm.

An affordable range of 47 congees, served at marble-topped tables recalling a 1950s coffee shop.

Top Flight Mongolian BBQ

Map 5, I6. 04-01 Park Mall, 9 Penang Rd. Dhoby Ghaut MRT.
Ⓣ 3344888.

Daily 11.30am–2.30pm & 6–10pm.

Choose from an array of meats, vegetables and sauces, which are then cooked for you on a hot griddle in the open kitchen. Unlimited visits to the food bar cost under $16 (lunchtime) and $28 (dinner), including starters, and desserts.

VEGETARIAN CHINESE

Though their menus often feature "mock" meat dishes, the following selection of Chinese restaurants are all strictly **vegetarian.** They all use ingredients like yam, bean curd, mushrooms, water chestnuts and nuts to such imaginative effect that they'll appeal even to confirmed meat eaters.

Fut Sai Kai Restaurant

Map 4, C3. 147 Kitchener Rd. Bus #65, #66, #81, #97, #103, #139 or #147. ⊤ 2980336. Tues–Sun 10am–9pm.

Old-fashioned Cantonese restaurant with a strongly Oriental atmosphere and fiery red decor; $20 is sufficient for two. Bean curd forms the backbone of Chinese vegetarian cooking, though, oddly, it reaches your table shaped to resemble meat or fish.

Happy Realm Vegetarian Food Centre

Map 3, A11. 03-16 Pearl's Centre, 100 Eu Tong Sen St. Outram Park MRT. ⊤ 2226141. Daily 11am–8.30pm.

"The way to good health and a sound mind", boasts the restaurant's card; tasty and reasonably priced vegetarian dishes.

Kwan Yim Vegetarian Restaurant

Map 4, D10. 190 Waterloo St. Bugis MRT. ⊤ 3382394. Daily 8am–8.30pm.

A huge display of sweet and savoury *pow* is the highlight of this unfussy establishment, sited close to Bencoolen Street.

Lingzhi Restaurant

Map 5, C5. B1-17/18 Orchard Towers, 400 Orchard Rd. Orchard MRT; bus #36. ⊤ 7343788. Daily 11am–10pm.

A real treat, where skewers of vegetables served with satay sauce are the highlight of an imaginative menu; there's also a takeaway counter.

As you'd expect of a nation so enamoured with cutting edge technology, Singapore boasts numerous cafés offering email and Internet access. The emphasis is on the Internet, rather than the café side of the business, so don't expect to be spoilt for choice on the eating and drinking front. Most have nothing more than a fridgeful of soft drinks and a modest selection of pastries on display. Web access typically costs around $5 per hour, or $3 per half-hour. For more details, see p.262.

RESTAURANTS AND COFFEE SHOPS: VEGETARIAN CHINESE

AMERICAN, NORTH AND SOUTH

Cha Cha Cha

Map 8, F4. 32 Lorong Mambong, Holland Village. Buona Vista MRT; bus #7 or #105. ☎ 4621650.

Daily 11.30am–11pm.

Classic Mexican dishes ($10–22) are served in this vibrantly coloured restaurant; outside are a few open-air patio tables, ideal for posing with a bottle of Dos Equis beer, but book ahead for these.

Chico's N Charlie's

Map 5, D5. 05-01 Liat Towers, 541 Orchard Rd. Orchard MRT. ☎ 7341753.

Daily 11am–11pm.

Faithfully re-created Mexican decor and food ($11–38), as well as a good-value set lunch ($15 for main course, soup, garlic bread, dessert and coffee or tea).

Billy Bombers

Map 4, F11. 02-52 Bugis Junction, 200 Victoria St. Bugis MRT. ☎ 3378018.

Daily 11.30am–2.30pm & 6.30–10.30pm.

Shades of Arnold's diner in *Happy Days*: reasonably priced burgers and bowls of chilli eaten in speakeasy booths upholstered in red leather.

Bobby Rubino's

Map 3, H2. B1-03 Fountain Court, CHIJMES, 30 Victoria St. City Hall MRT; bus #171 or #190. ☎ 3375466.

Daily 12.30–4pm & 6–10pm.

Ribs are the speciality, but steaks, burgers and other big-boy platters are available; eschew the "wine-rack" partitions and rough-hewn red-brick interior and make for the terrace, superbly located below CHIJMES' looming convent.

Dan Ryan's Chicago Grill

Map 5, B6. B1-01 Tanglin Mall, 91 Tanglin Rd. Bus #105, #123 or #174. ☎ 7383800.

Daily 11am–midnight.

Chug back a Budweiser and get stuck into "American portions" of ribs, burgers and chicken in a dining room that's crammed with Americana; main courses cost around $15.

Ponderosa

Map 3, H3. 02-20 Raffles City Shopping Centre, 252 North Bridge Rd. City Hall MRT. ☎3344926.

Daily noon–10.30pm.

The perfect cure for vitamin deficiency – chicken, steak and fish dishes come with baked potato, sundae, and as much salad as you can eat, all for $24.90.

Seah Street Deli

Map 3, I2. *Raffles Hotel*, 1 Beach Rd. City Hall MRT; bus #56 or #171. ☎3371886.

Daily 11am–10pm, Fri & Sat till 11pm.

New York-style deli boasting mountainous sandwiches, at around $10 each. Huge

crayons, bagels and wristwatches on the walls make this the most un-colonial establishment in *Raffles Hotel*.

EUROPEAN

- - - - - - - - - - - - - - - - - -

Le Beaujolais

Map 3, D11. 1 Ann Siang Hill. Bus #51, #103, #124, #166, #174 or #190. ☎2242227.

Daily 11am–11pm.

Charming wine bar, stacked on two floors above one of Singapore's last remaining hills, serving cold cuts and salads and featuring a strong wine list. If you can't land one of a handful of alfresco seats, head upstairs, where you might just as well be in a Parisian café.

PUB FOOD

Flag & Whistle Pub, 10 Duxton Hill (Map 3, B13); ☎2231126. Ploughman's lunches and sandwiches for less than $12 – see p.224.

J.J. Mahoney Pub, 58 Duxton Rd (Map 3, C13); ☎2256225. Fish and

chips, and chicken and chips for under $10 – see p.224.

Molly Mallone's, 42 Circular Rd, Boat Quay (Map 3, F8). Irish stews, oysters and bar snacks – see p.219.

Gordon Grill

Map 5, E3. *Goodwood Park Hotel*, 22 Scotts Rd. Newton or Orchard MRT. ☏ 7301744.

Daily noon–3pm & 7–11pm.

Upmarket restaurant lent a Scottish feel by the tartan decor and the haggis with tatties: excellent food – but at a price. Set lunch ($32) is your best bet.

J P Bastiani

Map 3, D5. 01-12 Clarke Quay, 3a River Valley Rd. Raffles Place MRT; bus #124, #174 or #190. ☏ 4330156.

Daily 11.30–3pm & 6.30–11pm.

This venue has come a long way since it started out as a pineapple cannery in the nineteenth century. Today it's as sleek and sophisticated as any bar-restaurant in Singapore. After an apéritif downstairs (see p.223), head up to the dining room and choose from the well-conceived Mediterranean menu – or, on a Sunday, opt for the champagne brunch ($43 per person).

Milano's

Map 3, F5. Funan the IT Mall, North Bridge Rd. City Hall MRT; bus #124 or #166.

Daily 11.30am–11.30pm.

Their "All you can eat – all day, every day" policy makes *Milano's* unbeatable value: choose from soups, pizzas, pastas and salad. Then choose again. And again. $11 a head.

Da Paolo

Map 3, C13. 66 Tanjong Pagar Rd. Tanjong Pagar MRT; bus #103, #124, #145 or #166. ☏ 2247081.

Mon–Fri 11.30am–2.30pm & 7–10.30pm, Sat & Sun 7–10.30pm.

Serves great home-made pasta, or splash out on authentic meat and fish dishes washed down with one of a range of northeastern Italian wines (from $40); three-course weekday set lunches are reasonable value at around $25.

Pasta Fresca

Map 3, F8. 30 Boat Quay. Raffles Place MRT; bus #51, #124, #145, #166, #174 or #190. ☏ 5326283.

Daily 11am–10pm.

HIGH TEA AND TIFFIN

Many of Singapore's swisher hotels advertise that most colonial of traditions, **high tea**, in the local press; below are a few of the more permanent choices. Typically, a Singapore high tea comprises local and Western snacks, both sweet and savoury. If you really want to play the part of a Victorian settler, Singapore's most splendid food outlet at the *Raffles* still serves **tiffin** – the colonial term for a light curry meal (derived from the Hindi word for luncheon).

Alkhaff Mansion, 10 Telok Blangah Green (Map 8, H5; Redhill MRT, then bus #145; or bus #124); ☎2786979. The Verandah Bar hosts a sweet and savoury local high tea on Saturday and Sunday only (2.30–4.30pm).

Café l'Espresso, *Goodwood Park Hotel*, 22 Scotts Rd (Map 5, E3; Newton or Orchard MRT); ☎7377411. A great array of English cakes and pastries. Daily 2.30–6pm.

Café Vienna, *Royal Holiday Inn – Crowne Plaza*, 25 Scotts Rd (Map 5, D4; Orchard MRT); ☎7377966. Tremendously popular with Singaporeans, so get there early and queue to avoid disappointment. Mon–Fri 3–5.30pm, Sat & Sun 3–6pm.

Hilton Lounge, *Hilton Hotel*, 581 Orchard Rd (Map 5, D5; Orchard MRT); ☎7372233. Afternoon tea ($22) at the *Hilton* is taken overlooking Orchard Road from the second-floor mezzanine lounge. Daily noon–5pm.

Tiffin Room, *Raffles Hotel*, 1 Beach Rd (Map 3, I2; City Hall MRT; bus #56 or #171); ☎3371886. Tiffin lunch (noon–2pm) and dinner (7–10pm) both cost over $30 per person, though the spread of edibles and the charming colonial surroundings make them worth considering. Between tiffin sittings, high tea ($25) is served (3.30–5pm).

Match up fresh pasta (made at the owner's own factory) and a sauce from the menu, and sit out on the riverside terrace. Around $20 a head, drinks extra.

Paulaner Bräuhaus
Map 2, K6. 01-01 Millennia Walk, 9 Raffles Blvd. Bus #36 or #71. ☎ 3377123.
Dinner 11am–2.30pm & 6.30–9.30pm, then drinks only. German theme restaurant-cum-brewery, serving generous platters of *wurst*, *kartoffeln* and *sauerkraut*; two

pay $60, including a *stein* of beer each.

FILIPINO

Kabayan Filipino Restaurant
Map 5, E5. 03-25 Lucky Plaza, 304 Orchard Rd. Orchard MRT.
Daily 10am–9pm.
Big, dark chamber crammed with tables to cater for the Sunday melee of Filipino maids; dishes are laid out buffet-style, and best washed down with San Miguel beer.

INDIAN AND NEPALI

In the same way as the Chinese, immigrants from north and south India brought their own cuisines with them, which vary in emphasis and ingredients though all utilize *daal* (lentils), chutneys, yoghurts and sweet and sour *lassis* (yoghurt drinks); neither north nor south Indians eat beef. **North Indian** food tends to rely more on meat, especially mutton and chicken, and uses breads – *naan*, *chapatis*, *parathas* and *rotis* – rather than rice. The most famous style of north Indian cooking is *tandoori* – named after the clay oven in which the food is cooked – and you'll commonly come across *tandoori* chicken – marinated in yoghurt and spices and then baked.

    South Indian (and **Sri Lankan**) food tends to be spicier and more reliant on vegetables. Its staple is the *dosai* (pan-cake), often served at breakfast time as a *masala dosai*, stuffed with onions, vegetables and chutney, and washed down with *teh tarik*. Indian Muslims serve the similar *murtabak*, a grilled *roti* pancake with egg, onion and minced meat. Many south Indian cafés turn to serving *daun pisang* at lunchtime, usually a vegetarian meal where rice is served on banana leaves and small, replenishable heaps of various vegetable curries are placed alongside; in some places, meat and fish are on offer, too.

Though Indian food outlets span the island, you'll find the highest concentration of really good ones in Little India. South Indian Muslim restaurants also tend to cluster on North Bridge Road in the Arab Quarter, where you'll find tasty *biriyanis* and *murtabaks*.

Azmi Muslim Food Stall
Map 4, B6. 168-170 Serangoon Rd. Bus #65, #66, #81, #97, #103, #139 or #147.
Daily 10am–9pm.
Set within the *Thye Chong Restaurant* on the corner of Norris Road, *chapatis* are hand-cooked on a griddle in front of you. Brains, liver and goats' legs are served, as well as more conventional dishes (of which the best is the *keema* curry) on the accompanying curry menu.

Annalakshmi Restaurant
Map 3, G4. *Excelsior Hotel & Shopping Centre*, 5 Coleman St. City Hall MRT; bus #124 or #166. ☎ 3399993.

Daily 11.30am–3pm & 6–9.30pm.

Terrific north and south Indian vegetarian food in sumptuous surroundings, with all profits going to *Kala Mandhir*, an Indian cultural association next door. Many of the staff are volunteers from the Hindu community, so your waiter might just be a doctor or a lawyer. From $10 a dish.

Banana Leaf Appolo
Map 4, A7. 56–58 Race Course Rd. Bus #65, #66, #81, #97, #103, #139 or #147.
☎ 2938682.
Daily 10.30am–10pm.
Recently refurbished and

RESTAURANTS AND COFFEE SHOPS: INDIAN AND NEPALI

resplendent in marble (though eating with your hands is still the order of the day), this is a pioneering fish-head curry restaurant where a wide selection of south Indian dishes are all served on banana leaves. Fish-head curry, $30 for two people.

Cashmir

Map 5, F5. 04-28 Ngee Ann City, 391 Orchard Rd. Orchard MRT. ⊤ 7355506.
Daily 11.30am–3pm & 6.30–11pm.
Superb pan-Indian cuisine in a bright and airy room embellished with marble columns and Moghul-style archways.

Gandhi Eating House

Map 4, A7. 29 Chandler Rd. Bus #65, #66, #81, #97, #103, #139 or #147.
Daily 9am–9.30pm.
Many locals reckon this open-fronted place at the back of the Race Course Road restaurants is knocking out the best chicken curries in Little India; meals come on banana leaves, water in metal jugs.

Gorkha Grill

Map 3, C11. 21 Smith St. Bus #51, #103, #124, #166, #174 or #190. ⊤ 2270806.
Daily 11.30am-11.30pm.
There are fish, mutton and chicken dishes galore at this enchanting Nepali place, but be sure to start with *momo* (minced chicken dumplings) and end with *kheer*, or Nepali rice pudding, a tasty blend of cream, rice and cardamom. If the murals of mountains and votive flags leave you wanting to see Nepal, speak to owner Dan, who leads treks from Kathmandu, and can book ahead for you.

Islamic Restaurant

Map 4, G6. 791–797 North Bridge Rd. Bus #7, #107, #130, #145 or #197. ⊤ 2987563.
9.30am–9.30pm; closed Fri.
Aged Muslim restaurant manned by a gang of old men who plod solemnly up and down between the tables. It boasts the best chicken *biriyani* in Singapore, cooked in the traditional way – heated from above and below with charcoal. $10 for two.

Kinara

Map 3, F7. 57 Boat Quay. Raffles Place MRT; bus #51, #124, #145, #166, #174 or #190. ☎5330412. Daily noon–2.30pm & 6.30–10.30pm.

Exquisite restaurant boasting antique fittings imported from the subcontinent; a marvellous view of the river from upstairs, and elegantly presented Punjabi dishes. Around $50 for two.

Komala Vilas

Map 4, B8. 76–78 Serangoon Rd. Bus #65, #66, #81, #97, #103, #139 or #147. ☎2936980. Daily 7am–10pm.

A cramped, popular vegetarian establishment specializing in fifteen varieties of *dosai*. The "South Indian Meal", served upstairs on a banana leaf, is great value at $4.50.

Madras New Woodlands Restaurant

Map 4, B7. 12–14 Upper Dickson Rd. Bus #65, #66, #81, #97, #103, #139 or #147. ☎2971594. Daily 8am–11pm.

Functional, canteen-style place serving up decent vegetarian food at bargain prices. House specialities are the Thali set meal ($4) and the VIP Thali ($6); samosas, bahjis and other snacks are available after 3pm, and there's a big selection of sweets, too. Recommended.

Maharani

Map 5, D4. 01-03 Scotts Walk, 25 Scotts Road. Orchard MRT. ☎2358840. Daily noon–3pm & 6.30–11pm.

Orchard Road's pioneering north Indian restaurant has moved from its original premises, but the food has suffered no loss in quality. The menu grades each dish's "heatiness" from one- to three-star. Around $25 a head, with beer.

Moti Mahal Restaurant

Map 3, C12. 18 Murray St. Tanjong Pagar MRT; bus #103, #124, #145 or #166. ☎2214338. Daily 11am–3pm & 6.30–10.30pm.

Not cheap, but one of Singapore's very best Indian

RESTAURANTS AND COFFEE SHOPS: INDIAN AND NEPALI

restaurants, serving tasty tandoori dishes in pleasant surroundings. The special is *murg massalam*, a whole chicken stuffed with rice ($50; order in advance).

Muthu's Curry Restaurant

Map 4, A7. 76–78 Race Course Rd. Bus #65, #66, #81, #97, #103, #139 or #147. ⓣ 2932389.
Daily 10am–10pm.
Rough-and-ready south Indian restaurant with no menu, but famous for its fish-head curry.

Orchard Maharajah

Map 5, G5. 25 Cuppage Terr, Cuppage Rd. Somerset MRT. ⓣ 7326331.
Daily 11.30am–3pm & 6.30–11pm.
Set in a wonderful old Peranakan house, this splendid north Indian restaurant has a large terrace and a tempting menu that includes the sublime fish *mumtaz* – fillet of fish stuffed with minced mutton, almonds, eggs, cashews and raisins – worth the extra few

dollars. The set lunch is good value at $16.

Selera Restaurant

Map 4, B9. 15 Mackenzie Rd. Bus #65, #66, #81, #97, #103, #139 or #147. ⓣ 3385687.
Daily noon–11.30pm.
The best curry puffs – curried meat and boiled egg folded into pastry – in Singapore. Two for around a dollar.

Sri Vijayah

Map 4, B9. 229 Selegie Rd. Bus #65, #66, #81, #97, #103, #139 or #147. ⓣ 3361748.
Daily 6am–10pm.
Hole-in-the-wall vegetarian joint offering unbeatable value for money: $3 buys a replenishable mountain of rice and vegetable curries, and there's a mouth-watering display of sweetmeats at the front door.

Taj Jazzaurant

Map 4, B8. 02-01 Little India Arcade, 48 Serangoon Rd. Bus #65, #66, #81, #97, #103, #139 or #147. ⓣ 2914680.
Daily 11.45am–2.45pm & 6–10pm.
Fine north and south Indian

food (south coast prawn and *brinjal* curry at $12, and *naan pasinda*, leg of lamb in yoghurt, for $18) until 10pm, after which the bar continues to serve.

INDONESIAN

Similar to Malay cuisine (see below), **Indonesian** cookery is characterized by its use of fragrant, aromatic spices and sweet, peanut-based sauces. Specialities to look out for are *nasi padang* – a hot, dry style of cooking that hails from Sumatra – and *rijstaffel*, a Dutch-influenced concept that works along the same lines as a buffet, except that in this case the buffet comes to your table.

Alkaff Mansion
Map 8, H5. 10 Telok Blangah Green. Redhill MRT, then bus #145; or bus #124. ℡ 2786979. Daily noon–midnight.
Built in the 1920s as a weekend retreat for the Alkaff family, this splendidly restored mansion offers a superb *rijstaffel* ($66): ten dishes served by a line of ten women in traditional *kebayas*. Or just have a beer in the bar, worth the exorbitant price for an hour or two of colonial grandeur.

House of Sundanese Food
Map 3, F7. 55 Boat Quay. Raffles Place MRT; bus #51, #124, #145, #166, #174 or #190. ℡ 5343775.
Mon–Fri 11am–2.30pm & 5–10pm, Sat & Sun 5–10pm.
Spicy salads and barbecued seafood characterize the cuisine of Sunda (West Java), served here in simple yet tasteful surroundings. Try the tasty *ikan sunda* (grilled Javanese fish) – an $18 fish feeds two to three people.

Kintamani
Map 3, A6. *Apollo Hotel*, 405 Havelock Rd. Bus #64 or #123. ℡ 7332081.
Daily noon–3pm & 6.30–10.30pm.
Balinese umbrellas, statues, batiks and temple bricks frame

a menu that spoils you for choice: *soto ayam madura* (chicken and ginger broth), *ikan bakat* (grilled fish, Sundanese-style) and the inevitable satay make great starts, after which you could do far worse than *udung bali*: king prawns cooked in chilli and soya bean sauce.

Rendezvous Restaurant

Map 4, C13. 02-02 Hotel Rendezvous, 9 Bras Basah Rd. Dhoby Ghaut MRT. ⓣ 3397508. Daily 11am–9.30pm.

Revered *nasi padang* joint that still turns out lip-smacking curries, *rendangs* and *sambals*; the weighing machine in the corner is an unusual touch.

Rumah Makan Minang

Map 4, G7. 18a Kandahar St. Bus #7, #107, #130, #145 or #197. Daily noon–2.30pm & 6–10.30pm.

Fiery *nasi padang* – highly spiced Sumatran cuisine – in the heart of the Arab Quarter; $4 ensures a good feed, while the popular barbecued fish costs $3.

Sanur Restaurant

Map 5, G5. 04-17/18 Centrepoint, 176 Orchard Rd. Somerset MRT. ⓣ 7342192. Daily 11.30am–2.45pm & 5.45–10pm.

Hearty, reasonably priced food served by waitresses in traditional batik dress; the beef *rendang* is terrific. It's best to book ahead.

Tambuah Mas Indonesian Restaurant

Map 5, C5. 04-10, Tanglin Shopping Centre, 19 Tanglin Rd. Bus #105, #123 or #174. ⓣ 7333333. Daily 11.30am–2.30pm & 6–10.30pm.

Friendly restaurant, approached through a Minangkabau-style entrance, which offers *padang* food and a smattering of Chinese dishes.

INTERNATIONAL

Compass Rose Restaurant

Map 3, I3. 69th floor, *Westin Stamford Hotel*, 2 Stamford Rd. City Hall MRT. ⓣ 3388585.

Daily noon–2.30pm &
6.30–10.30pm.

An expensive place with a
panoramic view of central
Singapore. Buffet lunch ($48)
is the cheapest way to
experience the international
cuisine.

Don Noodle Bistro

Map 5, B6. 01-16 Tanglin Mall,
163 Tanglin Rd. Bus #105, #123
or #174. ⓣ 7383188.
Daily 11.30am–10.30pm.
Minimalist yet chic, *Don* is
something of a paradox – a
Western-style take on the
noodle bar, imported back to
the East. The menu is not
country-specific, meaning that
you can enjoy Indonesian
kway teow goreng while your
dining companion tucks into
Japanese *ramen* noodles.

Hot Stones

Map 3, F7. 53 Boat Quay.
Raffles Place MRT; bus #51,
#124, #145, #166, #174 or #190.
ⓣ 5345188.
Daily noon–2.30pm &
6–10.30pm.
A healthy and novel twist on
dining: steaks, chicken and
seafood grilled at table on

non-porous Alpine rock
heated to 200° – no oil or fat,
but bags of flavour.

Louis' Oyster Bar

Map 3, F7. 36 Boat Quay.
Raffles Place MRT; bus #51,
#124, #145, #166, #174 or #190.
ⓣ 5330534.
Mon–Fri 11am–1am, Sat & Sun
5pm–1am.
The Louis in question is Louis
Armstrong, who beams down
from all the walls. Oysters cost
around $18 per half-dozen,
but the "High Society
Platter" (crayfish, crab,
mussels, oysters and prawns
on ice; $55 for two) is hard to
resist.

Nooch

Map 5, D5. 02-16 Wheelock
Place, 501 Orchard Rd. Orchard
MRT. ⓣ 2350880.
Mon–Fri noon–3pm &
6–10.30pm, Sat & Sun
noon–11pm.
The blurb on its menu calls
this cool and popular,
crescent-shaped joint
overlooking Orchard
Boulevard a
"nondestinational" restaurant
– meaning that the idea is to

order and scoff your MSG-free Thai or Japanese noodles on the double, and be on your way. The *tub tim krob*, or chestnuts in syrup and coconut milk, is a good way to douse the fires after a Thai *tom yam* soup. Recommended.

Olive Tree

Map 4, F11. *Hotel Intercontinental*, 80 Middle Rd. Bugis MRT. ☎ 3387600. Daily 11.30am–2.30pm & 6–10.30pm.

Anything goes in this stylish joint with a sun-kissed, Mediterranean theme: kick off with *bruschetta* or *gambas ceviche* (prawns marinated in tomato sauce, lime juice and olive oil), move on to *merguez* sausages with couscous, complemented by a Lebanese durum wheat salad, and end with Andalusian chocolate mousse. Buffet-style set lunches ($40) and dinners ($50) ease the choosing process.

Top of the M

Map 5, F5. 39th floor, *Mandarin Hotel*, 333 Orchard Rd. Orchard MRT. Daily noon–3pm & 6.30–10.30pm.

Singapore's highest revolving restaurant also features a buffet (around $50) that revolves, monthly, through the cuisines of Europe; at night, the lights of the city below are pure *Blade Runner*. Book ahead at the weekend.

Pizza Hut has branches at Centrepoint, Plaza Singapura and Wisma Atria all on Orchard Road; their Tuesday evening "All you can eat" package ($8) offers great value. Shakey's (Shaw Towers, Beach Road) runs a delivery service on ☎ 7484848 – as in "send for it, for it, for it".

JAPANESE

Elegantly presented and subtly flavoured, **Japanese** cuisine is dominated by fish, which crops up in classic dishes such as sushi (raw fish wrapped in rice and seaweed) and *sashimi* (sliced or cubed raw fish). Other dishes that merit a try include teriyaki (chicken in a sweet sauce) and *teppanyaki* (grilled slices of meat or seafood), but bear in mind that Japanese food doesn't come cheap.

Inagiku

Map 3, I3. 3rd floor, *Westin Plaza Hotel*, 2 Stamford Rd. City Hall MRT. ☎ 3388585.
Mon–Sat noon–2.30pm & 6.30–10.30pm.
More of a maze than a restaurant, with four sections serving expensive, quality tempura, *teppanyaki*, sushi, and an à la carte menu – the latter the cheapest alternative.

Japanese stalls

Map 4, F11. *Food Junction*, B1, Seiyu Department Store, Bugis Junction, 200 Victoria St. Bugis MRT.
Daily 10am–9pm.
Sumo has *sashimi*, tempura and teriyaki sets around $9, while nearby *Express-Teppanyaki*'s "big value meal" ($6.20) offers a choice of meats and vegetables flash-fried on the U-shaped hot bar.

Sakae Sushi

Map 5, D5. 02-13 Wheelock

Place, 501 Orchard Rd. Orchard MRT. ☎ 7376281.
Daily noon-10pm.
Cheery sushi and *sashimi* bar, bang in the centre of Orchard Road, where lunch sets start from $12. Diners choose to sit up at the conveyor-belt bar, or at diner-style booths around the restaurant's outer walls.

Senbazuru

Map 3, D5. *Hotel New Otani*, 177a River Valley Rd. Raffles Place MRT; bus #124, #174 or #190. ☎ 3383333.
Daily 11.30am–2.30pm & 6.30–10.30pm.
If the wide menu proves too mind-boggling, choose from the selection of set lunches; for real gastronomes, there's the *kaiseki ryori*, or traditional eleven-course meal.

Sushi Tei

Map 8, F4. 20 Lorong Mambong, Holland Village. Buona Vista MRT; bus #7 or

---

For inexpensive Japanese sushi and *sashimi*, head for
Diamaru in the Liang Court Shopping Complex, or Yaohan, in
Plaza Singapura.

#105. ☎ 4632310.
Daily 11.30am–2.30pm &
6–10pm.

A cross-fertilization of Tokyo sushi bar and airport baggage reclaim: diners snatch sushi ($1.50–$4) from the conveyor belt looping the bar.

Tatsu Sushi
Map 3, H2. 01-16, CHIJMES, 30 Victoria St. City Hall MRT; bus #171 or #190. ☎ 3325868.

Mon-Sat noon–2.30pm &
6.30–11pm.

Four years old now, Tatsu is already a veteran of the notoriously fluid CHIJMES restaurant scene. Owner Ronny Chia's culinary expertise, and the high quality of ingredients used (all fish is flown in from Japan) have resulted in a clientele that's around 75 percent Japanese.

KOREAN

Newcomers to **Korean** food will find it both robust and exciting – perhaps this has something to do with the amount of ginseng in every dish. Meat features prominently on a Korean menu, and is often cooked by diners them- selves on a table barbecue, or *bulgogi*. Another speciality is *kim chi,* or spicy pickled cabbage. For liquid refreshment, try the OB beer.

Haebok's Korean
Restaurant
Map 3, C13. 44–46 Tanjong Pagar Rd. Tanjong Pagar MRT; bus #103, #124, #145 or #166. ☎ 2239003.

Daily 11.30am–3pm &
5.30–10.30pm.

All the standard dishes, served by lukewarm staff in a plain dining room. If you aren't acquainted with Korean food, plastic models of the meals available displayed in the front window lend a few pointers.

Korean Restaurant Pte Ltd

Map 5, H5. 05-35 Specialists' Centre, 277 Orchard Rd. Somerset MRT. ⓣ 2350018. Daily 11am–11pm.
Singapore's first Korean restaurant, beautifully furnished and serving up a wide range of dependably good dishes at $16–20 per dish.

Seoul Garden Korean Restaurant

Map 2, K6. 03-119 Marina Square, 6 Raffles Blvd. Bus #36 or #71. ⓣ 3391339. Mon–Fri 11am–3pm & 5.30–10.30pm, Sat & Sun 11am–10.30pm.
Entertaining, busy restaurant with daily set lunches from $7.90; best value is the all-you-can-eat Korean barbecue – a buffet of twenty seasoned meats, seafoods and vegetables cooked by customers at their tables.

MALAY AND NONYA

Malay cuisine is based on rice, often enriched with coconut milk, which is served with a dizzying variety of curries and *sambal*, a condiment comprising pounded chillies blended with *belacan* (shrimp paste), onions and garlic. Other spices which characterize Malay cuisine include ginger and *galangal* (a root similar to ginger), coriander, lemon grass and lime leaves. Malaysia's most famous dish is satay, but the classic way to sample Malay food is to eat *nasi campur*, a buffet of steamed rice served with an array of accompanying dishes; other popular dishes include *nasi goreng* (mixed fried rice with meat, seafood and vegetables); and *rendang* (slow-cooked beef, chicken or mutton in lemon grass and coconut).

Pork, of course, is taboo to all Muslims, but it has been married with Malay cooking in **Nonya** cuisine, which evolved as a result of the intermarriage of early Chinese immigrants and local Malays. Typical Nonya dishes incorporate elements and ingredients from Chinese, Malay and Thai cooking, the end product tending to be spicier than Chinese food. Chicken, fish and seafood forms the backbone of the cuisine, along with pork. Noodles (*mee*) flavoured with chillies, and rich curries made from rice flour and coconut cream, are common. A popular dish is *laksa*, noodles in spicy coconut soup served with seafood and chopped beansprouts. Other popular dishes include *ayam buah keluak*, chicken cooked with "black" nuts; and *otak-otak*, fish mashed with coconut milk and chilli paste and steamed in a banana leaf.

Bengawan Solo

Map 5, G5. Centrepoint, 176 Orchard Rd. Somerset MRT. Map 3, H10. Clifford Centre, 24 Raffles Place. Raffles Place MRT.

Daily 10am–8pm.

Excellent cake shops, specializing in Malay *kueh* (cakes).

Bintang Timur Restaurant

Map 5, E4. 02-08/13 Far East Plaza, 14 Scotts Rd. Orchard MRT. ⑦2354539.

Daily 11am–9.45pm.

A perennial favourite, thanks to its reliable cooking; sticks of satay here are bigger than usual, so don't over-order.

Around $12 a head without beer.

Blue Ginger

Map 3, C14. 97 Tanjong Pagar Rd. Tanjong Pagar MRT; bus #103, #124, #145 or #166. ⑦2223928.

Daily 11.30am–3pm & 6.30–11pm.

Housed in a renovated shophouse, this trendy Peranakan restaurant is proving a yuppy favourite, thanks to dishes such as *ikan masal assam gulai* (mackerel simmered in a tamarind and lemon-grass gravy), and that benchmark of Nonya cuisine, *ayam buah keluak* – braised chicken with Indonesian black nuts.

RESTAURANTS AND COFFEE SHOPS: MALAY AND NONYA

Guan Hoe Soon

Map 7, C4. 214 Joo Chiat Rd,
Katong. Bus #16 or #33.
Ⓣ3442761.
11am–3pm & 6–9.30pm; closed
Tues.

Fifty years old, and still
turning out fine Nonya
cuisine; try the *chen dool*
(coconut milk, red beans,
sugar, green jelly and ice), a
refreshing end to a meal.
Around $35 for two, with
beer.

Mum's Kitchen

Map 7, C4. 314 Joo Chiat Rd.
Bus #16 or #33. Ⓣ3460969.
Daily 11am–10pm.

The emphasis here, as you'd
imagine, is on home-cooked
food, Nonya-based, though
with other Asian incursions.
House speciality Mum's
Curry is wonderful, and best
chased down by home-made
barley water; special business
lunches (Mon–Fri) offer
three courses at $18 for two
people.

Nonya & Baba Restaurant

Map 3, B3. 262 River Valley

Rd. Bus #32, #54 or #139.
Ⓣ7341382.
Daily 11.30am–10pm.

Greatly respected Nonya
restaurant lent character by its
marble tables and tasteful
decor; the *otak-otak* and the
ayam buah keluak are both
terrific; other dishes cost
around $7 a head.

Peranakan Inn

Map 7, C4. 210 East Coast Rd.
Bus #14. Ⓣ4406195.
Daily 11am–3pm & 6–9.30pm.

As much effort goes into the
food as went into the
renovation of this immaculate,
sky-blue shophouse
restaurant, which offers
authentic Nonya favourites at
reasonable prices; around $8 a
dish.

Spring Blossoms Café

Map 4, D13. *Bayview Inn*, 30
Bencoolen St. Bus #7, #14, #36,
#97, #124, #166, #174 or #190.
Ⓣ3372882 ext 281.
Sat & Sun noon–5pm.

This faceless hotel café's buffet
lunch is a great introduction
to Nonya cuisine, and very
reasonable at around $15.

RESTAURANTS AND COFFEE SHOPS: MALAY AND NONYA

213

THAI AND VIETNAMESE

You'll be thankful for a cooling bottle of Singha beer after you've done battle with a fiery **Thai** meal. Popular dishes include *tom yam* (a challengingly spicy prawn soup), green curry, fishcakes, chicken feet salad, and pineapple fried rice – which isn't fried rice with pineapple in it, but whole pineapple with fried rice inside. **Vietnamese** cuisine betrays Chinese, Thai, and French influences. Soups, *chao tom* (prawn paste barbecued on sugar cane) and spring rolls are perennial favourites, and are best washed down with Saigon's own "33" beer.

Cuppage Thai Food Restaurant

Map 5, G5. 49 Cuppage Terr. Somerset MRT. ☎ 7341116. Daily 11am–3pm & 6–11pm. Nondescript inside, but boasting a great outdoor terrace, this cheap and cheerful restaurant offers quality Thai dishes for around $8.

Diandin Leluk

Map 3, D6. 01-07 Riverside Point, 30 Merchant Rd. Raffles Place MRT; bus #51, #124, #145, #166, #174 or #190. Daily 11am–11pm. A very ordinary Thai restaurant in many ways, the Diandin Leluk offers one unique selling point – a frontage, on the opposite bank to Clarke Quay, on the Singapore River. Its soups, curries and salads are passable.

Indochine

Map 3, D11. 49 Club St. Bus #51, #103, #124, #166, #174 or #190. ☎ 3230503. Mon–Sat noon–2.30pm & 6–10pm. Owned by a Laos-born Australian, Indochine is one of Singapore's most elegant restaurants, its beautiful fixtures complemented by a truly great menu embracing Vietnamese, Laotian and Cambodian cuisine. Try the Laotian *Larb Kai* (spicy chicken salad) or the *Nha Trang* roast duck and mango salad. The *chao tom* (minced prawn wrapped round sugarcane) is also mouthwatering.

Pimai Thai

Map 4, F11. *Hotel Inter Continental*, 80 Middle Rd. Bugis MRT. ☎ 4311064. Daily noon–3pm & 6–10.30pm.

High-quality Thai cuisine served by attentive staff in traditional garb; the à la carte menu has treats like *hor mok talay* (steamed seafood soufflé) and *pha phow*, red sea bass fillet wrapped in banana leaves – or opt for the great eight-course set lunch (from $32; min two people).

Pornping Thai Seafood Restaurant

Map 2, M3. 01-96/98 Golden Mile Complex, 5001 Beach Rd. Bus #82 or #100. ☎ 2985016. Daily 10am–10pm.

Set in a complex known locally as "Thai Village" and always full of Thais waiting to catch buses home. All the standard dishes at cheap prices – $25 buys a meal for two, washed down with Singha beer.

Shingthai Palace

Map 4, G12. 36 Purvis St. City Hall MRT; bus #56 or #171. ☎ 3371161. Daily 11am–2pm & 6–10pm.

Good but characterless restaurant off Beach Road serving reasonably priced Thai dishes; try the *peek kai sord sai* (chicken wings with asparagus, prawns, mushrooms and meat). Around $15–20 a head.

Sukhothai

Map 3, F7. 47 Boat Quay. Raffles Place MRT; bus #51, #124, #145, #166, #174 or #190. ☎ 5382422. Daily 6.30–11pm, also Mon–Fri noon–3pm.

Chef's recommendations include fried cotton fish topped with sliced green mangoes, but you can't go far wrong whatever you plump for; the dining room is rather understated, so take advantage of the riverside tables.

Thanying Restaurant

Map 3, D5. Blk D, Clarke Quay. Raffles Place MRT; bus #124, 174 or #190. ☎ 3361821. Daily 11.30am–2.30pm & 6.30–10.30pm.

RESTAURANTS AND COFFEE SHOPS: THAI AND VIETNAMESE

One of the few Clarke Quay ventures really to take off, thanks to friendly staff, a large menu and generous portions.

Viet Cafe
Map 3, B4. 01-76 UE Square, Unity St. Bus #124, #174 or #190. ⓣ 3336453.
Daily noon–3am.

The heady aromas of Vietnamese *pho* (soup) – mint, basil and citrus – hang heavy in the air at the sleek *Viet Cafe*. Follow the pebble path which leads up to the balcony or, better still, sit out on the forecourt and enjoy the night air. Handy for a late-night snack after a beer along Mohamed Sultan Road.

Nightlife

Singapore's **nightlife** has gone from strength to strength over the past few years. The island's burgeoning bar and pub scene means there is now a wide range of drinking holes to choose from, with the Colonial District, Boat Quay and Orchard Road areas offering particularly good **pub-crawl** potential. With competition so hot, more and more bars are turning to **live music** to woo punters, though this is usually no more than cover versions performed by local bands. That said, big-name groups do occasionally make forays into Southeast Asia, playing Bangkok, Kuala Lumpur and Jakarta as well as Singapore. **Clubs** also do increasingly brisk business. Glitzy and vibrant, they feature the latest imported pop, rock and **dance music**, though don't expect anything like a rave scene – Ecstasy isn't in the Singaporean dictionary.

BARS AND PUBS

With the **bars** and **pubs** of Singapore ranging from slick cocktail joints, through elegant colonial chambers to boozy dives, you're bound to find a place that suits you. Establishments open either in the late morning (to catch the lunchtime dining trade) or in the early evening, and usually close around midnight. On Friday and Saturday, opening hours almost invariably extend by an hour or two. Many serve snacks throughout the day, and a few offer more substantial dishes. It's possible to buy a small glass of beer in most places for around $6-7, but **prices** can be double or treble that amount, especially in the Orchard Road district. A glass of wine usually costs much the same as a beer, and spirits a dollar or two more. One way of cutting costs is to arrive in time for **happy hour** in the early evening, when bars offer local beers and house wine either at half price, or "one for one" – you get two of whatever you order, but one is held back for later.

Singaporeans adore **rock music**, and a plethora of bars pander to this, presenting nightly performances by local or Filipino cover bands. These are listed below, but for more details, see p.228. Also hugely popular is **karaoke**, which almost reaches an art form in some Singapore bars.

THE COLONIAL DISTRICT

Bar and Billiards Room

Map 3, I2. *Raffles Hotel*, 1 Beach Rd. City Hall MRT; bus #56 or #171.

Daily 11.30am–midnight.

A Singapore Sling ($18.50), in the colonial elegance of the hotel where the drink was invented by Ngiam Tong Boon in 1915, is a must on a visit to Singapore. Snacks are available through the afternoon, and playing billiards costs another $15 an hour.

Compass Rose Bar

Map 3, I3. 70th Floor, *Westin Stamford Hotel*, 2 Stamford Rd. City Hall MRT.

Daily 11am–12.30am.

Tasteful bar from whose floor-to-ceiling windows you can see as far as southern Malaysia; happy hour 5.30–8.30pm; minimum charge $15 after 8.30pm.

Lot, Stock and Barrel Pub

Map 4, G12. 29 Seah St. City Hall MRT; bus #56 or #171.

Daily 4pm–midnight.

Frequented by an early office

crowd and a late backpacker crowd (Beach Road's guesthouses are just around the corner), who come for the rock classics on the jukebox; happy hour 4–8pm.

Paulaner Bräuhaus
Map 2, K5. 01-01 Millenia Walk, 9 Raffles Blvd. Bus #36 or #71.
Daily noon–midnight.
Wurst and *sauerkraut* might be a priority upstairs, but down in the bar of this themed microbrewery, lager is very much in the forefront of the punters' minds; predictably busy around Oktoberfest-time.

BOAT QUAY

Bernie Goes to Town
Map 3, F7. 82a/b Boat Quay. Raffles Place MRT; bus #51, #124, #145, #166, #174 or #190. ⓣ 5363533.
Mon–Thurs & Sun 11am–1am, Fri & Sat 3pm–3am.
This laid-back, roadhouse-style joint is just a short walk down Boat Quay from the yuppy haunt of *Harry's*, but a whole world away from it in terms of

atmosphere. Reggae, blues and R&B are the preferred sounds here, and there is a live band nightly. Beers and margheritas are discounted during happy hour (3–8pm).

Escobar
Map 3, F8. 37 Boat Quay. Raffles Place MRT; bus #51, #124, #145, #166, #174 or #190.
Daily noon–2am.
Latino grooves, best enjoyed by secreting yourself among the cool people who inhabit the waterfront terrace; bar snacks are uninspiring except for the decent *calamares*.

Harry's Quayside
Map 3, F8. 28 Boat Quay. Raffles Place MRT; bus #51, #124, #145, #166, #174 or #190. ⓣ 5383029.
Daily 11am–1am.
There's live jazz and R&B Tuesday to Saturday in this upmarket place, and a blues jam every Sunday evening. Light lunches are served and prices are lower in the early evening.

Molly Malone's
Map 3, F8. 42 Circular Rd.

BARS AND PUBS: BOAT QUAY

Raffles Place MRT; bus #51,
#124, #145, #166, #174 or #190.
☏ 5345100.
Daily 11am–1am.
With Kilkenny and Guinness
($12 a pint) on tap, sounds
courtesy of Van Morrison and
the Pogues, and a menu
offering Connemara oysters
and Irish stew, hardly your
quintessential Singaporean
boozer, but a good crack
nonetheless, when full. Happy
hour (11am–8pm) knocks a
couple of bucks off a pint.

Mambo No. 5
Map 3, F7. 60 Boat Quay.
Raffles Place MRT; bus #51,
#124, #145, #166, #174 or #190.
Daily 3pm–2am.
Cramped and sweaty bar,
rocking over the weekend,
whose DJ's catholic tastes
embrace soul, Motown, funk,
hip-hop, reggae and R&B;
not the place for a quiet chat.

LITTLE INDIA AND AROUND

Leisure Pub
Map 4, B10. B1-01 Selegie

Centre, 189 Selegie Rd. Bus
#65, #66, #81, #97, #103, #139
or #147.
Daily 5pm–midnight.
Tame but endearing darts-
orientated establishment
that's ideal for a quiet chat
and handy for Bencoolen
Street; happy hour
3–8pm.

Pirate's Well Pub
Map 4, B10. 01-275 Selegie
Complex, 257 Selegie Rd. Bus
#65, #66, #81, #97, #103, #139
or #147.
Daily 5pm–midnight.
Indian-run hideaway
catering to the Little India
community; dim lighting
conjures a moody
ambience.

Taj Jazzaurant
Map 4, B8. 02-01 Little India
Arcade, 48 Serangoon Rd. Bus
#65, #66, #81, #97, #103, #139
or #147.
Disco daily 10pm–2am.
Once the plates and cutlery
have been cleared away (see
p.204), there's swinging Hindi
and Tamil dance music deep
into the night.

ORCHARD ROAD

Anywhere
Map 5, C5. 04-08/09 Tanglin
Shopping Centre, 19 Tanglin Rd.
Bus #105, #123 or #174.
℡ 7348233.
Mon–Sat 6pm–2am.
Tania, Singapore's most
famous covers band, plays
nightly to a boozy roomful of
expats that's at its rowdiest on
Friday nights; happy hour
Mon–Fri 6–8pm.

Cable Car Saloon
Map 5, G5. 17 Cuppage Rd.
Somerset MRT.
Mon–Sat 11.30am–2am, Sun
11.30am–12.30am.
Cable Car has upped sticks
from Tanjong Pagar in order
to join Orchard's in-crowd.
The intimate atmosphere is
the same, though, as is the
emphasis on cocktails on the
extensive drinks menu. Happy
hour 11.30am–8pm.

Excalibur Pub
Map 5, C5. B1-06 Tanglin
Shopping Centre, 19 Tanglin Rd.
Bus #105, #123 or #174.

Daily 11am–10.30pm.
Wonderfully cluttered and
cramped British-style pub, full
of weather-beaten expats.

Ice Cold Beer
Map 5, G5. 9 Emerald Hill.
Somerset MRT.
Daily 5pm–2am.
Noisy, hectic and happening
place where the beers are kept
on ice under the glass-topped
bar; there are regular
promotions, and there's a pool
table upstairs. Happy hour is
5–9pm.

No. 5 Emerald Hill
Map 5, G5. 5 Emerald Hill Rd.
Somerset MRT. ℡ 7320818.
Daily noon–2am.
Quite a pleasant Peranakan-
style bar-restaurant, if you can
stomach the posing bar staff,
and the constant crunch of
monkey nuts under foot.
There's nightly live jazz in the
upstairs bar. Happy hours
noon–9pm & 1–2am.

Observation Lounge
Map 5, F5. 38th floor, *Mandarin
Hotel*, 333 Orchard Rd. Orchard
MRT.

Mon–Thurs & Sun 11am–1am, Fri & Sat 11am–2am.

Swanky cocktail bar offering awesome views over downtown Singapore.

Saxophone

Map 5, G5. 23 Cuppage Rd. Somerset MRT. ☎ 2358385.

Daily 6pm–2am.

The coolest address in town, and a magnet for the beautiful people, who relax on the terrace to the sounds of the house jazz band. Happy hour 6–8pm.

The Sportsman

Map 5, D5. 02-01 Far East Shopping Centre. Orchard MRT.

Daily 11am–midnight.

One for homesick British footie fans, this: the walls are plastered with pictures of the likes of Gazza and Beckham, big matches are screened live, and Tiger beer is $5 a mug.

Snackworld

Map 5, G5. Cuppage Road. Somerset MRT.

Daily 11am–midnight.

Buy a bottle of Tiger from Snackworld and enjoy the music drifting over from

Saxophone without paying Saxophone prices – a great place to hang out.

Vintage Rock Cafe

Map 5, H5. 03-18 Cuppage Plaza, 5 Koek Rd. Somerset MRT.

Daily 5pm–midnight.

Friendly staff and locals, great R&B music on the speakers and cheapish beer: recommended. Happy hour 5–8pm.

Why? Pub

Map 5, E4. 04-06 Far East Plaza, 14 Scotts Rd. Orchard MRT.

Daily 2pm–midnight.

The budget prices in this tiny, lively pub – one of a clutch in this corner of Far East Plaza – attract big drinkers.

RIVER VALLEY ROAD
- -

Crazy Elephant

Map 3, D5. 01-07 Trader's Market, Clarke Quay. Raffles Place MRT; bus #124, #174 or #190.

Mon–Thurs & Sun 5pm–1am, Fri & Sat 5pm–2am.

The only bar with any real clout along Clarke Quay, playing decent rock music on the turntable between live sessions by the house band; decor comprises wood panelling and graffiti, but regulars prefer the tables out by the water's edge.

J P Bastiani

Map 3, D5. 01-12 Clarke Quay, 3a River Valley Rd. Raffles Place MRT; bus #124, #174 or #190.

Daily 6pm–1am.

With paintings on the walls, elegant furnishings and cigar-smoke-laden air, Bastiani oozes far more class than any of its Clarke Quay neighbours. Its central open courtyard is the bar's most serene spot.

The Mitre Hotel

Map 5, G7. 145 Killiney Rd. Somerset MRT.

Daily noon–midnight.

Marvellously shabby old hotel bar, with TV and dartboard, which recalls the Singapore of yore, before the arrival of air-con and karaoke machines.

Next Page Pub

Map 3, B3. 17 Mohamed Sultan Rd. Bus #32, #54 or #139.

Daily 3pm–1am.

Cool, popular pub which became the elder statesman of Mohamed Sultan Road when the *Front Page* burned down a while back. Decor is a mixture of Chinese wooden screens, lanterns and rough brick wall, and there's a pool table out back. A quieter annexe is planned for the shophouse next door; until then, the loud music might grate a little.

Wong San's

Map 3, B3. 12 Mohamed Sultan Rd. Bus #32, #54 or #139.

Daily 3pm–1am.

Stylish pub in a beautifully decorated Peranakan-style building, popular with local journalists and white-collar workers.

The Yard

Map 3, B3. 294 River Valley Rd. Bus #32, #54 or #139.

Daily 3pm–midnight.

This busy English pub was attracting a loyal crowd way

BARS AND PUBS: RIVER VALLEY ROAD

back when Mohamed Sultan Road was nothing more than a row of delapidated shophouses, and is still a great place for a beer. Bar snacks are available, and happy hour is 3–8pm.

CHINATOWN AND TANJONG PAGAR (DUXTON HILL)

Bar Sa Vahn

Map 3, E11. 49 Club St. Bus #51, #103, #124, #166, #174 or #190.
Daily 5pm–1am.
You know a bar means business when it counts a six-metre waterfall among its fixtures and fittings. Candle-lit, and crammed with Buddha effigies, scatter cushions and plants, the Sa Vanh (the name means "Heaven" in Lao) is a chilled-out bar, if ever there was one. The cool acid-jazz sounds round things off nicely. Happy hour 5–8pm. Upstairs is sister establishment the *Indochine* restaurant (p.214).

Flag and Whistle Public House

Map 3, B13. 10 Duxton Hill. Tanjong Pagar MRT; bus #103, #124, #145 or #166.
Daily 11am–midnight.
Predictable British pub, complete with Bass beer, bar snacks and a large Union Jack. Happy hour 11am–8pm.

J.J. Mahoney Pub

Map 3, C13. 58 Duxton Rd. Tanjong Pagar MRT; bus #103, #124, #145 or #166.
Open Mon–Thurs & Sun 5.30pm–2am, Fri & Sat 4.30pm–3am.
A popular haunt for karaoke-hungry local yuppies; the bar serves Bass beer and snacks throughout the night; happy hour 11am–8pm, doesn't include Bass.

Lang Kwai Fong

Map 3, D8. 50 Eu Tong Sen St. Bus #33, #54, #124 or #190.
Open Mon–Sat 7pm–3am.
While it's a crime to see a building (the Thong Chai Medical Institute – see p.89) of such cultural importance and architectural worth turned into a bar, it must be

said that the end result is most impressive – a blend of flashing lights, gleaming bars and elegant Chinese fittings. Happy hour is daily from 6 to 9pm.

DISCOS AND NIGHTCLUBS

Unlike their London and New York counterparts, Singaporean **nightclubs** are, on the whole, refreshingly unpretentious, their customers more intent on enjoying themselves than on posing. European and American dance music dominates (though some play Cantonese pop songs, too), and many feature live bands playing cover versions of current hits and pop classics.

Clubs tend to open around 9pm, though some start earlier in the evening with a happy hour. Indeed, the difference between bars and discos has recently begun to blur, and some now include bars or restaurants that kick off at lunchtime. Most have a **cover charge**, at least on busy Friday and Saturday nights, which fluctuates between $10 and $30, depending on what day it is and what sex you are; it almost invariably entitles you to a drink or two. It's worth checking the local press to see which venues are currently in favour; a scan through *8 Days* or *IS* magazines will bring you up to date. Singapore also has a plethora of extremely seedy **hostess clubs**, in which Chinese hostesses working on commission try to hassle you into buying them an extortionately expensive drink. Fortunately, they are easy to spot: even if you get beyond the heavy wooden front door flanked by brandy adverts, the pitch darkness inside gives the game away.

Boom Boom Room
Map 4, F10. 02-04, 3 New Bugis St. Bugis MRT. ℡ 3398187.

Daily 9pm–2am; cover charge Tues–Sat.

The nightly comedy and dance show is tame by old

Bugis Street standards, though still well attended and enjoyed by locals and tourists.

Brix

Map 5, E4. 10–12 Scotts Rd. Orchard MRT. ☎ 7307107.
Daily 9pm–2am.
Formerly known as *Brannigan's*, this large basement bar has shed its pick-up joint reputation, roughed up its decor a bit, and moved up into the premier league of Singapore clubs. There's loud R&B nightly.

Chinois Chinois

Map 5, F6. 02-01, 8 Grange Rd. Somerset or Orchard MRT. ☎ 7339555.
Mon–Fri 6pm–3am, Sat & Sun 8pm–3am.
Huge Cantonese nightclub, where cover charges apply throughout the week.

Sparks Disco

Map 5, F5. 7th Floor, Ngee Ann City, 391 Orchard Rd. Orchard MRT. ☎ 7356133.
Daily Mon–Sat 6pm–3am.
Soccer-pitch-sized and multi-chambered nightspot whose

slick Art Deco fittings are aimed squarely at the yuppie market. Three live bands play jazz, pop and Canto-pop.

Sugar

Map 3, B3. 13 Mohamed Sultan Rd. Bus #32, #54 or #139. ☎ 8360010.
Mon–Sat 8pm–3am.
If Elton John were to decorate Marie Antoinette's bedroom it'd probably look something akin to the front bar at Sugar, currently one of Singapore's coolest nightspots. Most of the dancing goes on out back, though, where Singapore's beautiful people dance to house and garage.

Sultan of Swing

Map 3, B6. 01-01 Central Mall, 5 Magazine Rd. Raffles Place MRT; bus #124, #174 or #190. ☎ 5570828.
Daily 5pm–2am.
Popular *Sultan of Swing* draws a substantial enough crowd of young executives to fill the huge dance hall that lies behind the quieter wine bar out front. There's a

retro Eighties theme to the music till midnight, after which house sets in. Cover charges apply Sat & Sun only.

Tajie

Map 3, B3. 27 Mohamed Sultan Rd. Bus #32, #54 or #139. ☎ 8870007.

Daily 7pm–1am (late-night extension imminent).

"Chinese funky" is how its staff describe this popular bar-cum-disco, whose decor comprises rough brick walls and red Chinese lanterns. The actual dance floor at *Tajie* (the name means "big sister" in Chinese) is modest – most punters prefer to dance where they stand. Music is a mixture of house and trance; cover charges apply at weekends only.

Venom

Map 5, D4. 12-01 Pacific Plaza, Orchard Rd. Orchard MRT.

Tues–Sun 8pm–3am.

Dress code at *Venom* is stated as "very trendy, casual", a phrase which neatly sums up this immensely popular,

industrial-chic club overlooking the Orchard Road district.

Vibes

Map 5, C5. Orchard Hotel, 442 Orchard Rd. Bus #105, #123 or #174. ☎ 7355893.

Tues–Sun 8pm–2am.

You'll be tripping over local execs and media darlings if you come down to *Vibes*. Music is a blend of Motown, R&B and acid jazz. Happy hour is daily 6–10pm.

Vogue

Map 3, B6. 01-01 Central Mall, 7 Magazine Rd. Raffles Place MRT; bus #124, #174 or #190.

Daily 8pm–2am.

Smaller and more intimate than neighbouring *Sultan of Swing*, *Vogue* plays exclusively techno music. Cover charges apply throughout the week.

Zouk

Map 2, F6. 17–21 Jiak Kim St. Bus #51 or #64. ☎ 7382988.

Mon–Sat 6pm–3am.

Singapore's trendiest club, fitted out to create a

DISCOS AND NIGHTCLUBS

Mediterranean feel. Famous DJs like Paul Oakenfold guest occasionally. Happy hour 8–9pm.

LIVE MUSIC

Singapore is too far off the European and North American tour trail to attract many big-name **Western performers**, but there are occasional forays to rally the troops – Eric Clapton, Deep Purple, Michael Jackson, Alanis Morissette and Mariah Carey have all visited in recent years. Concerts of this calibre are usually staged at the Singapore Indoor Stadium, and exhaustively covered by the local press for weeks beforehand. **Local bands** do exist and some aren't at all bad, but these are more likely to perform in community centres, rather than decent venues. Rivalling Western music in terms of popularity in Singapore is **Canto-pop**, a bland hybrid of Cantonese lyrics and Western disco beats whose origins lie in the soundtracks of 1950s Cantonese movie musicals; Hong Kong Canto-pop superstars visit periodically, and the rapturous welcomes they receive make their shows quite an experience.

No matter who else is in town, you can always catch a set of cover versions at one of Singapore's bars and clubs; the main venues are picked out below. If you like middle-of-the-road **rock** music, you'll be in your element, as scores of local and Filipino bands nightly belt out Bryan Adams and Eagles hits. **Jazz** and **blues** ensembles are also popular. For more low-key musical accompaniment, go to any of the swankier hotels in town, and you're bound to find a resident pianist crooning Sinatra standards.

The most exhaustive lists of what's on are to be found in the weekly magazine, *8 Days*, the fortnightly *IS* and monthly *Where Singapore,* though the "Life!" section of the *Straits Times* is also worth a scan.

VENUES

Anywhere

See p.221.

Good-time rock music by local favourites Tania.

Bernie Goes to Town

See p.219.

Reggae, blues or R&B played live.

Crazy Elephant

See p.222.

Live blues and rock throughout the week.

Harry's Quayside

See p.219.

Live jazz Wed–Sat, and a blues jam Sun evening.

Molly Malone's

See p.219.

Two guitar'n'fiddle sets nightly.

No.5 Emerald

See p.221.

Live jazz upstairs nightly.

Saxophone

See p.222.

Slick jazz played on a cramped stage behind the bar.

Singapore Indoor Stadium

Map 7, A4. Stadium Road. Kallang MRT; bus #16. ⓣ 3442660.

The usual venue for big-name bands in town; tickets are available through Sistic or Ticketcharge (see p.231).

World Trade Centre

Map 8, I6. 1 Maritime Square. Bus #97, #143 or #166. ⓣ 3212187.

Hosts international acts from time to time, as well as presenting free local gigs in its amphitheatre (check press for details).

LIVE MUSIC: VENUES

Entertainment and the arts

O f all the performing arts, **drama** gets the best showing in Singapore, the island's theatres staging
productions that range from English farces to contemporary productions by local writers. **Dance** – Western
or Asian – is more of a rarity, and events crop up only periodically, though you could time your trip to coincide with
the annual **Singapore Festival of Arts** in June. **Asian
culture** is showcased in Singapore's major venues from time
to time, but tends to appear more often on the street than
in the auditorium, particularly around the time of the bigger festivals. **Cinema** is big business in Singapore, with up-
to-the-minute Asian and Western movies all drawing big
crowds, and the annual **Singapore International Film
Festival** in April.

INFORMATION, LISTINGS AND TICKETS

For **information** on cultural events and performances,
pick up a copy of either the *Singapore Straits Times* (whose

TICKETING AGENCIES

Both agencies are open daily 10am–8pm; Ⓦ *www.sistic.co.sg*; Ⓦ *www.ticketcharge.net*

Sistic

Far East Square, 43 Pekin St. Map 3, F10.

Parco Bugis Junction, 200 Victoria St. Map 4, F1.

Raffles City Shopping Centre. Map 3, I3.

Scotts Shopping Centre, 6 Scotts Rd. Map 5, E5.

Singapore Indoor Stadium, Stadium Road. Map 7, A4.

Specialists' Shopping Centre, 277 Orchard Rd. Map 5, H5.

Takashimaya, Ngee Ann City, 391 Orchard Rd. Map 5, F5.

Victoria Concert Hall, Parliament Lane. Map 3, H7.

Ticketcharge

Centrepoint, 176 Orchard Rd. Map 5, G5.

Substation, 45 Armenian St. Map 3, F2.

Funan the IT Mall,109 North Bridge Rd. Map 3, F5.

Forum the Shopping Mall, 583 Orchard Rd. Map 5, C5.

daily "Life!" supplement has a good "what's on" section), *8 Days* magazine, the fortnightly – and free – *IS* magazine, or *Where Singapore*, which is monthly, and also free. Alternatively, phone the venue's box office – all the relevant numbers are given below. **Sistic** ☏3485555 and **Ticketcharge** ☏2962929 are Singapore's central ticketing agencies; see box for details. The cost of a ticket to a cultural performance in Singapore usually starts at around $10, though international acts command substantially higher prices.

CLASSICAL MUSIC

At the epicentre of the **Western** classical music scene in Singapore is the **Singapore Symphony Orchestra**. Performances by this 85-member, multinational orchestra take place at the Victoria Concert Hall and often feature guest soloists, conductors and choirs from around the world; occasional **Chinese** classical music shows are included in the programme. From time to time, ensembles from the orchestra also give **lunchtime concerts**. In addition, the Singapore Symphony Orchestra gives occasional free performances in Singapore's parks, while Sentosa Island also hosts regular Sunday concerts – the shows are free, but the usual Sentosa entry fee applies.

Nanyang Academy of Fine Arts Chinese Orchestra
Map 4, E11. 111 Middle Rd. Bugis MRT. ☎ 3382790. Chinese classical and folk music.

Singapore Symphony Orchestra
Map 3, H7. Victoria Concert Hall, Empress Place. Raffles Place MRT; bus #97 or #167. ☎ 3381230.
Performances on Friday and Saturday evenings throughout the year.

CULTURAL PERFORMANCES

If you walk around Singapore's streets for long enough, you're likely to come across some sort of streetside **cultural event**, most commonly a **wayang**, or Chinese opera, played out on tumbledown outdoor stages that spring up overnight next to temples and markets, or just at the side of the road. Wayangs are highly dramatic and stylized affairs, in which garishly made-up and costumed characters enact popular Chinese legends to the accompaniment of the crashes of cymbals and gongs. Wayangs take place throughout the year, but the best time to catch one is during the Festival of the Hungry Ghosts, when they are held to entertain passing spooks, or during the Festival of the Nine Emperor Gods (see p.243). The STB may also be able to help you track down a wayang, and as usual the local press is worth checking.

Another fascinating traditional performance, **lion dancing**, takes to the streets during Chinese New Year, and **puppet theatres** appear around then, too.

At the Chinese Opera Teahouse, 5 Smith St (daily 10am–10pm; ☎ 3234862; map 3, C11; bus #51, #103, #124, #166, #174 or #190), $15 buys you Chinese tea and an opera performance with subtitles in English.

The Kala Mandhir cultural association, based at the *Excelsior Hotel* on Coleman Street, is dedicated to perpetuating traditional **Indian** art, music and dance. Less spontaneous displays of Asian culture can be seen at **theme parks** such as Asian Village on Sentosa Island (see p.136) and the Malay Cultural Village (see p.117).

FILM

With over fifty **cinemas** on the island, you should have no trouble finding a movie that appeals to you, and at a price ($5–8) that compares favourably with Europe and America. As well as Hollywood's latest blockbusters, a wide range of **Chinese**, **Malay** and **Indian movies**, all with English subtitles, are screened. Chinese productions tend to be a raucous blend of slapstick and martial arts, while Malay and Indian movies are characterized by exuberant song and dance routines. Cinema-going is a popular pastime so, if you plan to catch a newly released film, turn up early – and

FILM

take a jumper along, as air-con units are perpetually on full blast. Be prepared, also, for a lot of noise during shows: Singaporeans tend to talk all the way through subtitled movies, and the rustling of a bag of popcorn pales next to the sound of melon seeds being cracked and crunched. The most central cinemas are listed below, but check the local press for a full rundown of any special events or one-offs that might be taking place.

For **Western films** in their original language, the Alliance Française, 1 Sarkies Rd (℡7378422; map 5, E2), screens free French films every Tuesday (7.15pm) and Wednesday (9.15pm) and holds an annual film festival in November. There are also regular presentations at the British Council (see "Directory" on p.260 for address) and the Goethe Institute, 05-01, 163 Penang Rd (℡7354555; map 5, I6).

The **Singapore International Film Festival** takes place in April. Now an annual event, it screens over 150 films and shorts – mostly by Asian directors – over two weeks. Smaller festivals are occasionally mounted by the Singapore Film Society.

Cathay Cinema
Map 4, B13. 2 Handy Rd. Dhoby Ghaut MRT. ℡3383400. Singapore's oldest cinema, now a multi-screen affair.

Cathay Cineleisure Orchard
Map 5, F6. 8 Grange Rd. Somerset or Orchard MRT. ℡2358386. Central and recently renovated cinema, with a swish new shopping centre constructed around it.

Jade Classics
Map 4, H11. 4th floor, Shaw Leisure Gallery, 100 Beach Rd. Bugis MRT. ℡2942568. Like the Picture House, this screens slightly more cerebral movies than most.

Lido Cineplex
Map 5, D5. Level 5, Shaw

FILM

House, 1 Scotts Rd. Orchard MRT. ⓉY7324124.
Five screens, including the luxurious Lido Classic.

The Picture House
Map 4, B13. Cathay Building, 2 Handy Rd. Dhoby Ghaut MRT. Ⓣ3383400.
A new cinema, pricier than most, which screens less mainstream new releases.

Yangtse
Map 3, A11. Pearl Centre, 100 Eu Tong Sen Rd. Outram Park MRT. Ⓣ2237529.
Located in the heart of Chinatown, this place shows Western and Oriental films.

THEATRE AND THE PERFORMING ARTS

Singapore has a modest but thriving **drama** scene, with most local productions debuting at either the Black Box, Substation or Drama Centre, and graduating to the Victoria Theatre if they are successful. Prices of tickets range from about $15 to $45. Foreign companies occasionally visit, and usually perform at the Victoria or Kallang theatres. Performances of **dance** take place from time to time – most notably by the Singapore Dance Theatre (Ⓣ3380611), which periodically performs classical and contemporary works at various venues, and even in local parks.

Singapore's annual **Festival of the Arts** attracts class acts from all over the world. A schedule of events is published in May, a month before the festival begins so, unless you are in Singapore for quite a while, you'll probably have trouble getting tickets for the more popular events. However, an accompanying **fringe festival** takes place concurrently, and its programme always includes free street and park performances. In addition, Singapore hosts a biennial Festival of Asian Performing Arts in odd years, which showcases the cultures of neighbouring nations.

The Black Box
Map 3, E2. Fort Canning Centre, Cox Terrace, Fort Canning Park. Dhoby Ghaut MRT. ⓣ3384077.
Local productions by the Theatreworks Company.

Boom Boom Room
Map 4, E10. 02-04, 3 New Bugis St. Bugis MRT; bus #51, #133 or #190. ⓣ3398187.
Stand-up comedy hasn't really taken off in Singapore, though the Boom Boom Room's vaguely saucy revue, featuring a camp Malay comedian whose jokes are delivered in broad Singlish (Singaporean English), is worth checking out.

Drama Centre
Map 3, E3. Canning Rise. Dhoby Ghaut MRT. ⓣ3360005.
Drama by local companies.

Hilton-British Airways Playhouse
Map 5, D5. *Hilton Hotel*, 581 Orchard Rd. Orchard MRT. ⓣ7372233.
Light comedy from London's West End theatres.

Jubilee Hall
Map 3, I2. *Raffles Hotel*, 1 Beach Rd. Raffles City MRT. ⓣ3371886.
Occasionally stages retro plays.

Kallang Theatre
Map 7, A4. 1 Stadium Walk. Kallang MRT; bus #14 or #16. ⓣ3454888.
Hosts visiting companies such as the Bolshoi Ballet, and touring musicals like *Chicago*.

The Substation
Map 3, F2. 45 Armenian St. City Hall MRT; bus #7, #14, #36, #124, #167 or #190. ⓣ3377800.
Self-styled "home for the arts" with a multipurpose hall that presents drama and dance, as well as art, sculpture and photography exhibitions.

Victoria Theatre
Map 3, H7. 9 Empress Place. Raffles Place MRT. ⓣ3377490.
Visiting performers and successful local performances that graduate here from lesser venues.

THEATRE AND THE PERFORMING ARTS

Festivals

With so many ethnic groups and religions represented in Singapore, you'll be unlucky if your trip doesn't coincide with some sort of **festival**, either secular or religious. Religious celebrations range from exuberant, family-orientated pageants to blood-curdlingly gory displays of devotion; secular events tend to comprise a carnival with a cast of thousands. Below is a chronological round-up of Singapore's major festivals, with suggestions of where best to enjoy them. Most of them have no fixed **dates**, but change annually according to the lunar calendar. We've listed rough timings, but for specific dates each year it's a good idea to check with the STB which produces a monthly round-up of festivals in Singapore.

Some, but by no means all, festivals are also public holidays, when many shops and restaurants may close. For a full list of public holidays, see p.32.

JANUARY–MARCH

THAIPONGGAL

Mid-Jan A Tamil thanksgiving festival marking the end of the rainy season and the onset of Spring. In Hindu homes, rice is cooked in a new pot and allowed to boil over, to symbolize prosperity. At the Sri Srinivasa Perumal Temple on Serangoon Road, food is prepared against a cacophony of drums, bells, conch shells and chanting, offered up to the gods, and then eaten by devotees as a symbol of cleansing.

CHINESE NEW YEAR

Jan–Feb Singapore's Chinese community springs spectacularly to life to welcome in the new lunar year. The festival's origins lie in a Chinese legend telling of a horned monster which was awoken by the onset of Spring, terrorizing nearby villagers until they discovered it could be held at bay by noise, light and the colour red. Essentially, Chinese New Year is a family affair – old debts are settled, friends and relatives visited, mandarin oranges exchanged, red envelopes (*hong bao*) containing money given to children, and red scrolls and papers bearing the character *fu* pasted to front doors as a sign of good fortune. Even so, there's still plenty to see in Chinatown, whose streets are ablaze with lanterns and fairy lights. Chinese opera and lion and dragon dance troupes perform in the streets, while ad hoc markets sell sausages and waxed ducks, pussy willow, chrysanthemums, lanterns and mandarin oranges; particularly splendid is the flower market that sets up on open ground at the junction of Neil and Kreta Ayer roads. On and along the Singapore River, the Hong Bao Special takes place, an extravaganza of floats, fireworks, music, dance and stalls that lasts for a couple of weeks. SBC's annual televised Lunar New Year Countdown is broadcast live from an outdoor location in Chinatown, and is well worth looking out for in the press. Colourful parades of stilt-walkers, lion dancers and floats along Orchard Road celebrate the Chingay (literally, "gaily decorated float") holiday, part of the New Year festivities, though nowadays a multicultural affair.

THAIPUSAM

Jan/Feb Not for the faint-hearted, this Hindu festival sees entranced penitents walking the three kilometres from Little India's Sri Perumal Srinivasa Temple to the Chettiar Temple on Tank Road, carrying kavadis – elaborate steel arches decorated with peacock feathers and attached to their skin by hooks and prongs – and with skewers spiked through their cheeks and tongues, to honour the Lord Murugan. Some join the procession to pray for assistance, others to give thanks for heavenly aid already granted. Coconuts are smashed at the feet of the penitents for good luck as they set off, and friends and relatives jig around them en route, singing and chanting to spur them on.

HARI RAYA HAJI

Feb/March An auspicious day for Singapore's Muslims, who gather at mosques to honour those who have completed the Haj, or pilgrimage to Mecca (birthplace of Muhammad); goats are sacrificed, and their meat given to the needy.

APRIL—AUGUST

QING MING

April Ancestral graves are cleaned and restored, and prayers and offerings of joss sticks, incense papers and food made by Chinese families at the beginning of the third lunar month, to signal the onset of spring and a new farming year.

VESAK DAY

May Saffron-robed monks chant sacred scriptures at packed Buddhist temples, and devotees release caged birds to commemorate the Buddha's birth (May), enlightenment and the attainment of Nirvana; in the evening, candle-lit processions are held at temples. Race Course Road's Temple of a Thousand Lights is a good place to view the proceedings.

BIRTHDAY OF THE THIRD PRINCE

May Entranced mediums cut themselves with swords to honour the birthday of the Buddhist child god Ne Zha, who is said to carry a magic bracelet and a spear, and to ride the wind; their blood is wiped on much sought-after paper charms at temples around the state.

DUMPLING FESTIVAL

May/June Stalls along Albert Mall sell traditional pyramid-shaped Chinese dumplings in the run-up to the Dumpling Festival, celebrated on the fifth day of the fifth lunar month. The festival commemorates Qu Yuan, a Chinese scholar who drowned himself in protest against political corruption. Local people, it is said, tried to save him from sea creatures by beating drums, disturbing the waters with their oars, and throwing in rice dumplings to feed them, but to no avail.

SINGAPORE ARTS FESTIVAL

June Annual celebration of world dance, music, drama and art, utilizing venues around the state, with events lasting several weeks.

DRAGON BOAT FESTIVAL

June/July Rowing boats, bearing a dragon's head and tail, their crews spurred on by the pounding of a great drum in the prow, race biennially across Marina Bay to commemorate Qu Yuan (see above). Next in 2002.

SINGAPORE NATIONAL DAY

August 9 Singapore's gaining of independence in 1965 is celebrated with a national holiday and a huge show at either the Padang or the National Stadium, featuring military parades and fireworks.

FESTIVAL OF THE HUNGRY GHOSTS

August Sometimes called *Yue Lan*, this festival is held to appease the souls of the dead released from Purgatory during the thirty days of the seventh lunar month, and so forestall unlucky events. Chinese street operas are held, and joss sticks – some the size of a man – red candles and paper money are burnt outside Chinese homes. Paper effigies of worldly goods such as houses, cars and servants are sometimes burnt, too. Elsewhere, marquees are set up in the street to hold festive banquets, followed by auctions of pieces of charcoal, cake and flowers – all thought to be auspicious.

APRIL–AUGUST

SEPTEMBER–DECEMBER

BIRTHDAY OF THE MONKEY GOD

Sept (also Feb) To celebrate the birthday of one of the most popular deities in the Chinese pantheon, mediums possessed by the Monkey God's spirit pierce themselves with skewers and dispense charms written in their own blood at the Monkey God Temple on Seng Poh Road, while a sedan chair possessed by the god himself is carried by worshippers. Elsewhere street operas and puppet shows are performed – look out for ad hoc canopies erected near Chinese temples.

MOON CAKE FESTIVAL

Sept Also known as the Mid-Autumn Festival (held on the fifteenth day of the eighth lunar month), when Chinese people eat and exchange moon cakes (made from sesame and lotus seeds and stuffed with red bean paste or a duck egg) to honour the fall of the Mongol Empire – plotted, so legend has it, by means of messages secreted in cakes. Another, simpler explanation is that the cakes represent the full moon, at its brightest at this time of year. Moon cake stalls spring up across Singapore two weeks before the festival, but particularly in Chinatown.

LANTERN FESTIVAL

Sept Strictly speaking a subset of the Moon Cake Festival (above), the Lantern Festival is celebrated over two weeks in the Chinese Gardens (see p.126), where children parade with gaily coloured lanterns and cultural shows; lion and dragon dances are a common sight.

NAVARATHIRI

Sept–Oct Hindu temples such as the Chettiar Temple on Tank Road, and Chinatown's Sri Mariamman Temple, devote nine nights to classical dance and music in honour of Dhurga, Lakshmi and Saraswathi, the consorts of the Hindu gods Shiva, Vishnu and Brahma. Visitors are welcome at the nightly performances that take place at temples across the island. On the tenth night, a silver horse is carried at the head of a procession from Tank Road, taking in River Valley, Killiney and Orchard roads and Clemenceau Avenue.

THIMITHI

Sept–Nov Another dramatic Hindu ceremony, this one sees devotees proving the strength of their faith by running across a four-metre-long pit of hot coals at the Sri Mariamman Temple in Chinatown. Outside the temple, devotees in their hundreds line up awaiting their turn, and building up their courage by dancing, shouting and singing.

FESTIVAL OF THE NINE EMPEROR GODS

Oct The nine-day sojourn on earth of the Nine Emperor Gods, thought to cure ailments and bring good health and longevity, is celebrated at the Kiu Ong Yiah Temple on Upper Serangoon Road by Chinese opera and mediums cavorting in the streets. Capping the festival is a procession, during which effigies of the nine gods are carried in sedan chairs.

PILGRIMAGE TO KUSU ISLAND

Oct Locals visit Kusu Island (see p.138) in their thousands to pray for good luck and fertility at the Tua Pekong

Temple and the island's Muslim shrine. The pilgrimage commemorates the ancient tale of a turtle that turned itself into an island to save two shipwrecked sailors.

DEEPAVALI (DIWALI)

Oct/Nov Serangoon Road is festooned with fairy lights during this, the most auspicious of Hindu festivals, celebrating the victory of the Lord Krishna over Narakasura, and thus of light over dark. Oil lamps are lit outside homes to attract Lakshmi, the goddess of prosperity, and prayers are offered at all temples.

RAMADAN

Oct–Dec Muslims spend the ninth month of the Islamic calendar fasting in the daytime in order to intensify awareness of the plight of the poor and to identify with the hungry. Many also abstain from drinking, smoking and sex. The fast is broken nightly with delicious Malay sweetmeats served at stalls outside mosques. The biggest collection of stalls sets up along Bussorah and Kandahar streets, outside the Arab Quarter's Sultan Mosque, though the lights, bustling bazaar and Malay Village of Geylang (see p.117) also warrant a visit. Muslims mark Hari Raya Puasa, the end of Ramadan, by feasting, donning their best traditional clothes and visiting family and friends. (Begins late Nov in 2000, mid-Nov in 2001, early Nov in 2002, late Oct 2003.)

CHRISTMAS

December 25 Singapore's central shopping centres vie annually for the best decorations in town, making Christmas a particularly colourful and atmospheric time for shopping.

Shopping

For many stopover visitors, Singapore is synonymous with **shopping**, though – contrary to popular belief – prices are not rock bottom across the board, due to the consistently strong Singaporean dollar and a rising cost of living. Good deals can be found on watches, cameras, electrical and computer equipment, fabrics and antiques, and cut-price imitations (Rolexes, Lacoste polo shirts, and so on) are rife, but many other articles offer no substantial saving. Choice and convenience, though, make the Singapore shopping experience a rewarding one, with scores of shopping centres and department stores meaning that you're rarely more than an air-conditioned escalator ride away from what you want to buy. What's more, come during the annual **Great Singapore Sale** (usually between May and July), and you'll find seriously marked-down prices in many outlets across the island.

THE ART OF SHOPPING IN SINGAPORE

Unless you're in a department store, prices are negotiable, so be prepared to **haggle**. If you're planning to buy something pricey – a camera, say, or a stereo – it's a good idea to pay a visit to a reputable department store and arm yourself with the correct retail price, so you'll know if you're being ripped off. Asking for the "best price" is always a good start to negotiations; from there, it's a question of technique, but be realistic – shopkeepers will soon lose interest if you offer an unreasonably low price. Moving towards the door of the shop often pays dividends: it's surprising how often you'll be called back. And don't be hurried into a purchase, but shop around until you're content with the deal you've secured.

Usual shopping hours are daily 10am–9pm, though some shopping centres, especially along Orchard Road, stay open until 10pm. The only exception to this is the Christian-owned C. K. Tang's, which closes on Sunday.

DEPOSITS, GUARANTEES AND REFUNDS

Deposits shouldn't be required unless you're having clothes made up by a tailor – don't trust any other shops if they ask you to part with cash before you receive your purchase. If you buy any electrical goods, make sure you get an international, not a national, **guarantee**, and that it's dated and endorsed by the shop. Guarantees should detail the model and serial number of your purchase. It's also important to check that the product's **voltage** and cycle is compatible with that of your home country – especially if you're from Canada or the USA. Even if you are not buying something that warrants a guarantee, make sure you leave with a **receipt** – larger stores will produce one as a matter of course, though in small outlets you may have to ask for itemized proof of purchase. **Refunds**, while often possible in department stores for faulty goods, are unusual in small shops, but if you wish to make an official complaint (see p.247), a receipt will be required.

A goods and services **tax** (GST), introduced in 1994, has added a three percent sales tax to all goods and services, but tourists can claim a refund on purchases of $300 or over (receipts of $100 or more can be pooled) at retailers displaying a blue and grey **Tax Free Shopping** sticker. Ask retailers to draft you a Tax Free Shopping Cheque, which you can then redeem subsequently at the airport.

Should you have a complaint which you can't resolve with a particular store, contact the Retail Promotions Centre on ☎ 4502114. Or you can go to Singapore's Small Claims Tribunal, Subordinate Courts, Apollo Centre, 2 Havelock Rd ☎ 5356922, which has a fast-track system for tourists; it costs $10 to have your case heard.

CUSTOMS, SHIPPING AND INSURANCE

If you are buying in bulk, or purchasing products made of materials such as crocodile skin or ivory, be aware of **customs** regulations back home – your nation's consulate should be able to tell you what you can and can't import. Any weapons (including the *kris*, or Malay ceremonial sword) going through Singapore customs must have an export permit issued by the Police Arms and Explosives Branch, Block J, Ladyhill Road (☎ 7344162). Larger stores will usually pack and ship items home for you, or you can go to the General Post Office (see p.264) – in either case, be sure to arrange **insurance**.

ANTIQUES, ARTS AND CRAFTS

Singapore bulges with stores selling Asian antiques, arts and crafts, ranging from Bornean wooden effigies to Korean chests, and from Chinese snuff bottles to Malaysian pewterware. If it's **antiques** you're after, trawling through Tanglin Shopping Centre at the western end of Orchard Road, or

Holland Road Shopping Centre in Holland Village (see p.125), is a good start. Slightly more central, Cuppage Road also has two or three antique shops that warrant a browse. Watten Rise, northwest of Orchard Road, is a happy hunting ground for **antique furniture** – get off bus #171 when you see the Chinese High School on your left, and cross over Bukit Timah Road, or try the area around the junction of River Valley and Tank roads, and at Clarke Quay.

Arts and crafts can be found everywhere, but again there are specific areas worth heading for. Chinatown boasts a glut of souvenir stores stocking interesting goods beside the usual tack, and is nowadays the home of the relocated Singapore Handicraft Centre (see below). At Marina Square there are daily demonstrations of traditional arts and crafts, while Arab Street is good for robust basketware and leatherware.

Antiques of the Orient
Map 5, C5. 02-40 Tanglin Shopping Centre, 19 Tanglin Rd. Bus #105, #123 or #174.
Specialists in antiquarian books, maps and prints.

China Mec
Map 3, I3. 03-31/32 Raffles City Shopping Centre, 250 North Bridge Rd. Raffles City MRT.
Vast selection of Beijing cloisonné goods – patterned bowls, statues and other articles decorated with copper inlays and enamel.

De Lin Buddhist Artifacts Center
Map 4, D11. 01-35 Fortune Centre, 190 Middle Rd. Bugis MRT; bus #81.
Sells effigies, trinkets, necklaces, books and other Buddhist-related goods.

Eng Tiang Huat
Map 3, B3. 284 River Valley Rd. Bus #32, #54 or #139.
Oriental musical instrument shop whose owners like nothing better than to demonstrate their stock; also wayang costumes and props.

Far East Inspirations

Map 3, D10. 33 Pagoda St. Bus #32, #54 or #139.

The classiest of several antique shops along Pagoda Street, carrying Asian furniture, porcelain-based lamps, prints and watercolours.

Funan Stamp and Coin Agency

Map 3, F5. 03-03 Funan the IT Mall, 109 North Bridge Rd. City Hall MRT; bus #124 or #166.

As you'd expect, old coins and stamps.

House of Zhen

Map, 3, D11. 252 South Bridge Rd. Bus #51, #103, #124, #166, #174 or #190.

This expansive store at South Bridge's junction with Temple Street, matches the famous Katong Antiques House (below), in its range of antiques, collectables and furniture. Members of staff are friendly and knowledgeable.

Jasmine Fine Arts

Map 5, H5. 04-14 Orchard Point, 160 Orchard Rd. Somerset MRT.

Appealing artwork from China; next door is the Orchard Point Exhibition Hall, and there are many other outlets on the same floor.

Katong Antiques House

Map 7, C4. 208 East Coast Rd. Bus #14.

Dark, cluttered Aladdin's cave of Asian collectables; through its swing doors are tiffin carriers, Peranakan slippers and clothes, and Chinese porcelain. Keeps rather erratic hours.

Lopburi

Map 5, B6. 01-04 Tanglin Place, 91 Tanglin Rd. Bus #105, #123 or #174.

Seriously fine – and seriously expensive – antique Buddhas and Khmer sculptures, as well as some old silk textiles.

Min Ching Antique House

Map 3, D5. Clarke Quay. Raffles Place MRT; bus #124, #174 or #190.

Antique Chinese furniture, screens, *kan* tables for smoking opium, and pieces made from rare *huanghuali* wood.

ANTIQUES, ARTS AND CRAFTS

National Museum Shop
Map 3, F2. 53 Armenian St (the Substation). City Hall MRT; bus #7, #14, #36, #124, #167 or #190.
Map 3, G1. 71 Bras Basah Rd (the Singapore Art Museum). City Hall MRT; bus #171, #190 or #197.
A potpourri of books, prints, souvenirs and artefacts homing in on Singapore's cultural heritage.

New Ming Village
Map 8, D5. 32 Pandan Rd. Jurong East MRT, then bus #78. Ming and Qing dynasty porcelain reproductions made by hand, according to traditional methods – most fascinating is the painstaking work of the painters. This is not a place to come unless you are dead set on buying some porcelain.

One Price Store
Map 5, G5. 3 Emerald Hill Rd. Somerset MRT.
This venerable old shop, fronted by a jungle of potted plants, carries everything from carved camphorwood chests to Chinese snuff bottles.

Poh Hwa Stamp Maker
Map 3, D9. 02-50 Hong Lim Complex, Blk 531 Upper Cross St. Bus #51, #103, #124, #166, #174 or #190.
Handmade and inexpensive rubber stamps.

Rasha Collections
Map 8, F3. 03-32 Holland Road Shopping Centre, 211 Holland Ave. Buona Vista MRT; bus #7 or #105.
Antique woodwork and brasswork, cushions and jewellery.

Rishi Handicrafts
Map 4, H8. 58 Arab St. Bus #7, #107, #130, #145 or #197.
Leather sandals, necklaces, briefcases, belts and knick-knacks.

Risis
Map 5, A6. Botanic Gardens, Cluny Road. Bus #7, #106 or #174.
Specializes in jewellery made by gold-plating real orchids.

Selangor Pewter
Map 8, D5. 32 Pandan Rd. Jurong East MRT, then bus #78.
Map 3, I3. 02-38 Raffles City

ANTIQUES, ARTS AND CRAFTS

Shopping Centre, 252 North Bridge Rd. City Hall MRT.
A store masquerading as something more cultural, with its "museum" of pewterware and free demonstrations all increasing the pressure to buy.

Singapore Handicraft Centre
Map 3, C9. Chinatown Point, 133 New Bridge Rd. Bus #33, #54, #124 or #190.
This place gathers around fifty souvenir shops under one roof, making it a handy one-stop shopping point.

Sun Craft
Map 5, C5. 02-08 Tanglin Shopping Centre, 19 Tanglin Rd. Bus #105, #123, #174.
Work by well-known local artists, using a range of different media.

Tong Mern Sern Antiques
Map 3, D5. Blk D Clarke Quay. Raffles Place MRT; bus #124, #174 or #190.
A potpourri of ancient bits and bobs – postcards, abacuses, lamps – from Singapore's past.

Wong's Collections
Map 3, D11. 3 Ann Siang Hill. Bus #51, #103, #124, #166, #174 or #190.
Sells everything from antique furniture and wartime food coupons to matchboxes and MRT cards.

Zhen Lacquer Gallery
Map 3, C13. 17 Duxton Rd. Tanjong Pagar MRT; bus #103, #124, #145 or #166.
Boxes, bowls, trays and paintings whose exquisite polished finish is crafted from the resin of the lacquer tree.

BOOKSHOPS

Times bookshops stock a wide choice of titles, and crop up all over town, with branches at 04-08/15 Centrepoint, 175 Orchard Rd (Map 5, G5) and 02-24/25 Raffles City Shopping Centre, 252 North Bridge Rd (Map 3, I3). **MPH** shops are also well stocked, especially the flagship

BOOKSHOPS

store on Stamford Road (Map 3, G2). For **secondhand books**, your best bet is to check out the shelves in the backpacker crashpads of Bencoolen Street.

Books Kinokuniya
Map 5, F5. 03-10/15 Ngee Ann City, 391 Orchard Rd. Orchard MRT.
Singapore's largest bookstore by a long way, with an excellent selection of novels and magazines; branch at Sogo Department Store, 3rd floor, Raffles City Shopping Centre, 250 North Bridge Rd.

Borders
Map 5, D5. 01-00 Wheelock Place, 501 Orchard Rd. Orchard MRT.
US chain of bookstores, boasting an in-house cafe.

Packir Mohamed & Sons
Map 5, H5. 01-20/21 Orchard Plaza, 150 Orchard Rd. Somerset MRT.
Boasts a huge selection of magazines, both local and Western.

Pro Saint Book Store
Map 4, F12. 02-77 Bras Basah Complex, 231–233 Bain St. City Hall MRT; bus #56 or #171.
Books bought, sold and exchanged.

Select Books
Map 5, C5. 03-15 Tanglin Shopping Centre, 19 Tanglin Rd. Bus #105, #123 or #174.
A huge array of specialist books on Southeast Asia.

Sunny Bookshop
Map 5, E4. 03-02 Far East Plaza, 14 Scotts Rd. Orchard MRT.
New and secondhand English- and Chinese-language books.

ELECTRONIC EQUIPMENT

Electronic equipment remains reasonably priced in the duty-free city of Singapore, but don't expect miracles.

BOOKSHOPS

What's more impressive than Singapore's prices is its range of goods – whether you want to buy a clock, a computer, a camera or even a karaoke machine, some or other store is bound to stock the model you're after. Singaporeans love all things hi-tech, and entire shopping centres specialize in electronics, making comparing prices and models a breeze. Orchard Road's Lucky Plaza is the focal point for **cameras**, with nearby Orchard Plaza and Far East Plaza also crammed with stores. You'll find the galleries of Sim Lim Tower and Sim Lim Square, around the intersection of Bencoolen Street and Rochor Road, teeming with stores selling **electronic goods** galore, from transistor radios to state-of-the-art TVs and VCRs. Also worth exploring is Plaza Singapura, whose department store Yaohan is a good place to check the going rates. For **computers** and **software**, the Funan IT Mall, 109 North Bridge Rd, boasts a choice second to none, though nearby Peninsula Plaza specializes in this field too. Haggling is the norm in electrical goods shops, and all the rules laid out on p.245 apply – as do the warnings about checking compatibility and ensuring you get an international guarantee.

The best shopping centres in Orchard Road and Chinatown are listed on p.73 and p.88, respectively

---

JEWELLERY

Singapore's glut of stores selling precious stones and gold means that **jewellery** prices remain competitive. Goldsmiths, in particular, are abundant, and their **gold** is of a consistently high quality – usually 22 or 24 carat. Prices of gold jewellery are affected, to some extent, by the craftsmanship involved, though primarily it's the weight and current market rate which dictate cost. Goldsmiths aplenty are to be found in Chinatown's People's Park Complex, and at the Pidemco Centre, 95 South Bridge Rd, where the entire first floor is a jewellery mart. Little India's Serangoon Road has a wide choice too, while in Orchard Road you'll find gold worked by international designers. Orchard Road is also the place to find high-quality **pearls**, **precious stones** and **jade**, or try Arab Street and Chinatown. Patronizing one of the array of reliable dealers listed in the STB's *Merchants of the Gold Circle* guide will ensure you get good quality, though as ever, bargaining is essential.

Chu's Jade Centre
Map 3, C9. 01-53/54 Chinatown Point, 133 New Bridge Rd. Bus #33, #54, #124 or #190.
Semiprecious stones, huge clusters of freshwater pearl necklaces, and exquisite jade sculptures.

CT Hoo
Map 5, C5. 01-22 Tanglin Shopping Centre, 19 Tanglin Rd. Bus #105, #123 or #174.
Pearl specialists up at the western end of Orchard Road.

Je T'aime
Map 5, I6. 120 Oxley Rise. Somerset MRT.
International designs in gold.

Jewel of India
Map 4, B7. 94 Serangoon Rd. Bus #65, #66, #81, #97, #103, #139 or #147.
Importers of hand-crafted gold jewellery – one of many along Serangoon Road.

Larry's
Map 5, F5. 'B' Tower, 01-17 Ngee Ann City, 391 Orchard Rd. Orchard MRT.
Hong Kong-designed gold, and precious gems – or have something tailor-made.

Richard Hung Jewellers
Map 5, E5. 01-24 Lucky Plaza, 304 Orchard Rd. Orchard MRT.
Well-regarded jewellers, based in central Orchard Road, where staff are all qualified gemologists.

JEWELLERY

Singapore Gems and Metals Co
Map 8, H4. 7 Kung Chong Rd. Redhill MTR.
Phone ahead to arrange a viewing of the cutting and polishing process in the workshop, before moving on to the well-stocked showroom.

MUSIC

CDs and tapes of all the latest mainstream and classical Western releases are universally available, as well as of a surprising number of independent ones. In addition, most music stores stock a wide library of **Canto–pop** releases, though to check out some **Indian sounds** you'll have to go to Serangoon Road, and for Malay artists you'll want to make for the Joo Chiat Complex. **Thai pop** – often very good – is available at stores in the Golden Mile Complex on Beach Road. Tapes cost around $10, and CDs around $20–25, but one or two smaller stores slash prices considerably.

Beethoven Record House
Map 5, G5. 03-41 Centrepoint, 176 Orchard Rd. Somerset MRT.
Classical sounds.

HMV Singapore
Map 5, F5. 01-11 The Heeren Shops, 260 Orchard Rd. Orchard MRT.
Global music chain, now in Singapore, and offering good deals on latest releases.

Lata Music Centre
Map 4, A7. 42 Race Course Rd. Bus #65, #66, #81, #97, #103, #139 or #147.
Large selection of Indian music on tape.

Roxy Records
Map 3, F5. 03-36 Funan the IT Mall, 109 North Bridge Rd. City Hall MRT; bus #124 or #166.
Discerning CD store with a good collection of indie albums and new releases.

MUSIC

Sing Disc Sounds

Map 3, I3. 03-29a Raffles City Shopping Centre, 252 North Bridge Rd. Raffles City MRT.

A modest selection of CDs, but at prices that are consistently a dollar or two below those in the major chains.

Supreme Record Centre

Map 5, G5. 03-28 Centrepoint, 175 Orchard Rd. Somerset MRT.

One of the widest pop music selections in Singapore, plus a selection of imports from England and the USA.

Tower Records

Map 5, D4. 4th floor, Pacific Plaza, Orchard Road. Orchard MRT.

Wide choice of music on CD only.

CLOTHES AND TEXTILES

Having a suit made up at one of the scores of **tailors** operating in Singapore, while not as cheap as in Bangkok, is still a money-saving exercise. The trick is to have a very clear idea of the style you want, and several days in hand for having alterations made. At the measuring stage, ensure the tailor knows exactly what design you want – it helps if you have a photo or catalogue clipping of the sort of suit you have in mind. A **deposit** is required at this stage, but don't be persuaded into paying the full cost until you've had as many fitting sessions as are necessary for the suit to be tailored to your satisfaction. Orchard Road's shopping centres boast the greatest numbers of tailors – try Far East Plaza, Far East Shopping Centre, Lucky Plaza or Orchard Plaza; otherwise, Peninsula Plaza has several options, or check out the pricier hotel-arcade tailors.

For something a little more ethnic, you'll find Singapore is exactly the hotbed of Asian **fabrics** you'd expect it to be. The streets of the Arab Quarter, and the markets of Geylang Serai stock the greatest choice of fabrics, including vast selections of Malaysian and Indonesian **batik.** Batik is produced by applying hot wax to a piece of cloth with either a pen or cotton stamp; when the cloth is dyed, the wax resists the dye and a pattern appears, a process that can be repeated many times to build up colours. The traditional way to wear batik is as a **sarong** – a rectangular length of cloth wrapped around the waist and legs to form a sort of skirt, worn by both males and females. The exquisite style of fabric known as **songket** is a step up in price from batik. Made by handweaving gold and silver thread into plain cloth, songket is used to make sarongs, headscarves and the like. Silk, too, is abundant: Chinese, Japanese and Thai silks are all available, or there are the primary-coloured silk **saris** of Little India's fabric stores.

As well as ethnic fabrics, Singapore is also a great place to stock up on cheap and cheerful **travelling gear** such as T-shirts and shorts. **Carpets** – both new and antique – from all over the world are competitively priced in Singapore.

Aljunied Brothers
Map 4, H8. 91 Arab St. Bus #7, #107, #130, #145 or #197. Map 5, E5. 04-75 Lucky Plaza, 304 Orchard Rd. Orchard MRT Batik lengths as well as ready-made clothes.

Amir & Sons
Map 5, E5. 03-01/7 Lucky Plaza, 304 Orchard Rd. Orchard MRT.
Fine carpets from Persia, Pakistan, Turkey and China.

Dakshaini Silks
Map 4, B6. 164 Serangoon Rd. Bus #65, #66, #81, #97, #103, #139 or #147.
Premier Indian embroidered silks.

Giordano
Map 5, G5. 3rd floor, Centrepoint, 175 Orchard Rd. Somerset MRT.
Budget fashion chain, with jeans and other clothes in bright colours.

CLOTHES AND TEXTILES

Goodwill Trading Co

Map 4, H8. 56 Arab St. Bus #7, #107, #130, #145 or #197. Indonesian batik sarongs heaped on varnished wood shelves.

Jim Thompson Silk Shop

Map 3, I2. 01-07 Raffles Hotel Arcade, 328 North Bridge Rd. City Hall MRT; bus #56 or #171. Though businessman Jim Thompson disappeared under mysterious circumstances in Malaysia's Cameron Highlands in 1967, his name is still a byword for quality silk.

Marks and Spencer

Map 5, D5. B1/B2 Wheelock Place, 501 Orchard Rd. Orchard MRT. Fashions and underwear for men and women (as well as toiletries and food).

The Orientalist

Map 5, B5. 10 Tanglin Rd. Bus #105, #123 or #174.

Imposing address at western end of Orchard Road, offering absolutely vast range of carpets from Persia, Pakistan, India and Turkey.

Sithi Vinayagar Co

Map 4, B7. 72 Serangoon Rd. Bus #65, #66, #81, #97, #103, #139 or #147. Raw Thai and embroidered silks.

S.S. Bobby Traders

Map 4, H8. 57 Arab St. Bus #7, #107, #130, #145 or #197. Indian, Chinese and Thai silks, linen and lace.

Stockmart

Map 5, H5. 02-21/22 Orchard Point, 160 Orchard Rd. Somerset MRT. Dirt-cheap jeans, dresses, shirts, T-shirts and shorts.

CLOTHES AND TEXTILES

Directory

AIRLINES The main airlines are listed below. You'll find any others in the phone directory.

Aeroflot, 01-02/02-00 Tan Chong Tower, 15 Queen St ⓣ 3361757; Air Canada Singapore, 101 Thomson Rd, #01-08 United Square ⓣ 2561198; Air India, B1-10/12 UIC Building, 5 Shenton Way ⓣ 2259411; Air Lanka, 13-01a/b, 133 Cecil St ⓣ 2257233, PIL Building, 140 Cecil St ⓣ 2236026; Air New Zealand, 24-08 Ocean Building, 10 Collyer Quay ⓣ 5358266; American Airlines, 04-02 The Promenade, 300 Orchard Rd ⓣ 8397766; British Airways, 04-02 The Promenade, 300 Orchard Rd ⓣ 8397788; Cathay Pacific, 16-01 Ocean Building, 10 Collyer Quay ⓣ 5331333; Garuda, 13-03 United Square, 101 Thomson Rd ⓣ 2505666; KLM, 12-06 Ngee Ann City Tower A, 391a Orchard Rd ⓣ 7377622; Lufthansa, 05-07 Palais Renaissance, 390 Orchard Rd ⓣ 2455600; MAS, 02-09 Singapore Shopping Centre, 190 Clemenceau Ave ⓣ 3366777; Pelangi Air, 02-09 Singapore Shopping Centre, 190 Clemenceau Ave ⓣ 3366777; Philippine Airlines, 01-10 Parklane Shopping Mall, 35 Selegie Rd ⓣ 3361611; Qantas, Unit 06-05/08 The Promenade, 300 Orchard Rd ⓣ 7309222; Royal Brunei, 01-4a/4b/5 *Royal Holiday Inn Crowne Plaza*, 25 Scotts Rd ⓣ 2354672; Royal Nepal Airlines, 03-09 Peninsula Shopping Centre, 3 Coleman St ⓣ 3395535; Silkair, see Singapore Airlines ⓣ 2212221; Singapore Airlines, Airline House, 25 Airline Rd ⓣ 5423333, also 01-01 SIA Bldg, 77 Robinson Rd ⓣ 2238888; also at *Mandarin Hotel*, 333 Orchard Rd ⓣ 2297293

and Raffles City Shopping Centre, 252 North Bridge Rd
Ⓣ 2297274; SriLankan Airlines, 13-01a/b Keck Seng Tower, 133
Cecil St Ⓣ 2236026; Thai Airways, 02-00 The Globe, 100 Cecil St
Ⓣ 2249977; United Airlines, 44-02 Hong Leong Building, 16 Raffles
Quay Ⓣ 8733525.

AIRPORT ENQUIRIES The toll-free Changi airport flight information
number is Ⓣ 1-800/5424422.

AMERICAN EXPRESS Travel services at 18-01 The Concourse,
300 Beach Rd Ⓣ 2998133 and 01-04/05 Winsland House, 3 Killiney
Rd Ⓣ 2355788.

BANKS AND EXCHANGE All Singapore's banks change travellers'
cheques, with the UOB and Posbank charging the lowest
commission. Normal banking hours are Mon–Fri 10am–3pm & Sat
11am–1pm. Licensed moneychangers also abound – particularly in
Arab Street and the Orchard Road shopping centres – and offer
more favourable rates.

BRITISH COUNCIL Napier Road, west of Orchard Road
Ⓣ 4731111.

CAR RENTAL Avis, *Boulevard Hotel*, 200 Orchard Blvd Ⓣ 7371668;
Changi airport Terminal 1 Ⓣ 5432331 and Terminal 2 Ⓣ 5428855;
Hertz, 01-20 Tanglin Shopping Centre, 19 Tanglin Rd Ⓣ 7344646;
Sintat, Terminals 1 & 2, Changi airport Ⓣ 5459086 or 5427288.

CHILDREN Theme parks and attractions offer significant
reductions in admission prices for children, often more than fifty
percent. Restaurants are generally welcoming of families, and
hotels can make special provision for children (see p.144). Nappies
and other baby supplies are widely available from pharmacies and
there's a branch of Mothercare at 01-34/39 Centrepoint, 176
Orchard Rd.

CREDIT CARD HELPLINES American Express Ⓣ 2998133; Diners
Club Ⓣ 2944222; Mastercard and Visa Ⓣ 1-800/3451345.

DENTISTS Listed in the *Singapore Buying Guide* (equivalent to the Yellow Pages) under "Dental Surgeons" and "Dentist Emergency Service".

DEPARTURE TAX A $15 tax is levied on all flights out of Singapore.

DISABLED TRAVELLERS *Access Singapore,* an informative booklet published by the National Council of Social Service, details hotels, banks, shopping centres and hospitals with facilities for the disabled. For a copy of the booklet write to the council at 11 Penang Lane or call ℡ 3361544. Singapore is an accessible city for travellers with disabilities as hefty tax incentives are provided for developers who include access features for the disabled in new buildings. However, life is made a lot easier if you can afford to pay for more upmarket hotels. Getting around the city can be a problem: buses are not accessible to wheelchairs and there are no lifts in the MRT system. However, two taxi companies, TIBS and City Cab (see p.48 for details), have several cabs big enough to take a wheelchair. There are acoustic signals at most street crossings.

DOCTORS There is no free outpatient service for tourists in Singapore. If you need treatment, try Rochor OPD, Prinsep Street ℡ 3362425, or Maxwell Road OPD, 03-00, 4 Kadayanallur St ℡ 2216611. That said, you'll find clinics in most shopping centres – there are scores in both the Tanglin Shopping Centre and the Specialists Shopping Centre.

DRUGS It's very unwise to have anything to do with drugs of any description in Singapore. The penalties for trafficking drugs in or out of the country are severe in the extreme – foreigners have been executed in the past – and if you are arrested for drugs offences you can expect no mercy and little help from your consular representatives.

ELECTRICITY Singapore's mains electricity is 220–240 volts, 50 Hertz.

DENTISTS—ELECTRICITY

EMAIL AND INTERNET ACCESS Singapore boasts numerous cafés offering email and Internet access, typically costing $5 an hour, $3 for a half-hour, among them: *Cyberarena*, 39 Cuppage Terrace ⊤7381540 (Map 5, D5; daily 10am–11.30pm); *Cyberia* 02-28 Far East Shopping Centre, 45 Orchard Rd ⊤7321309 (Map 5, D5; daily 11am–11pm); *e-den,* 02-08 Wheelock Place ⊤8870178 (Map 5, D5; daily noon–midnight); *PICity@Capitol*, 01-19 Capitol Bldg, 11 Stamford Rd ⊤3389289 (Map 3, H3; daily 10am–10pm); *Travel Café,* 50 Prinsep St ⊤3389001 (Map 4, C12; Mon–Thurs & Sun 11am–11pm, Fri & Sat 11am–2am).

EMBASSIES AND CONSULATES
Australia ⊤8384100; Brunei ⊤7339055; Canada ⊤3253200; France ⊤4664866; Germany ⊤7371355; India ⊤7376777; Indonesia ⊤7377422; Ireland ⊤2768935; Malaysia ⊤2350111; New Zealand ⊤2359966; Philippines ⊤7373977; Sri Lanka ⊤2544595; Thailand ⊤7372644; UK ⊤4739333; USA ⊤4789100; Vietnam ⊤4625938.

EMERGENCIES Police ⊤999; Ambulance and Fire Brigade ⊤995 (all toll-free); larger hotels have doctors on call at all times.

GAY SINGAPORE Homosexuality is illegal and convictions carry sentences of between ten years and life imprisonment. There is a small underground scene but don't expect to find venues advertised.

GOLF Singapore has a number of golf courses, several of them truly world-class. All the clubs listed here allow non-members to play upon payment of a green fee, though all will be bulging with members at the weekend. Green fees average out at around $75, but you'll pay far more than this at the island's poshest country clubs. At the Parkland Golf Driving Range, 920 East Coast Parkway ⊤3451111, one hundred balls costs $5 on weekdays before 3.30pm, and $6 after 3.30pm and at the weekend. Changi Golf Club, 20 Netheravan Rd ⊤5455133 (Map 7, H1); Jurong Country Club, 9 Science Centre Rd ⊤5685188 (Map 8, C4);

Keppel Club, Bukit Chermin Road ☎ 2735522 (Map 8 H6); Raffles Country Club, 450 Jalan Ahmad Ibrahim ☎ 8617655 (Map 1, B5); Seletar Country Club, 3 101 Seletar Club Rd ☎ 4814745 (Map 6, G4); Sentosa Golf Club, 27 Bukit Manis Road, Sentosa Island ☎ 2750022 (see map p.132).

HOSPITALS Singapore General, Outram Road ☎ 2223322, Alexandra Hospital, Alexandra Road ☎ 4735222, and National University Hospital, Kent Ridge ☎ 7795555 are all state hospitals and all have outpatient departments.

IMMIGRATION DEPARTMENT For visa extension enquiries, contact the Singapore Immigration and Registration Department, 10 Kallang Rd (Mon–Fri 9am–5pm; ☎ 3916100).

LAUNDRY Washington Dry Cleaning, 02-22 Cuppage Plaza, 5 Koek Rd (Mon–Sat 9am–7.45pm); Washy Washy, 01-18 Cuppage Plaza, 5 Koek Rd (Mon–Sat 10am–7pm).

LEFT LUGGAGE A 24-hr luggage storage service is available in the arrival and departure halls of both terminals at Changi airport. Charges are $3 for the first 24hr; $4 per day for subsequent days. Oversized or awkwardly shaped baggage is charged at a higher rate.

LIBRARY Singapore National Library for books and information on Singapore is beside the National Museum on Stamford Road (Mon 11am–8pm, Tues–Fri 9am–8pm, Sat 9am–5pm, Sun 1–5pm).

NEWSPAPERS As well as dailies in Chinese, Malay and Tamil, Singapore has two morning English-language newspapers, the *Straits Times*, a decent broadsheet, with good coverage of international events, and the *Business Times*, dealing mainly with commercial and financial news. In addition, an amusingly tame tabloid, the *New Paper*, hits the streets every afternoon, although there's little of real interest in it for non-Singaporeans. All three are owned by Singapore Press Holdings which is careful to steer well clear of any criticism of the government.

GOLF–NEWSPAPERS

OFFENCES Singapore is known locally as fine city. There's a fine of $500 for smoking in public places such as cinemas, trains, lifts, air-conditioned restaurants and shopping malls, and one of $50 for "jaywalking" – crossing a main road within 50m of a pedestrian crossing or bridge. Littering carries a $1000 fine, with offenders now issued Corrective Work Orders and forced to do litter-picking duty; eating and drinking on the MRT could cost you $500. Other fines include those for urinating in lifts (legend has it that some lifts are fitted with urine detectors), not flushing a public toilet and chewing gum (which is outlawed in Singapore).

PHARMACIES Guardian pharmacy has over forty outlets, including ones at Centrepoint, 176 Orchard Rd; Raffles City Shopping Centre, 252 North Bridge Rd; and Clifford Centre, 24 Raffles Place. Usual hours are 9am–6pm, but some stay open until 10pm.

POLICE Tanglin Police Station, 17 Napier Rd, off Orchard Road ☎ 7330000; come here to report stolen property. In an emergency, dial ☎ 999.

POST OFFICES The GPO (Mon–Fri 8am–6pm, Sat 8am–2pm) is beside Paya Lebar MRT; all poste restante is held here (take your passport with you, and be sure to have the staff check under first names as well as family names, as misfiling is common). There are countless other post offices across the state, with usual hours of Monday to Friday 8.30am–5pm and Saturday 8.30am–1pm, though postal services are available until 9pm at the Comcentre on Killiney Road.

SAMARITANS ☎ 1-800/2214444.

SWIMMING All hotels of a certain size in Singapore have swimming pools, but if you're in budget accommodation, you'll have to opt either for the beach or for a public pool. The island's longest stretch of beach lies along the East Coast Park, but you'll find the waters off Sentosa's sands much cleaner. Singapore's twenty or so public pools are listed in the *Yellow Pages*. The most central of these is

OFFENCES—SWIMMING

the River Valley Swimming Complex opposite the *New Otani Hotel* on River Valley Road, though the Katong Swimming Complex on Wilkinson Road, and Buona Vista Swimming Complex on Holland Drive, are better. For something more adventurous, try Sentosa's Fantasy Island (p.136).

TELEPHONES Local calls from private phones in Singapore cost next to nothing; calls from public phones cost 10c for three minutes, with the exception of Changi airport's free courtesy phones. Note that many businesses in the city have mobile phone numbers – usually prefixed 9 – and these are expensive to call. Singapore has no area codes – the only time you'll punch more than seven digits for a local number is if you're dialling a toll-free (T 1-800) number or a pager. Card phones are taking over from payphones in Singapore: cards are available from the Comcentre on Killiney Road, and post offices, as well as 7-Elevens, stationers and bookshops and come in denominations rising from $2. International calls can be made from all public cardphones. Otherwise, use a credit-card phone. IDD calls made from hotel rooms in Singapore carry no surcharge. Calling abroad from Singapore dial 00 plus the country code plus the area code minus the initial zero. Useful country codes include: UK 44, USA and Canada 1, Australia 61, New Zealand 64. For directory enquiries, call T 100 and for IDD information call T 100 or T 1607, or T 104 for international enquiries.

THOMAS COOK Travel services at 01-02a Singapore Land Tower, 50 Raffles Place (Mon–Fri 9am–5pm, Sat 9am–1pm; T 5350111).

TIME Singapore is eight hours ahead of GMT, sixteen hours ahead of US Pacific Standard Time, thirteen hours ahead of Eastern Standard Time, and two hours behind Sydney.

TIPPING Tipping is not customary in Singapore. Restaurants, however, automatically add a service charge and government tax (around fifteen percent) to bills.

SWIMMING–TIPPING

TOUR OPERATORS

All the following arrange sightseeing tours of Singapore (see p.50 for details).

Gray Line of Singapore ☎ 3318203; Holiday Tours ☎ 7382622; RMG Tours ☎ 2201661; SAFE and Mansfield Travel Group Pte Ltd (helicopter tours) ☎ 2280962; SH Tours ☎ 7349923; Singapore Sightseeing ☎ 3323755.

TRAVEL AGENTS All the following are good for discounted air fares and buying bus tickets to Malaysia and Thailand: Airpower Travel, 131a Bencoolen St ☎ 3346571; Eastern & Oriental Express ☎ 3923500; Harharah Travel, 1st floor, 171a Bencoolen St ☎ 3372633; STA Travel, Cuppage Terrace ☎ 7377188.

VACCINATIONS Vaccinations can be arranged through the Government Vaccination Centre, Institute of Health, 226 Outram Rd ☎ 3572222.

WOMEN'S HELPLINE Women's helpline AWARE ☎ 1-800/7745935.

CONTEXTS

CONTEXTS

A brief history of Singapore

W hat little is known of Singapore's **ancient history** relies heavily upon legend and supposition. Third-century Chinese sailors could have been referring to Singapore in their account of a place called Pu-Luo-Chung, or "island at the end of a peninsula". In the late thirteenth century, **Marco Polo** reported seeing a place called Chiamassie, which could also have been Singapore: by then the island was known locally as Temasek – "sea town" – and was a minor trading outpost of the Sumatran Srivijaya empire. The island's present name comes from the Sanskrit *Singapura*, meaning "Lion City", and was first recorded in the sixteenth century. A legend narrated in the Malay annals (the *Sejarah Melayu*) told how a Sumatran prince saw a lion while sheltering on the island from a storm; the annals reported that the name had been in common use since the end of the fourteenth century.

Throughout the fourteenth century, Singapura felt the squeeze as the Ayuthaya and Majapahit empires of Thailand and Java struggled for control of the Malay peninsula. Around 1390, a Sumatran prince called **Paramesvara** threw off his allegiance to the Javanese Majapahit Empire and fled from Palembang to present-day Singapore. There, he murdered his host and ruled the island until a Javanese offensive forced him to flee north, up the peninsula, where he and his son, **Iskandar Shah,** subsequently founded the Melaka sultanate. A grave on Fort Canning Hill (see p.65) is said to be that of Iskandar Shah, though its authenticity is doubtful. With the rise of the Melaka sultanate, Singapore devolved into an inconsequential fishing settlement; a century or so later, the arrival of the Portuguese in Melaka forced Malay leaders to flee southwards to modern-day Johor Bahru for sanctuary, and a Portuguese account, in 1613, of the razing of an unnamed Malay outpost at the mouth of Sungei Johor marked the beginning of two centuries of historical limbo for Singapore.

Sir Stamford Raffles and the founding of Singapore

By the late eighteenth century, with China opening up for trade with the West, the **British East India Company** felt the need to establish outposts along the Straits of Melaka to protect its interests. Penang was secured in 1786, but with the Dutch expanding their rule in the East Indies (Indonesia), a port was needed further south. Enter visionary colonial administrator **Thomas Stamford Raffles** (see p.280 for full biography). In 1818, the governor-general of India authorized Raffles, then lieutenant-governor of Bencoolen (in Sumatra), to establish a British colony at the southern tip of the Malay Peninsula; early the next year, he stepped ashore on the northern bank of the Singapore River, accompanied by Colonel William Farquhar, who was a former Resident of Melaka and was fluent in Malay.

At the time, inhospitable swampland and tiger-infested jungle covered Singapore, and its population is generally thought to have numbered around 150, although some historians suggest it could have been as high as a thousand. Raffles recognized the island's potential as a deep-water harbour, and immediately struck a treaty with **Abdul Rahman**, *temenggong* (chieftain) of Singapore, establishing a British trading station there. The Dutch were furious at this British invasion of what they considered was their territory, but Raffles – who still needed the approval of the sultan of Riau-Johor for his outpost, as Abdul Rahman was only an underling – disregarded Dutch sensibilities. Realizing that the sultan's loyalties to the Dutch would make such approval impossible, Raffles approached the sultan's brother, Hussein, recognizing him as the true sultan, and concluded a second treaty with both the *temenggong* and His Highness the **sultan Hussein Mohammed Shah**. The Union Jack was raised, and Singapore's future as a free trading post was set.

Strategically positioned at the foot of the Straits of Melaka, and with no customs duties levied on imported or exported goods, Singapore's expansion was meteoric. The population had reached ten thousand by the time of the first census in 1824, with Malays, Chinese, Indians and Europeans arriving in search of work as coolies and merchants. In 1822, Raffles set about drawing up the demarcation lines that divide present-day Singapore. The area south of the Singapore River was earmarked for the Chinese; a swamp at the mouth of the river was filled and the commercial district established there, while Muslims were settled around the Sultan's Palace in today's Arab Quarter. The Singapore of those times was a far cry from the pristine city of the late twentieth century. "There were thousands of rats all over the district" wrote Abdullah bin Kadir, scribe to Stamford Raffles, "some almost as large as cats. They were so big that they used to attack us if we went out walking at night and many people were knocked over."

SIR STAMFORD RAFFLES AND THE FOUNDING OF SINGAPORE

The early boom years

In 1824, Sultan Hussein and the *temenggong* were bought out, and Singapore ceded outright to the British. Three years later, the fledgling state united with Penang and Melaka (by now under British rule) to form the Straits Settlements, which became a British crown colony in 1867. For forty years the laissez-faire economy boomed, though life was chaotic and disease was rife. More and more immigrants poured onto the island and by 1860 the population had reached eighty thousand, with each arriving ethnic community bringing its attendant cuisines, languages and architecture. **Arabs, Indians, Javanese** and **Bugis** (from Sulawesi) all came, but most populous of all were the **Chinese**, who arrived in numbers from the southern provinces of China and settled quickly, helped by the clan societies (*kongsis*) already establishing footholds on the island. The British, for their part, erected impressive Neoclassical theatres, courts and assembly halls, and in 1887 Singapore's most quintessentially British establishment – the **Raffles Hotel** – opened for business.

By the end of the nineteenth century, the opening of the Suez Canal and the advent of steamships had consolidated Singapore's position at the hub of international trade in the region, with the port becoming a major staging post on the Europe–East Asia route. In 1877, **Henry Ridley** began his one-man crusade to introduce the rubber plant into Southeast Asia, a move which further bolstered Singapore's importance: the island soon became the world centre of rubber exporting. This status was further enhanced by the slow but steady drawing of the Malay Peninsula under British control – a process begun with the Treaty of Pangkor in 1874 and completed in 1914 – which meant that Singapore gained further still from the mainland's tin-

and rubber-based economy. Between 1873 and 1913, trade increased eightfold, a trend which continued well into the twentieth century.

Singapore's Asian communities found their political voice in the 1920s: in 1926, the **Singapore Malay Union** was established, and four years later, the Chinese-supported **Malayan Communist Party (MCP)** appeared. But pro-independence activity had still not achieved its goal when the spectre of war reared its head in 1942.

The Japanese invasion and years of occupation

In 1942, the bubble burst. In December 1941, the Japanese had bombed Pearl Harbor and invaded the Malay Peninsula. Less than two months later they were at the top of the causeway, safe from the guns of "Fortress Singapore", which pointed south from what is now Sentosa Island. The inhabitants of Singapore had not been prepared for an attack from this direction and on February 15, 1942, the fall of Singapore (which the Japanese then renamed Syonan, or "Light of the South") was complete.

Three and a half years of brutal Japanese rule ensued, during which thousands of civilians were executed in vicious anti-Chinese purges and Europeans were either herded into **Changi Prison**, or marched up the peninsula to work on Thailand's infamous "Death Railway". Less well known is the vicious campaign, known as **Operation Sook Ching**, mounted by the military police force, or *Kempeitai*, during which upwards of twenty-five thousand Chinese males between eighteen and fifty years of age were shot dead at Punggol and Changi beaches as enemies of the Japanese.

THE BATTLE FOR SINGAPORE

The possibility of Singapore having no landward defences no more entered my mind than that of a battleship being launched without a bottom.

Sir Winston Churchill.

The hills and jungles of northern and western Singapore were the setting of the battle for "the strongest British bastion east of Suez". Popular wisdom had it that a Japanese attack could come only from the sea: the view of one British intelligence officer, that "the Japanese are very small and short-sighted and thus totally unsuited physically to tropical warfare", embodied the complacency and self-delusion of the Allied Command under **Lieutenant-General Arthur Percival.**

Events were to prove the British wrong. On December 8, 1941, Japanese forces led by **General Tomoyuki Yamashita** – the "Tiger of Malaya" – landed on Malaya's northeastern coast at Kota Bharu. By the end of January they had reached Johor Bahru, a kilometre away from Singapore. Judging that the Japanese attack would focus on the northeast coast of Singapore, Percival deployed what few defences were at his disposal there, leaving the scant Australian presence guarding the northwest stretched to breaking point.

From his command room in JB's istana, Yamashita oversaw a week's bombing of Singapore. Then, on February 7, 1942, the **invasion** began, with Japanese Imperial Guards mounting an attack on Pulau Ubin, northeast of Singapore. On the following day, Yamashita ordered intensive bombing of the coastline west

The postwar years

In 1945, Singapore passed back into British hands, but things were never to be the same. Singaporeans now wanted a say in the governing of their island. A year later, the Straits Settlements were dissolved, and Singapore became a

of the causeway. Having softened up their point of invasion, the Japanese used collapsible launches and the cover of darkness to attack the area west of what is now Sungei Buloh Reserve. Allied troops quickly withdrew in disarray, and by the following morning the Japanese had probed eight kilometres inland. After another landing a day later, this time at the mouth of the Kranji River, the Imperial Army began its two-pronged offensive.

Tengah Airfield (then 5km north of Jurong Lake) fell on February 9, and the following day saw Yamashita take his first steps on Singaporean soil and **establish command** near the airfield, as his troops pushed towards MacRitchie and Peirce reservoirs, the city's only sources of water.

Between February 11 and 14, **decisive victories** were won by the Japanese at Bukit Timah Hill and a few hundred metres from today's Haw Par Villas at Pasir Panjang Village, where a brigade of Malays made a heroic 48-hour stand before being all but wiped out. By February 14, Singapore was as good as lost – a fact that made the massacre of two hundred patients and staff at the Alexandra Hospital (northwest of Mount Faber) all the more appalling. Faced with further loss of life – and unaware to what extent Japanese supplies were stretched – Percival travelled up Dunearn Road to the Ford Motor Factory at Bukit Timah Village, where Yamashita was now based, and **surrendered** on Sunday, February 15. Winston Churchill called the British surrender "the worst disaster and the largest capitulation in British history"; it later transpired that the Japanese forces had been outnumbered and their supplies hopelessly stretched immediately prior to the surrender.

crown colony in its own right. Island politics, though, remained closely linked with those of the Peninsula for the next nineteen years.

Across the causeway, Malay nationalists set up the **United Malays National Organization (UNMO)** in 1946,

THE POSTWAR YEARS

whose main tenet was that Malays should retain special privileges over Chinese and Indians in Malaya. The pressure they brought to bear on the British government resulted, in February 1948, in the establishment of the Federation of Malaya, which brought together all the states of Peninsular Malaya, but not Singapore, whose inclusion would have led to ethnic Malays being in a minority. Protests erupted in Singapore at this exclusion, with the **Malayan Democratic Union (MDU)** calling for integration with Malaya – a position that commanded little support among the Chinese population. Singapore's first ever elections, a month later, were boycotted by the MDU.

Chinese opposition to the Federation of Malaya on the mainland ignited the **Communist Emergency**, an MCP-led guerrilla struggle lasting from 1948 until 1960, whose aim was to turn Singapore and Malaysia into a republic; in Singapore, the MCP was outlawed, and a state of emergency declared.

In the 1950s Singapore's progress towards independence slowly gathered momentum. In 1953 the British government appointed a commission to review the island's constitution, and though still flawed (only 25 of a legislative assembly of 32 were voted in), the elections of April 1955 were the most representative seen so far on the island. **David Marshall**, leader of the victorious **Labour Front**, became chief minister.

By 1957, the Federation of Malaya had achieved independence, and that same year, the British government agreed to the establishment of an elected, 51-member legislative assembly in Singapore. Full internal self-government was achieved in May 1959, when the **People's Action Party (PAP)**, led by Cambridge law graduate **Lee Kuan Yew**, won 43 of the 51 seats. Lee became Singapore's first prime minister, and quickly looked for the security of a merger with neighbouring Malaya. For its part – and despite reservations about aligning with Singapore's pre-dominantly Chinese population – anti-Communist Malaya feared that extremists within the PAP would turn Singapore into a Communist base, and accordingly preferred to have the state under its wing.

In 1963, Singapore combined with Malaya, Sarawak and British North Borneo (modern day Sabah), to form the **Federation of Malaysia**. The alliance, though, was an uneasy one. Differences soon developed between Lee Kuan Yew and the mainland's Malay-dominated **Alliance Party** over the lack of egalitarian policies. Although the PAP had dominated recent elections, many Chinese were concerned that Malays exercised too great a control over the federa-tion. Tensions rose on the island and ugly racial incidents developed into full-scale riots, in which several people were killed. Within two years Singapore was asked to leave the federation, in the face of outrage in Kuala Lumpur at the PAP's attempts to break into Peninsular politics in 1964.

Hours after announcing Singapore's full independence, on August 9, 1965, a tearful Lee Kuan Yew described the event, on national TV, as "a moment of anguish". One hundred and forty-six years after Sir Stamford Raffles had set Singapore on the world map, the tiny island, with no natural resources of its own, faced the prospect of being consigned to history's bottom drawer of crumbling colonial ports.

Independence

Against all the odds, Lee's personal vision and drive trans-formed Singapore into an Asian economic heavyweight. Political alignments were made to maximize business oppor-tunities, and the economy grew fast: per capita income increased an astonishing fourfold between 1965 and 1977, with huge profits being made in financial services, hi-tech

INDEPENDENCE

manufacture, information technology and the petroleum industry. The high taxes these boom areas produced were used to bolster the island's infrastructure and housing, and by 1980, the impossible had been achieved: Singapore stood on the verge of becoming a **Newly Industrialized Economy (NIE)**, along with Hong Kong, Taiwan and South Korea.

But these developments were achieved at a price. Heavy-handed **censorship of the media** was introduced, and offences such as dropping litter were punished in a draconian style with offenders submitted to the public humiliation of forced litter duty. Most disturbing of all was the government's attitude towards political opposition. When the opposition **Worker's Party** won a by-election in 1981, the candidate, J.B. Jeyaretnam, found himself charged with several criminal offences, and chased through the Singaporean law courts for the next decade. The archaic **Internal Security Act** still grants the power to detain without trial anyone the government deems a threat to the nation, which kept political prisoner **Chia Thye Poh** under lock and key from 1966 until 1998 for allegedly advocating violence. Population policies, too, have brought criticism from abroad. These began in the early 1970s, with a **birth control campaign** which proved so successful that it had to be reversed: the 1980s saw the introduction of the "Go For Three" project, which offered tax incentives for those having more than two children in an attempt to boost the national – and some say, more specifically the Chinese Singaporean – birth rate. Lee Kuan Yew also made clear his conviction that Singapore's educated elite should intermarry, thereby breeding the sort of babies that would serve the country well in the future.

At times, Singapore tries so hard to reshape itself that it falls into self-parody. "We have to pursue this subject of fun very seriously if we want to stay competitive in the twenty-first century", was the reaction of government minister, George Yeo, when challenged on the fact that some foreigners found Singapore dull. Whether Singaporeans will continue to suffer their government's foibles remains to be seen. Adults beyond a certain age remember how things were before independence, and, more importantly, before the existence of the MRT system, housing projects and savings schemes. Their children and grandchildren have no such perspective, however, and telltale signs – presently nothing more extreme than feet up on MRT seats, or jaywalking – suggest that the government can expect more dissent in future years. Already a substantial brain drain is afflicting the country, as Singaporeans with skills to offer choose to move abroad in the pursuit of a more liberal environment.

Singapore today

The man charged with leading Singapore into the new millennium is **Goh Chok Tong**, who became prime minister upon Lee's retirement from that post in 1990. Goh has made it clear that he favours a more open form of government, though whether he will be able to break the mould set by Lee – who still looms over the political scene in his role as senior minister, and whose son, **Brigadier-General Lee Hsien Loong**, is deputy prime minister – remains open to question.

Recent events do suggest that Goh has a mandate for change. In the 1991 elections he suffered the relative setback of seeing an unprecedented four opposition members voted into parliament. However, in the elections of January 1997 (which the PAP had won even before the polling stations opened as opposition candidates contested fewer than half of the seats), he clawed back two of these seats, partly thanks to insinuations that constituencies failing to return their PAP candidate would drop down the waiting list for housing estate renovations. Singapore's next general elections are due by mid-2002.

SINGAPORE TODAY

Sir Stamford Raffles

Let it still be the boast of Britain
to write her name in characters of light;
let her not be remembered as the tempest
whose course was desolation,
but as the gale of spring reviving
the slumbering seeds of mind and
calling them to life
from the winter of ignorance and oppression.
If the time shall come
when her empire shall have passed away,
these monuments will endure when her triumphs
shall have become an empty name.

his verse, written by **Sir Stamford Raffles** himself,
speaks volumes about the man whom history
remembers as the founder of modern Singapore.
Despite living and working in a period of imperial arro-
gance and self-motivated land-grabbing, Raffles maintained
an unfailing concern for the welfare of the people under his

governorship, and a conviction that British colonial expansion was for the general good. He believed Britain to be, as Jan Morris says in her introduction to Maurice Collis's biography Raffles, "the chief agent of human progress . . . the example of fair Government".

Fittingly for a man who was to spend his life roaming the globe, Thomas Stamford Raffles was born at sea on July 6, 1781 on the *Ann*, whose master was his father Captain Benjamin Raffles. By his fourteenth birthday, the young Raffles was working as a clerk for the **East India Company** in London, his schooling curtailed because of his father's debts. Even at this early age, Raffles' ambition and self-motivation was evident as, faced with a lifetime as a clerk, he resolved to educate himself, staying up through the night to study and developing a hunger for knowledge which would later spur him to learn Malay, amass a vast treasure-trove of natural history artefacts and write his two-volume *History of Java*.

Abdullah bin Kadir, Raffles' clerk while in Southeast Asia, describes him in his autobiography, *The Hikayat Abdullah*: "He was broad of brow, a sign of his care and thoroughness; round-headed with a projecting forehead, showing his intelligence. He had light brown hair, indicative of bravery; large ears, the mark of a ready listener . . . He was solicitous of the feelings of others, and open-handed with the poor. He spoke in smiles. He took the most active interest in historical research. Whatever he found to do he adopted no half-measures, but saw it through to the finish."

Raffles' diligence and hard work showed through in 1805, when he was chosen to join a team going out to Penang, then being developed as a British entrepôt; overnight, his annual salary leapt from £70 to £1500. Once in Southeast Asia, Raffles' rise was meteoric. By 1807 he was named **chief secretary to the governor in Penang** and soon

Lord Minto, the governor-general of the East India Company in India, was alerted to his Oriental expertise. Meeting Minto on a trip to Calcutta in 1810, Raffles was appointed **secretary to the governor-general in Malaya**, a promotion quickly followed by the **governorship of Java** in 1811. Raffles' rule of Java was wise, libertarian and compassionate, his economic, judicial and social reforms transforming an island bowed by Dutch rule.

Post-Waterloo European rebuilding saw the East Indies returned to the Dutch in 1816 – to the chagrin of Raffles, who foresaw problems for British trade should the Dutch regain their hold on the area. From Java, Raffles transferred to the **governorship of Bencoolen**, on the southern coast of Sumatra, but not before he had returned home for a break, stopping at St Helena en route to meet Napoleon ("a monster"). While in England he met his second wife, Sophia Hull (his first, Olivia, had died in 1814), and was knighted.

Raffles and Sophia sailed to Bencoolen in early 1818, Sophia reporting that her husband spent the four-month journey deep in study. Once in Sumatra, Raffles found the time to study the region's flora and fauna as tirelessly as ever, discovering the **rafflesia arnoldii** – "perhaps the largest and most magnificent flower in the world" – on a jungle field trip. By now, Raffles felt strongly that Britain should establish a base in the Straits of Melaka. Meeting Hastings (Minto's successor) in late 1818, he was given leave to pursue this possibility and in 1819 duly sailed to the southern tip of the Malay Peninsula, where his securing of **Singapore** early that year was a daring masterstroke of diplomacy.

For a man whose name is inextricably linked with Singapore, Raffles spent a remarkably short time on the island. His first stay was for one week, and the second for three weeks, during which time he helped delineate the new settlement (see p.270): "Looking a century or two ahead so as to provide for what Singapore may one day become," as Raffles himself later put it. Subsequent sojourns in Bencoolen ended tragically with the loss of four of his five children to tropical illnesses, while his own health also began to deteriorate. Raffles visited Singapore one last time in late 1822; his final public duty there was to lay the foundation stone of the Singapore Institution (later the **Raffles Institution**), an establishment created to educate local Malays, albeit upper-class ones. From Singapore, Raffles and Sophia travelled back to Bencoolen to pick up their personal effects, and from there journeyed home to Europe. The *Fame*, on which they set sail on February 2, 1824, caught fire 80km out to sea, claiming no lives but destroying Raffles' vast collection of natural history specimens and notes.

By August 1824, Raffles was back in England. Awaiting news of a possible pension award from the East India Company, he spent his free time founding the London Zoo and setting up a farm in Hendon. But the new life Raffles had planned for Sophia and himself never materialized. Days after hearing that a Calcutta bank holding £16,000 of his capital had folded, his pension application was refused; worse still, the Company was demanding £22,000 for over-payment. Three months later, the brain tumour that had caused Raffles headaches for several years took his life on July 4, 1826. Buried at Hendon, he was honoured by no memorial stone – the vicar had investments in slave plantations in the West Indies and was unimpressed by his friendship with William Wilberforce. Only in 1832 was Raffles commemorated, with a statue in Westminster Abbey.

Religion

otal **freedom of worship** is enjoyed in Singapore, whose multicultural society is reflected in the wide range of creeds that it supports. Over half of the population of 3.87 million follow Chinese religions – mostly Buddhism, but with elements of Taoism and Confucianism. Malays, who make up fourteen percent of the population, are predominantly Muslim, while the nation's Indians are either Hindu, Muslim or Sikh. In addition, one in ten Singaporeans are Christians: most are Protestants, though all denominations are represented, and there's a large enough Jewish community to support two synagogues.

Below are overviews of the three main strands of belief in Singapore today: Chinese religions, Islam and Hinduism.

Chinese religions

Singaporean Chinese are mainly either **Buddhist, Taoist** or **Confucianist**, although in practice they are often a mixture of all three. These different strands of Chinese religion ostensibly lean in very different directions, but in practice the combination of the three comprises a system of belief which is first and foremost pragmatic. The Chinese use religion to ease their passage through life, whether in the spheres of work or family, while temples double as social centres, where people meet and exchange views.

Buddhism

Buddhism states that the suffering of the world can only be achieved by attaining a state of personal enlightenment, or nirvana, through meditation. The founder of Buddhism, **Siddhartha Gautama**, was born a prince in Lumbini in present-day Nepal, around 500 BC. Shielded from knowledge of suffering and death for the first decades of his life, he subsequently renounced his pampered life and spent years in meditation, before finding enlightenment under a bodhi tree. At this point he became the Buddha or "Awakened One". (In Singapore and Southeast Asia he is called *Sakyamuni*, or "Holy Man of the Sakya tribe".) In his first sermon, Buddha taught the four noble truths: that suffering exists; that its source should be recognized; that one should strive for a cessation of suffering; and that this can be achieved by following the **Eightfold Path** – practising right views, intentions, speech, action, livelihood, effort, mindfulness and concentration. The Buddhist faith is split into two schisms: **Hinayana** (Lesser Vehicle) Buddhism, which teaches individuals how to attain enlightenment for themselves, and **Mahayana** (Greater Vehicle) Buddhism – favoured in Singapore – which teaches that, having reached enlightenment, followers should help others to do the same.

Taoism

Unity with nature is the chief tenet of Taoism, a philosophical movement dating from the sixth century BC, and propounded by the Chinese scholar **Lao Tze**. Taoism advocates that people follow a central path or truth, known as *Tao* or "The Way", and cultivate an understanding of the nature of things. This search for truth has often expressed itself in Taoism by way of superstition on the part of its

CHINESE RELIGIONS

devotees, who engage in fortune-telling and the like. The Taoist gods are mainly legendary figures – warriors, statesmen, scholars – with specific powers that can generally be determined by their form; others represent incarnations of the forces of nature.

Confucianism

Confucianism began as a philosophy based on piety, loyalty, humanitarianism and familial devotion. In the 2500 years since **Confucius**, its founder, died, it has transmuted into a set of principles that permeate every aspect of Chinese life. A blueprint for social and moral harmony, the Confucian ideology stresses one's obligation to family, community and the state, hinging on the individual's need to recognize his or her position in the social hierarchy and act accordingly – son must obey father, student must obey teacher, subject must obey ruler. Little wonder that Lee Kuan Yew has long advocated Confucian values in Singapore.

Chinese temples

The rules of **geomancy**, or **feng shui** (wind and water), are rigorously applied to the construction of **Chinese temples**, so that the buildings are placed to render them free from evil influences. Visitors wishing to cross the threshold of a temple have to step over a kerb that's intended to trip up evil spirits, and walk through doors painted with fearsome door gods; fronting the doors are two stone lions, providing yet another defence. Larger temples typically consist of a front entrance hall opening onto a walled-in courtyard, beyond which is the hall of worship, where joss (luck) sticks are burned below images of the deities. The most important and striking element of a Chinese temple is its roof. They are grand, multi-tiered affairs, with low, overhanging eaves, the ridges alive with auspicious creatures such as dragons and phoenixes and, less often, with miniature scenes from traditional Chinese life and legend. Temples are also normally constructed around a framework of huge, lacquered timber beams, adorned with intricately carved warriors, animals and flowers. More figures are moulded onto outer walls, which are dotted with octagonal, hexagonal or round grille-worked windows. *Feng shui* comes into play again inside the temple, with auspicious room numbers and sizes, colour and sequence of construction. Elsewhere in the temple grounds, you'll see sizeable ovens stuffed constantly with slowly burning fake money, prayer books and other offerings. Pagodas – tall, thin towers thought to keep out evil spirits – are common too.

Chinese temples play an important part in Chinese community life, and some hold occasional musical and theatrical performances, which can be enjoyed by visitors as well as locals. Temples are open from early morning to early evening and devotees go in when they like, to make offerings or to pray; there are no set prayer times. Visitors are welcome and larger temples have janitors who will show you round, although few speak good English.

Islam

Islam ("submission to God") was founded in Mecca in present-day Saudi Arabia by **Muhammad** (570–632 AD), the last in a long line of prophets that included Abraham, Moses and Jesus. Muhammad transmitted Allah's final and perfected revelation to mankind through the writings of the divinely revealed "recitation", the **Koran**. The official beginning of Islam is dated as 622 AD, when Muhammad and his followers, exiled from Mecca, made the **hijra**, or migration, north to Yathrib, later known as Medina, "City of the Prophet". The *hijra* marks the start of the Islamic calendar, 1 AH (Anno Hijra). All the central tenets of Islam are embodied in the Koran, with the most important known as the **Five Pillars of Islam**. The first pillar is *sha-hada* – the confession of faith, "There is no god but God, and Muhammad is his messenger." The *shahada* is recited at the *salat*, the second pillar, which enjoins the faithful to kneel five times daily and pray in the direction of Mecca. The other three tenets are: alms-giving to the local Muslim community (*zakat*); fasting during the ninth month of the Muslim lunar calendar, **Ramadan** (*saum* – see p.244); and the pilgrimage (**haj**) to Mecca, money and health allowing.

The first firm foothold made by Islam in Southeast Asia was the conversion of the court of Melaka, in modern-day Malaysia, in the early fifteenth century. One after another, the powerful Malay court rulers took to Islam, adopting the title sultan (ruler); nearby Singapore couldn't help but feel its influence. Today, almost all of Singapore's Malays are Muslims, as well as a proportion of its Indian population. The form of Islam practised is fairly liberal. Some, but not all, women wear long dress and headscarves, and certain taboos – like not drinking alcohol – are ignored by a growing number of Muslims.

Mosques

While only a small proportion attend the mosque every day, all Muslims converge on their nearest **mosque** on Friday – the day of prayer. Once there, the men wash their hands, feet and faces three times in the outer chambers, before entering the prayer hall to recite sections of the Koran. After this initial period, an **Imam** will lead prayers and, on occasions, deliver a sermon, in which the teachings of Muhammad will be applied to a contemporary context. Women cannot enter the main prayer hall during prayers and must congregate in a chamber to the side of the hall.

Visitors are welcome at certain times, provided that their shoulders and legs are covered. No non-Muslim is allowed to enter a mosque during prayer time or go into the prayer hall at any time, although it's possible to stand just outside and look in.

Hinduism

Hinduism reached the Malay Peninsula and Singapore long before Islam, brought by Indian traders more than a thousand years ago. Its base of support grew in the nineteenth century, when large numbers of indentured workers and convicts arrived from the subcontinent to labour on rubber estates and in construction.

Hinduism had no founder, but grew slowly over thousands of years. Its central tenet is the belief that life is a series of rebirths and reincarnations (*samsara*) that eventually leads to spiritual release (*moksha*). An individual's progress is determined by his or her *karma*, very much a law of cause and effect, in which negative decisions and actions slow up the process of upward reincarnation and positive ones accelerate it.

A whole variety of deities are worshipped, which on the surface makes Hinduism appear complex, but with only a loose understanding of the **Vedas** (the religion's holy books) the characters and roles of the main gods quickly become apparent. The deities you'll come across most often are the three manifestations of the faith's Supreme Divine Being: **Brahma the Creator**, **Vishnu the Preserver** and **Shiva the Destroyer**. Other enduring favourites among Hindus include: elephant-headed Ganesh, the son of Shiva, who is evoked before every undertaking except funerals; Vishnu's consort, the comely Lakshmi, worshipped as goddess of prosperity and wealth; and Saraswati, wife to Brahma, and seen as a goddess of purification, fertility and learning.

Hindu temples

Visitors are welcome to explore **Hindu temples**, but are expected to remove their shoes before entering. Step over the threshold and you enter a veritable Disneyland of colourful gods and fanciful creatures. The style is typically **Dravidian** (South Indian), as befits the largely Tamil population, with a soaring *gopuram*, or entrance tower, teeming with sculptures, and a central courtyard leading to an inner sanctum (off-limits to tourists) dedicated to the presiding deity. In the temple precinct, there are always busy scenes – incense burning, the application of sandalwood paste, and the *puja* (ritual act of worship).

Books

The majority of books about Singapore tend to be penned by Western visitors to the region, rather than by local writers. Only in the latter part of the twentieth century has writing about Singapore by Singaporeans themselves begun to gather momentum.

The best selection of local writing is available on the island itself, though Skoob Books of London is doing much to introduce Singaporean literature to the West. Some of the titles below are ostensibly concerned with Malaya or Malaysia, but all cast some light on Singapore, as the island's fortunes have always been closely linked with those of the Peninsula.

In the reviews below, publishers are listed in the format UK;US publisher, unless the title is available in one country only (in which case the country is specified), or if the publisher is the same in the UK and USA (in which case the publisher's name is given once); o/p signifies out of print.

Travel writing and exploration

John Bastin (ed), *Travellers' Singapore* (Penerbit Fajar Bakti).

Singapore-related vignettes from as early as 1819 and as late as the Japanese conquest of 1942.

Isabella Bird, *The Golden Chersonese* (OUP; Century; o/p).

Delightful epistolary romp through old Southeast Asia, penned by the intrepid Bird, whose adventures in the Malay states in 1879 ranged from strolls through Singapore's streets to elephant-back rides and encounters with alligators.

G.M. Gullick, *They Came To Malaya* (OUP). A cornucopia of accounts of people, places and events, written by the governors, planters and explorers who tamed Malaya and Singapore.

Rev G.M. Reith, *1907 Handbook to Singapore* (OUP; o/p). Intriguing period piece which illuminates early-twentieth-century colonial attitudes in Singapore: drill hall, gaol and docks are detailed, while the list of useful Malay phrases includes such essentials as "harness the horse" and "off with you".

Michael Wise (ed), *Travellers' Tales of Old Singapore* (In Print Publishing, UK). Identical in theme to Bastin's *Travellers' Singapore* (above), though Wise's selection of tales is the more catholic and more engrossing of the two.

Gavin Young, *In Search of Conrad* (Penguin, UK). Young plays detective and historian, tracing Joseph Conrad's footsteps around Southeast Asia in search of the stories and locations that inspired him. Young's time in Singapore takes him from the National Library to Bidadari cemetery in search of A.P. Williams – Conrad's Lord Jim.

History and politics

Abdullah bin Kadir, *The Hikayat Abdullah* (OUP, UK; o/p). Raffles' one-time clerk, Melakan-born Abdullah later turned diarist of some of the most formative years of Southeast Asian history; his first-hand account is crammed with illuminating vignettes and character portraits.

Barbara Watson Andaya and Leonard Andaya, *The History of Malaysia* (Macmillan; St Martin's Press). Unlike more paternalistic histories, penned by former colonists, this standard text on the region takes a more even-handed view, and finds time for cultural coverage.

David Brazil, *Street Smart Singapore* (Times Editions, Singapore). An Aladdin's cave of Singaporean history and trivia that remains fascinating throughout.

Maurice Collis, *Raffles* (Century; o/p). The most accessible and enjoyable biography of Sir Stamford Raffles: very readable.

Images of Asia series: Maya Jayapal's *Old Singapore* (OUP). Concise volume which charts the growth of the city-state, drawing on contemporary maps, sketches and photographs to engrossing effect.

Lee Kuan Yew, *The Singapore Story* (Singapore Press Holdings). Spanning the 42 years from his birth to Singapore's separation from Malaysia in 1965, the Granddaddy of contemporary Singapore's first volume of memoirs has drawn plaudits from the likes of Thatcher and Chirac, Keating and Kissinger. Essential reading for anyone wanting the inside track on Singapore's huge expansion over the past fifty years.

Nick Leeson, *Rogue Trader* (Warner; Little Brown). Leeson's own account of his beginnings, his ambitions and of the whirlpool of deceit in which he floundered as the result of his covert trading in Singapore. The inadequacies of Barings' systems and controls are revealed as contributing factors, though Leeson's apparent lack of penitence wins him little sympathy.

James Minchin, *No Man Is An Island* (Allen & Unwin; Paul & Co). A well-researched and at times critical study of Lee Kuan Yew, which refuses to kowtow to Singapore's ex-PM and is hence unavailable in Singapore itself, but gleefully sold in shops throughout Malaysia.

C. Mary Turnbull, *A Short History of Malaysia, Singapore & Brunei* (Graham Brash, Singapore). Informed introduction to the region, touching on the major issues that have shaped it. Its big brother, Turnbull's *History of Singapore 1819–1988* (OUP, UK), is, in contrast, as scholarly an approach to Singapore as you could wish for.

HISTORY AND POLITICS

C.E. Wurtzburg, *Raffles of the Eastern Isles* (OUP). A weighty and learned tome that's the definitive study of the man who founded modern Singapore; not for the marginally interested.

WWII and the Japanese Occupation

Noel Barber, *Sinister Twilight* (Arrow, UK). Documents the fall of Singapore to the Japanese, by re-imagining the crucial events of the period.

Russell Braddon, *The Naked Island* (Penguin, o/p; Simon & Schuster). Southeast Asia under the Japanese: Braddon's disturbing and moving first-hand account of the POW camps of Malaya, Singapore and Siam displays courage in the face of appalling conditions and treatment. Worth scouring secondhand stores for.

Peter Elphick, *Singapore The Pregnable Fortress* (Coronet, UK). Drawing on documents only made available in 1993, Elphick has produced the definitive history of the fall of

Singapore, showing the gaffes, low morale and desertion that led to it; a scholarly *tour de force*.

Culture and society

Culture Shock! Singapore (Kuperard; Graphic Arts Center Publishing). Cultural dos and don'ts for the leisure and business traveller to the region, spanning subjects as diverse as handing over business cards and belching after a fine meal.

Leslie Layton, *Songbirds in Singapore* (OUP, US; o/p). A delightful examination of songbird-keeping in Singapore, detailing all facets of the pastime, from its growth in the nineteenth century to its most popular birds.

Tan Kok Seng, *Son Of Singapore* (Heinemann, US; o/p). Tan Kok Seng's candid and sobering autobiography unearths the underside of the Singaporean success story, telling of hard times spent as a coolie.

CULTURE AND SOCIETY

Literature

Charles Allen, *Tales from the South China Seas* (Futura, o/p; David & Charles). Memoirs of the last generation of British colonists, in which predictable Raj attitudes prevail, though some of the drama of everyday lives, often in inhospitable conditions, is evinced with considerable pathos.

Noel Barber, *Tanamera* (Hodder, UK). Romantic saga based in mid-twentieth-century Singapore.

Gopal Baratham, *Moonrise*; *Sunset* (Serpent's Tail). When How Kum Menon's fiancée is murdered while sleeping by his side in Singapore's East Coast Park, it seems everyone he knows has a motive. How Kum turns detective, and an engaging whodunnit emerges. In *A Candle or the Sun*, Baratham swallows hard and tackles the thorny issue of political corruption.

Anthony Burgess, *The Long Day Wanes* (Minerva; Norton). Burgess's Malayan trilogy – *Time for a Tiger*, *The Enemy in the Blanket* and *Beds in the East* – published in one volume, provides a witty and acutely observed vision of 1950s Malaya, underscoring the racial prejudices of the period. *Time for a Tiger*, the first novel, is worth reading for the Falstaffian Nabby Adams alone.

James Clavell, *King Rat* (Hodder; Dell). Set in Japanese-occupied Singapore, a gripping tale of survival in the notorious Changi Prison.

Joseph Conrad, *Lord Jim* (Penguin). Southeast Asia provides the backdrop to the story of Jim's desertion of an apparently sinking ship and subsequent efforts to redeem himself; modelled upon the sailor A.P. Williams, who lived and died in Singapore.

Alastair Dingwall (ed), *Southeast Asia Traveller's Literary Companion* (In Print Publishing, UK). Among the bite-sized essays in this gem of a book are enlightening segments on Malaysia and Singapore, into which are crammed biographies, a recommended reading list, historical, linguistic and literary backgrounds. Excerpts range

LITERATURE

from classical Malayan literature to the nations' leading contemporary lights.

J.G. Farrell, *The Singapore Grip* (Flamingo; o/p; Carrol & Graf). Lengthy novel – Farrell's last – of World War II Singapore in which real and fictitious characters flit from tennis to dinner party as the countdown to the Japanese occupation begins.

Skoob Pacifica Anthology No. 1 and No. 2 (Skoob). These two thorough compendia of writings from the Pacific Rim together comprise an invaluable introduction to the contemporary literatures of Singapore and Malaysia.

W. Somerset Maugham, *Short Stories Volume 4* (Mandarin; Penguin). Peopled by hoary sailors, bored plantation-dwellers and colonials with mutton chop whiskers and topees, Maugham's short stories resuscitate the Malaya of a century ago; quintessential colonial literature graced by an easy style and a steady eye for a story.

Southeast Asia Writes Back! Anthology (Skoob). A thorough compendium of writings from the Pacific Rim that provides a useful introduction to the contemporary literature of Singapore.

Paul Theroux, *Saint Jack* (Penguin; Ballantine, o/p). The compulsively bawdy tale of Jack Flowers, an ageing American who supplements his earnings at a Singapore ship's chandlers by pimping for Westerners; Jack's jaundiced eye and Theroux's rich prose open windows on Singapore's past.

Wildlife

G.W.H. Davison and Chew Yen Fook, *A Photographic Guide to Birds of Peninsular Malaysia and Singapore* (New Holland; R. Curtis). Well-keyed and user-friendly, these slender volumes carry oodles of glossy plates that make positive identifying a breeze.

Glossary

Baba Straits-born Chinese (male).

Bukit Hill.

Bumboat Small cargo boat.

Cheongsam Chinese dress with long slit up the side.

Chunan Plaster made from eggs, lime, sugar and coconut husks.

Expressway Motorway/freeway.

Five-foot way Covered verandah outside a shophouse.

Godown Riverside warehouse.

Gopuram Bank of sculpted deities over entrance to a Hindu temple.

Haj Trip to Mecca.

Halal Something that's permissible by Islam.

Hawker centre A cluster of food stalls gathered under one roof and sharing common tables.

Istana Palace.

Jalan Road.

Kampung Village.

Kavadi Steel frames hung from the bodies of Hindu devotees during Thaipusam.

Keramat Auspicious Malay site.

Kongsi Chinese clan association.

Kris Wavy-bladed dagger.

Lorong Lane.

Mahjong A Chinese game with similarities to dominoes.

Mandi Asian method of bathing by dousing with water from a tank using a small bucket.

Masjid Mosque.

Nonya Straits-born Chinese (female); sometimes *Nyonya*.

Padang Field or square.

Peranakan Straits-born Chinese.

Pulau Island.

Ramadan Muslim fasting month.

Rotan Rattan cane; used in the infliction of corporal punishment.

Saree Traditional Indian woman's garment, worn in conjunction with a *choli* (short-sleeved blouse).

Singlish Singaporean English.

Shophouse Shuttered building with living space upstairs and shop space on ground floor.

Songkok Hat worn by Muslim males.

Sultan Ruler.

Tai chi Chinese martial art; commonly performed as an early-morning exercise.

Temenggong Chieftain.

Tiffin Lunch.

Tongkang Chinese sailing boat.

Trishaw Three-wheeled bicycles with a carriage for passengers.

Wayang Chinese opera.

Acronyms

CBD Central Business District.

JB Johor Bahru.

KL Kuala Lumpur.

MCP Malayan Communist Party.

MDU Malayan Democratic Union.

MRT Mass Rapid Transit system.

PAP People's Action Party.

SIA Singapore International Airline.

STB Singapore Tourist Board.

UNMO Malaysia's United Malays National Organization.

WTC World Trade Centre.

INDEX

Rough Guides
on the Web

www.travel.roughguides.com

We keep getting bigger and better! The Rough Guide to Travel Online
now covers more than 14,000 searchable locations. You're just a click
away from access to the most in-depth travel content, weekly
destination features, online reservation services, and an outspoken
community of fellow travelers. Whether you're looking for ideas for
your next holiday or you know exactly where you're going, join us online.

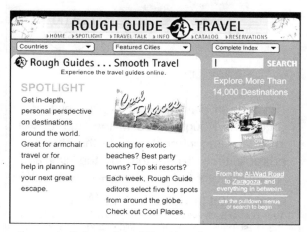

You can also find us on Yahoo!® Travel (http://travel.yahoo.com) and
Microsoft Expedia® UK (http://www.expediauk.com).

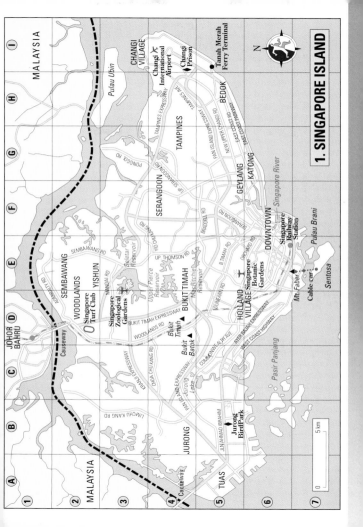

1. SINGAPORE ISLAND

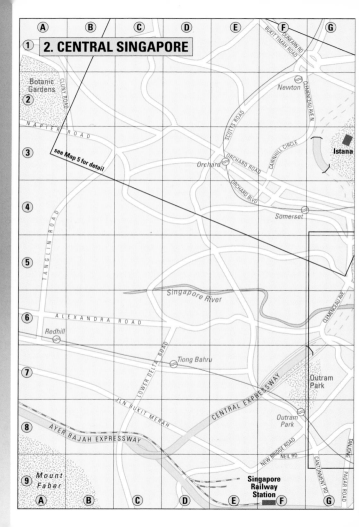

2. CENTRAL SINGAPORE

A **B** **C** **D** **E** **F** **G**

1

2 Botanic Gardens

3 see Map 5 for detail

Orchard

Newton

Istana

4 Somerset

5

6 ALEXANDRA ROAD

Redhill

Singapore River

7 Tiong Bahru

Outram Park

8 AYER RAJAH EXPRESSWAY

JLN BUKIT MERAH

LOWER DELTA ROAD

CENTRAL EXPRESSWAY

Outram Park

NEW BRIDGE ROAD

NEIL RD

9 Mount Faber

Singapore Railway Station

CLUNY ROAD

NAPIER ROAD

TANGLIN ROAD

BUKIT TIMAH ROAD

DUNEARN RD

CLEMENCEAU AVE

SCOTTS ROAD

ORCHARD ROAD

CAIRNHILL CIRCLE

ORCHARD BLVD

CLEMENCEAU AVE

TANJONG

CANTONMENT RD

PAGAR RD

A **B** **C** **D** **E** **F** **G**

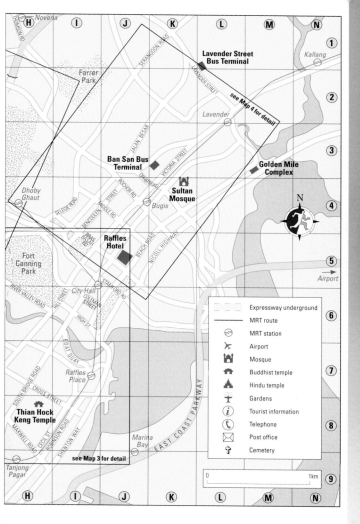

----	Expressway underground	
——	MRT route	
⊖	MRT station	
✈	Airport	
🕌	Mosque	
卍	Buddhist temple	
⛩	Hindu temple	
✝	Gardens	
(i)	Tourist information	
©	Telephone	
✉	Post office	
†	Cemetery	

see Map 4 for detail

see Map 3 for detail

0   1km

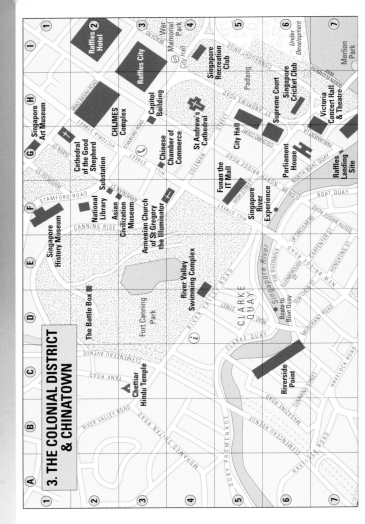

3. THE COLONIAL DISTRICT & CHINATOWN

Raffles Hotel
Raffles City
CHIJMES Complex
Capitol Building
Singapore Art Museum
Cathedral of the Good Shepherd
Substation
National Library
Asian Civilization Museum
Singapore History Museum
Chinese Chamber of Commerce
St Andrew's Cathedral
Capitol Building
City Hall
Singapore Recreation Club
Supreme Court
Singapore Cricket Club
Victoria Concert Hall & Theatre
The Battle Box
Armenian Church of St Gregory the Illuminator
Funan the IT Mall
Parliament House
Singapore River Experience
Raffles Landing Site
Fort Canning Park
River Valley Swimming Complex
Chettiar Hindu Temple
Clarke Quay
Boats to Boat Quay
Boat Quay
Riverside Point
Singapore River
Merlion Park
Padang
War Memorial Park
City Hall
Under Development

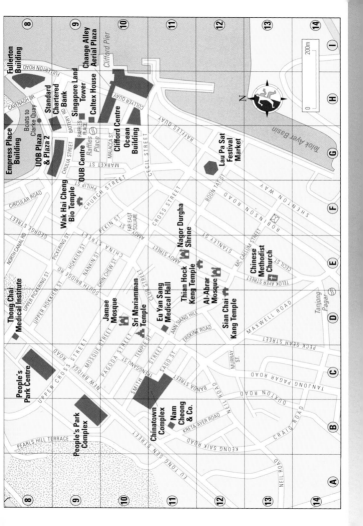

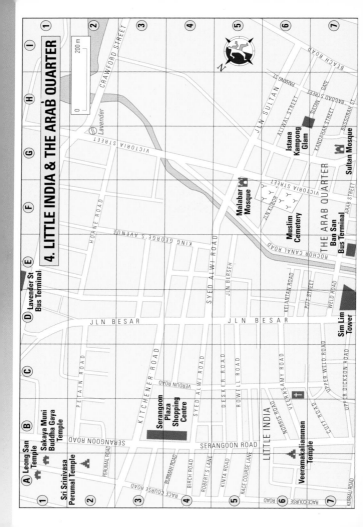

4. LITTLE INDIA & THE ARAB QUARTER

0   200 m

N

Little India & the Arab Quarter map labels:

- Leong San Temple
- Sakaya Muni Buddha Gaya Temple
- Sri Srinivasa Perumal Temple
- Lavender St Bus Terminal
- Serangoon Plaza Shopping Centre
- Malabar Mosque
- Istana Kampong Glam
- Muslim Cemetery
- Ban San Bus Terminal
- THE ARAB QUARTER
- Sultan Mosque
- LITTLE INDIA
- Veeramakaliamman Temple
- Sim Lim Tower

Streets:

- CRAWFORD STREET
- VICTORIA STREET
- JLN SULTAN
- PAHANG ST
- ALIWAL STREET
- BAGHDAD STREET
- KANDAHAR STREET
- BUSSORAH ST
- BEACH ROAD
- JLN KUBOR
- VICTORIA STREET
- ARAB STREET
- BOCHOR CANAL ROAD
- HORNE ROAD
- KING GEORGE'S AVENUE
- SYED ALWI ROAD
- JLN BERSEH
- KELANTAN ROAD
- PIT STREET
- WELD ROAD
- UPPER WELD ROAD
- JLN BESAR
- PETAIN ROAD
- KITCHENER ROAD
- VERDUN ROAD
- SYED ALWI ROAD
- DESKER ROAD
- ROWELL ROAD
- VEERASAMY ROAD
- UPPER DICKSON ROAD
- SERANGOON ROAD
- BURMAH ROAD
- BIRCH ROAD
- ROBERT'S LANE
- KINTA ROAD
- RACE COURSE LANE
- PERUMAL ROAD
- RACE COURSE ROAD
- NORRIS ROAD
- CUFF ROAD
- KERBAU ROAD

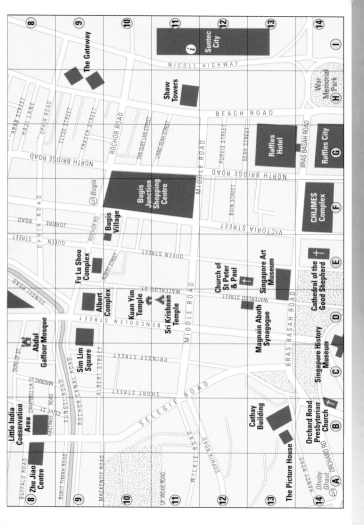

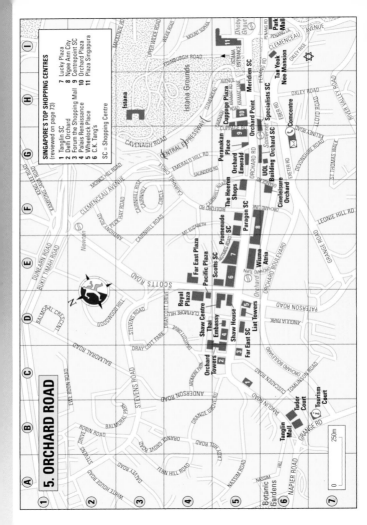

5. ORCHARD ROAD

SINGAPORE'S TOP SHOPPING CENTRES
(reviewed on page 73)

1 Tanglin SC
2 Delfi Orchard
3 Forum the Shopping Mall
4 Palais Renaissance
5 Wheelock Place
6 C.K. Tang's
7 Lucky Plaza
8 Ngee Ann City
9 Centrepoint SC
10 Orchard Plaza
11 Plaza Singapura

SC = Shopping Centre

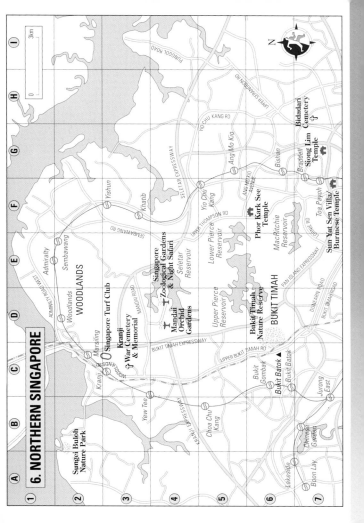

6. NORTHERN SINGAPORE

N

0   3km

Sungei Buloh Nature Park

Sembawang
Admiralty
Yishun
Khatib

WOODLANDS
Woodlands
Marsiling
Kranji

Singapore Turf Club

Kranji War Cemetery & Memorial

Mandai Orchid Gardens

Singapore Zoological Gardens & Night Safari

Seletar Reservoir

Upper Pierce Reservoir

Lower Pierce Reservoir

Yio Chu Kang

Ang Mo Kio

Bishan

Phor Kark See Temple

MacRitchie Reservoir

BUKIT TIMAH
Bukit Timah Nature Reserve

Sun Yat Sen Villa/ Burmese Temple

Braddell
Stong Lim Temple

Bidadari Cemetery

Toa Payoh

Bukit Gombak
Bukit Batok

Jurong East

Yew Tee
Choa Chu Kang

Lakeside
Boon Lay

Chinese Garden

PUNGGOL ROAD

UPPER SERANGOON RD

YIO CHU KANG RD

SELETAR EXPRESSWAY

SEMBAWANG RD

ADMIRALTY ROAD WEST

MANDAI ROAD

UPPER THOMSON RD

ANG MO KIO AVENUE

LORNG 1 RD

PAN ISLAND EXPRESSWAY

DUNEARN ROAD

BUKIT TIMAH ROAD

BUKIT TIMAH EXPRESSWAY

UPPER BUKIT TIMAH RD

KRANJI EXPRESSWAY

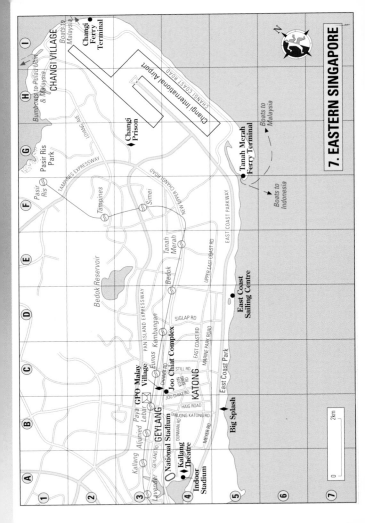

7. EASTERN SINGAPORE

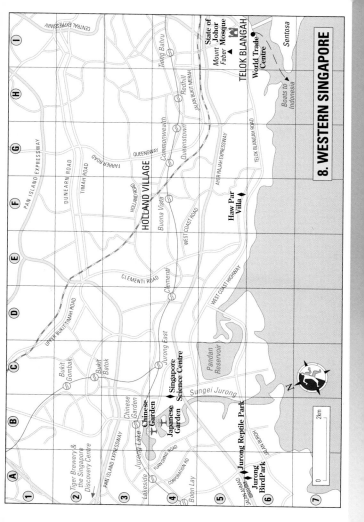

8. WESTERN SINGAPORE

CENTRAL EXPRESSWAY

Tiong Bahru

State of
Johor Mosque
Mount
Faber
TELOK BLANGAH

World Trade
Centre

Boats to
Indonesia

Sentosa

Redhill

JALAN BUKIT MERAH

Commonwealth

Queenstown

QUEENSWAY

AYER RAJAH EXPRESSWAY

TELOK BLANGAH ROAD

PAN ISLAND EXPRESSWAY

DUNEARN ROAD

FARRER ROAD

TIMAH ROAD

HOLLAND ROAD

HOLLAND VILLAGE

Buona Vista

WEST COAST ROAD

Haw Par
Villa

UPPER BUKIT TIMAH ROAD

Bukit
Gombak

Bukit
Batok

CLEMENTI ROAD

Clementi

WEST COAST HIGHWAY

Jurong East

Singapore
Science Centre

Pandan
Reservoir

Sungei Jurong

N

2km

0

Tiger Brewery &
the Singapore
Discovery Centre

Chinese
Garden

Chinese
Garden

Japanese
Garden

Jurong Lake

Lakeside

PAN ISLAND EXPRESSWAY

TUANDONG ROAD

CORPORATION RD

Boon Lay

Jurong Reptile Park

Jurong
BirdPark

JALAN AHMAD IBRAHIM

JALAN BURIH

9. THE MRT SYSTEM

Interchange ●

E12 Pasir Ris
E11 Tampines
E10 Simei
E9 Tanah Merah
E8 Bedok
E7 Kembangan
E6 Eunos
E5 Paya Lebar
E4 Aljunied
E3 Kallang
E2 Lavender
E1 Bugis
C2 City Hall
C1 Raffles Place
M1 Marina Bay

N14 Sembawang
N12 Yishun
N11 Khatib
N10 Yio Chu Kang
N9 Ang Mo Kio
N8 Bishan
N7 Braddell
N6 Toa Payoh
N5 Novena
N4 Newton
N3 Orchard
N2 Somerset
N1 Dhoby Ghaut

N15 Admiralty
N16 Woodlands
N17 Marsiling
N18 Kranji
N20 Yew Tee
N21 Choa Chu Kang
N22 Bukit Gombak
N23 Bukit Batok

W1 Tanjong Pagar
W2 Outram Park
W3 Tiong Bahru
W4 Redhill
W5 Queenstown
W6 Commonwealth
W7 Buona Vista
W8 Clementi
W9 Jurong East
W10 Chinese Garden
W11 Lakeside
W12 Boon Lay